Gender, Ethnicity, and Religion

Gender, Ethnicity, and Religion

Views from the Other Side

edited by
Rosemary Radford Ruether

FORTRESS PRESS
Minneapolis

Cover design: Brad Norr Design
Interior design: Beth Wright

Library of Congress Cataloging-in-Publication Data

Gender, ethnicity, and religion : views from the other side / edited by Rosemary Radford Ruether.
   p. cm.
Includes bibliographical references.
  ISBN 0-8006-3569-8 (pbk. : alk. paper)
  1. Sociology, Christian. I. Ruether, Rosemary Radford.
BT738 .G375 2002
261.8'34—dc21

                            2002013276

Manufactured in the U.S.A.
06   05   04   03   02   1   2   3   4   5   6   7   8   9   10

Contents

◨◨◨

Contributors   vii

Preface   ix
Rosemary Radford Ruether

Part One: Historical Precursors and Foremothers

1. Whiteness: The Workings of an Ideology in American
   Society and Culture   3
   Jacqueline Battalora

2. Climbing Jacob's Ladder: Alma Lillie Hubbard's Musical
   Career in New Orleans, 1900–1932   24
   Rosalind F. Hinton

3. The Poetry of Pauli Murray, African American Civil
   Rights Lawyer and Priest   45
   Elaine Caldbeck

4. The Lunch Counter Struggle, 1960–1963: Women
   Remapping Boundaries of Race, Gender, and Vocation   66
   Barbara R. I. Isaacs

Part Two: Contemporary Social Contexts for Struggle

5. Trying to Be God in the World: The Story of the Evangelical
   Women's Caucus and the Crisis over Homosexuality   99
   S. Sue Horner

6. Diaspora Economics: Filipino American Families and
   Globalization   125
   Jocelyn Eclarin Azada

7. The Garifuna *Dugu* Ritual in Belize: A Celebration
   of Relationships   144
   Barbara Flores

8. Across the Kitchen Table: Cuban Women Pastors
    and Theology   173
    Margarita M. W. Suárez

Part Three: Visions of New Possibility

9. Womanist Theology as Counter-Narrative   197
    Patricia-Anne Johnson

10. Claiming the "Fearsome Possibility": Toward a Contextual
    Christology of Disability   215
    Kimberly Anne Willis

11. The Nature of Nature: Ecofeminism and Environmental
    Racism in America   230
    Rita Lester

12. "To Make the Wounded Whole": Womanist Explorations
    of Reconciliation   247
    Stephanie Y. Mitchem

Contributors

◻◻◻

Jacqueline Battalora is a public-interest lawyer with Battalora & Associates, Chicago, and teaches courses in law and society at the University of Illinois at Chicago.

Rosalind F. Hinton is assistant professor of African American Religion at DePaul University in Chicago.

Elaine Caldbeck is a Theological Librarian at the United Library of Garrett-Evangelical and Seabury-Western Theological Seminaries. She sometimes teaches as an adjunct at Garrett and is an aspirant to the presbyterate of the Episcopal Church.

Barbara R. I. Isaacs is Lecturer of Religion in America for Loyola University Chicago's Department of Theology and serves as the corporate chaplain of the General Board of Pension and Health Benefits of the United Methodist Church in Evanston, Illinois.

S. Sue Horner is visiting associate professor of Women's Studies at North Park University, Chicago, and the author of a forthcoming book on the history of the contemporary evangelical feminist movement.

Jocelyn Eclarin Azada is currently a senior research analyst for the largest religious pension fund in the United States, the General Board of Pension and Health Benefits of the United Methodist Church. She has a master's degree from Garrett-Evangelical Theological Seminary, with special interests in economic ethics, liberation theology, and the possibilities for North–South dialogue.

Barbara Flores, a member of the Sisters of Charity of Nazareth, is a professor of theology at St. John's College in Belize and Assistant Director of Initial Formation for her order.

Margarita M. W. Suárez is an assistant professor in the Religion and Philosophy department of Meredith College, Raleigh, North Carolina, where she teaches courses in Religion and Culture, Global Christianities, and Liberation Theologies.

Patricia-Anne Johnson is assistant professor of Black Studies at California State University, Long Beach.

Kimberly Anne Willis received her Ph.D. from Northwestern University in Evanston, Illinois. She is the pastor of Marina United Methodist Church in Marina, California. Her research interest is disability and spirituality.

Rita Lester is assistant professor of religion at Nebraska Wesleyan University and is currently researching religious diversity in Lincoln, Nebraska, for the Harvard Pluralism Project.

Stephanie Y. Mitchem is associate professor of Religious Studies at University of Detroit Mercy and author of *Introducing Womanist Theology* (Orbis, 2002).

Preface

ROSEMARY RADFORD RUETHER

◻◻◻

The study of theology and the practice of religion have been transformed in recent years by incorporation of the experience of women from many social contexts, bringing new perspectives on gender in the contexts of race, ethnicity, sexual orientation, and disability. This volume highlights the exciting work of twelve young scholars working at this fruitful nexus.

In historical, social, and theological studies, new methodologies from cultural anthropology, social theory, and gender studies have emerged. They take lived religion explicitly into account and thereby illumine cultural values that emerge from many distinct contexts. These scholars and theologians are themselves working from these distinct standpoints. They are intently aware of their own cultural location, and they prize the culturally specific religious insights that arise from these contexts. Departing from an identification with the dominant elites in academic or ecclesial communities, the writers of this volume approach their topics from the marginalized communities in the churches, often not represented in theological schools.

Working from these many "other sides," the chapters in this volume shed particular light on the roles of religious agency in such communities as African Americans, Cuban and Belizan Caribbeans, and Filipinos. They look first at *particular historical moments of social transformation,* such as the lunch counter struggles of the 1960s and the splits created by the question of homosexuality in the evangelical feminist movement of the 1980s. They next illumine *the role of religious practices,* such as folk healing in Belize, religious music in black churches in New Orleans in the early twentieth century, and women's preaching in Cuban Protestant churches in the twenty-first century. Finally, the volume also offers *new theological perspectives,* arising from these many contexts—Afro-Caribbean, Cuban, womanism in the United States—as well as insights into sacramental theology and spirituality arising from the challenges of ecological crisis, the lives of people with disabilities, and the civil rights struggle.

I have been privileged to work with a unique cohort of wonderful students in the doctoral program of Garrett-Evangelical Theological Seminary and Northwestern University over the last twenty-five years. It is some of the best and most important research and writing of these former students, now colleagues, mostly in their doctoral theses, that is gathered here. All the writers are women, although I have had many excellent male students as well. All have done work in the general area of gender, religion, and ethnicity or alternative identities. All employ methods and perspectives other than those that arise from the dominant identity; that is, of white, non-disabled, heterosexual men.

The fact that all these chapters have issued from the research done for doctoral or master's degrees, in one case, at Garrett and Northwestern is, I think, a tribute to an extraordinarily creative cohort of students at institutions open to such research. It is this that we are celebrating in this volume. Clearly all of us wish to promote more such research and published work by women writing from perspectives other than the dominant identity. This book is a small step toward this end. These colleagues have been, and we hope will be, translating their work into independent monographs or journal articles as well.

These chapters bring together a great array of themes, although within the commonality I have mentioned above. Six of the chapters are on African American women or African American issues. Another chapter speaks of issues of homosexuality in homophobic churches. The other five chapters come from a Filipina perspective, a Belizan context, a Cuban context, a disability context, and an ecological context, although this latter chapter also relates to issues of racism. It is this commonality in speaking from or about "alternatives" that sparked our title, *Gender, Ethnicity, and Religion: Views from the Other Side*.

The volume has been arranged in three sections, each with four chapters. The first section groups studies that are primarily historical, focusing on the roots, precursors, and foremothers of the struggle for racial justice. The second section speaks of contemporary contexts of struggle and the third on visions of possibilities for a new church and society.

1. Struggles from the Past. The historical section opens with a lead chapter by Jacqueline Battalora, a professor of law and a public-interest lawyer in Chicago. Her theme is "whiteness," the ideology of calling a collection of people in the United States of different ethnicities, but all somewhat fair of skin, *white*. The purpose of this designation is not to find a common ethnic name for these people, although it is used as if it were an ethnic term. Rather, *white* is actually a term of "ethnic erasure." The distinct histories and ethnicities of people in this group—Irish, English, French, German, Italian, Jewish, Arab, and so forth—are erased by being made "white."

The purpose of this term is to privilege them in relation to all "non-white" or "colored" people. This is the dominant linguistic way of pointing to the fundamental racist pattern in the United States, divided between "white" people and people of "color." It is common in the U.S. to speak of a "color" problem, but obviously the actual problem of "color" racism comes from the "white" problem, the grouping of a privileged group on the basis of a socially constructed whiteness. "Whiteness" is an expandable category. Originally it meant English Protestants. Then it included Scotch, German, and Dutch Protestants. French and Irish Catholics and Jews were not included. But over time more people became "white," that is, entered the privileged group of whiteness, although actual prejudice against even these "others" has died slowly. We put this chapter first because it states the basic problem of race privilege in this country.

Rosalind F. Hinton and Elaine Caldbeck, both historians of African American life in the United States, have written chapters that recover the stories of important African American women leaders. Alma Lillie Hubbard, the subject of Hinton's chapter, was a pioneer in the union of classical European and black folk music in New Orleans. She became a national leader with a career that extended to Chicago and New York in the 1930s. In Hubbard we see the roots of black middle-class upward mobility through personal talent, nurtured through the basic institutions of the black community, family, church, and school.

Caldbeck's chapter is on the poetry of Pauli Murray, a well-known African American civil rights lawyer in Washington, D.C., in the late 1930s to 1960s. Murray was a key figure in the victory that won the inclusion of the word *sex* in affirmative action legislation in 1964. In her later years Murray went to theological seminary and was ordained an Episcopal priest, celebrating her first mass in the university chapel of Durham, North Carolina, a chapel donated by her white plantation master grandfather, where her black slave grandmother attended church sitting in the balcony. Murray is well known for this legal and ecclesiastical history, but her work as a poet is largely unknown. In her chapter Caldbeck recovers the work of Pauli Murray as an American epic poet of the struggle for racial and gender justice.

Barbara R. I. Isaacs, also an American historian, tells us the dramatic story of two groups of Methodist college students in the South, one from a white college and another from a black college, each of whom made the decision to participate in the sit-ins to desegregate lunch counters in the early 1960s. Isaacs details the ethical teaching each group of women had imbibed from their churches that impelled them to make this decision. She also shows how the black school, Bennett College in Greensboro, North Carolina, had the leadership of their president, Willa Player, who understood and supported the young women of the college; whereas the white students from Randolph-Macon Woman's College in Lynchburg, Virginia, was led by white men who were unwilling to take this risk and pilloried the young women who took the risk of action. Isaacs details the varied effects of this disparate relation to church and church-related college upon these young women from different racial backgrounds.

2. *Today's Struggles.* In the second section of the book we have chapters from four quite different social contexts. S. Sue Horner, also a historian and archivist of the Evangelical Women's Caucus, a feminist evangelical movement of the 1970s and 1980s, tells the story of how this movement arose and how it split and fell apart over the issue of homosexuality raised by some of its foremost leaders. The members of the caucus had been united in the shaping of an evangelical way of being feminist, but many were unable to extend this to the even more divisive issue of sexual orientation.

Jocelyn Eclarin Azada, a Filipina scholar of Filipino-American society, with a focus on the economic and social history of this community, focuses on the effects of globalization on Filipino-American families. She shows how traditional Filipino family values clash with the "ethic" demanded by global capitalism and how they "make do" by redefining family patterns in the hostile environment of the United States. She discusses how this situation creates intergenerational conflict and the loss of a sense of positive Filipino identity in the younger generation vis-à-vis parents who grew up in the Philippines. She suggests ways in which some Filipino families seek to create a new synthesis of American and Filipino values and ways of life.

Barbara Flores's chapter takes us outside the United States to the Garinagu people of Belize, Central America. This community was created in the era of the slave trade by a unique union of Carib Indians and escaped African slaves. Forced by the British out of their original home on St. Vincent Island, a major part of these "Black Caribs" made their way to Belize. There they created a distinct culture that brought together African and indigenous elements with their own distinct story of forced migration. The Garinagu practice a ceremony of social healing of the tensions that arise in the community from time to time. This Dugu ritual is vital to the well-being of the Garinagu but misunderstood and despised by their white Catholic church leaders. Barbara Flores, herself a religious sister and a Belizan, explores the profound worldview that lies behind this ritual and the pattern of its practice. Her goal is a new kind of Catholic catechetics that can accept and allow the Garinagu to integrate their traditional and Christian lives, thus overcoming the alienating effects of a colonizing religious socialization.

Margarita M. W. Suárez, a theologian teaching at Meredith College in Raleigh, North Carolina, takes us to another Caribbean island, Cuba. Of Cuban-American background herself, Suárez spent the better part of a year in Cuba researching Cuban Protestant women's preaching and pastoral leadership. With graphic vignettes, Suárez shows us the way in which these Protestant women, generally from conservative evangelical churches that have just begun to ordain women and that generally reject feminist and liberation theologies, are quietly injecting these more liberating understandings of the gospel into their communities through their actual practice of ministry.

3. *Struggles for the Future.* The third section of the book takes us to visions of new futures for women in different social contexts. Patricia-Anne Johnson, assistant professor in the Black Studies department at California State University, Long Beach, writes on "Womanist Theology as Counter-Narrative." Johnson's thesis is that womanism is the product of a series of counter-narratives in American life that stand against the dominant white male ideology of America as God's elect. These successive counter-narratives have included, most conspicuously, black preaching and the black church of the nineteenth century, and the civil rights and feminist movements of the 1960s. Womanism unites all these counter-narratives in a new context that makes the most excluded group, African American women, along with their history and struggles for survival, central. Womanist theology brings womanist consciousness into the church itself and its interpretation of the gospel.

Kimberly Anne Willis, a pastor in Marina United Methodist Church in Marina, California, writes from the perspective of people with disabilities and the disability movement, which is challenging exclusion of its people from mainstream society and church life. The theological branch of the disability movement has focused on both the practical ways that people with disabilities are excluded or hindered from full participation in the church and the ways its dominant theology subtly or blatantly reinforces a model of physical "wholeness" as normative for Christian wholeness and redemption.

Theological reflection from the perspective of people with disabilities in the church suggests some strikingly different approaches to key topics, such as Christology. As a people that worships a redeemer who was crucified and risen with the marks of his suffering in his feet, hands, and side, Christians can be said to worship a disabled Lord. Is it not time to recognize the implications of this for the relationship of the "able-bodied" and "disabled" in the church, rooted in a new understanding of the theology of Christian redemption? To be one with Christ as a disabled Lord includes all Christians. This is not just a "special treatment" of people with disabilities but a new theological perspective on the nature of the entire Christian community.

Rita Lester, professor of religious studies at Nebraska Wesleyan University in Lincoln, Nebraska, takes us to the issues of ecology and environmental racism. For years the ecology movement tended to focus on "wilderness" and a concept of nature defined as set apart from human beings, particularly from those in urban settings. African Americans and indigenous people dwelling in polluted areas of the city or on reservations often found little relevance in this "white" ecological perspective. But indigenous and African American people, particularly the women of these communities who see the environmental threat from the perspective of the daily lives of their families, have begun to redefine the ecological challenge. Looking through the lenses of environmental racism and ecofeminism overcomes the bifurcation between people and nature. The "mainstream" ecological movement is thus challenged to redefine itself in a way that locates its worldview in this deeper interconnection of racism, class, gender, and environmental devastation.

Our closing visionary chapter comes from Stephanie Y. Mitchem, professor of religious studies at the University of Detroit Mercy. Mitchem tells the story of the Detroit Metropolitan Black Women's Health Project, where urban working-class African American women began to grapple with the health issues of their community. In so doing they began to realize that they could not address the health needs of others without including their own health as well. As older African American women, they often bore the brunt of the bad health of their community by the very demands to serve the survival needs of their families. Putting themselves first in order to be able to serve others more effectively led to a whole new orientation to personal and communal well-being.

Mitchem puts this case study in the context of the theological work of black and womanist theologians. In Mitchem's closing words, "'to make the wounded whole' is to learn to live in polyphony, to cherish and nurture self and community. . . . In such a holistic view, reconciliation challenges all oppressive, dehumanizing systems, not merely restoring to former order, but rebalancing the old so that a new heaven and earth can begin." These words are a fitting conclusion not only to Mitchem's own chapter but to this whole volume, which seeks to bring together gender and religion from a "different side," the side of those often ignored or excluded by virtue of gender, race, ethnicity, sexual orientation, and disability. Our vision is not simply to include the excluded in the present "order" or rather disorder, but to create a kind of community, a new heaven and earth. This is the Christian vision of hope that is most ancient yet ever new.

Part One

◻◼◻

Historical Precursors and Foremothers

1.

Whiteness

The Workings of an Ideology in American Society and Culture

JACQUELINE BATTALORA

🔲🔲🔲

This chapter is concerned with issues of race and social justice. Its overarching concern can best be located within the field of social ethics, exploring why human connection across such socially constructed racial categories as white and black, among so many others, remains uncommon and difficult to sustain. One reason may lie in the pervasive yet unexamined culture of whiteness in America.

In the United States, race is explored through a lens that focuses on "whiteness." *Whiteness* refers to the meanings assigned to those classified racially as white or Caucasian. In other words, *whiteness* refers to what it means to be racialized white both as a matter of self-definition and as a matter of collective culture. What does it mean to me to identify as a white person? What has this racial classification meant for white people as a group within U.S. society? This exploration of meanings assigned to white skin utilizes tools and analyses derived from the academic field of critical race theory. Critical race theory evolved out of opposition to dominant conceptions of race, racism, equality, and law in the post–civil rights period. What emerged out of this opposition was a pattern of shared values, a sense of community, and a commitment to racial justice that shaped an identifiable theoretical tradition.[1] More recently, some scholars in this field have begun to examine law as a site of the social construction of white racial identity.[2]

Like other studies in the genre of critical race theory, this chapter is concerned with making whiteness visible as a racial construction. In addition, it explores how constructions of whiteness shape and constitute mainstream U.S. culture and society; it also seeks to develop ethical responses to such constructions and practices. This chapter begins with an exploration of the representational (addressing the meanings of whiteness) and moves into concerns that are epistemological (how we know what we know) and ethical (what ought to be done).

Working within the tradition of critical race theory, this approach is rooted in a conception of social justice that is concerned primarily with the ways in which various emotional, spiritual, psychic, symbolic, and material resources are made scarce to some racial groups and more available to others. It is also shaped by the ideals of liberty, justice, freedom, and equal opportunity that have functioned ideologically and symbolically as cornerstones of U.S. democracy. I do not use these ideals in a traditional way but seek to make use of our conceptions of liberty, justice, freedom, and equal opportunity by asking: For whom, how, and under what conditions do these concepts function? Through such efforts the ideals become nuanced concepts that function more as problematizing tools than as absolute truths within any given context. Through a combination of these concerns and a commitment to these ideals, a foundation for what I call a critical white racial ethic is given shape.

Conceptualizing Race

Race in U.S. society functions as a category of human classification, identity, and differentiation. The conceptualization of the term *race,* the existence of racial categories, and the meanings assigned to each of them are the result of complex social achievements. Race does not signify biological differences among groups of people but rather reflects these achievements or social constructions.[3] So if race is merely a reflection of constructed social meanings, why perpetuate them by addressing race at all? Race must be seen as relevant until it truly is no longer relevant in the real world of social interaction, including intimate relationships and institutional rules and practices.[4]

Imagine a day when the vast majority of parents racialized white, considering a (white) daughter's romantic relationship with a person racialized black, are concerned only that the couple treat each other with respect and loving care. On that day, historical constructions of race may no longer have relevance. Similarly, when studies of criminal justice practices no longer expose that whites receive lesser punishments than nonwhites with similar criminal records, then historical constructions of race may no longer have relevance in the social world.[5] Likewise, when studies of housing patterns no longer reveal that white people receive more access to safe neighborhoods with quality schools,[6] and when research on lending practices no longer shows that they are more likely to receive a bank loan than a similarly situated person who is racialized black or Hispanic, historical constructions of race may no longer be relevant.[7] Indeed, when "family values," a "good" neighborhood, or a "good" school are no longer cultural code words for "white," and when institutional practices no longer presume, in essence, the superiority of whiteness, then race may be deemed no longer relevant, in terms of imposing privileges and disadvantages in the world within which real bodies live and interact.

Until our society has transformed racially in such a way that the above disparities and anxieties no longer persist, it is imperative that race be directly and consistently addressed. It must, however, be addressed so as to capture the racial locations of whiteness. Nationally, race and racism have traditionally been thought of as being about black people. Depending on the region and historical moment, it has been about persons of American Indian, Mexican, Japanese, Korean, Puerto Rican, Chinese, Filipino, or Vietnamese descent, among others. In this traditional conception, race is external to, and therefore not centrally about, white people.[8] In such a conception, race equals nonwhite people. This traditional view also tends to conceive of racism as individual acts and prejudices, to the exclusion of social structural factors. Sociologist Ruth Frankenberg captures the traditional conception of race in this statement, slightly altered here: "Whiteness is not about me—I am not a racist." [9]

The traditional conception of race that this statement reflects excludes white people from being conceptualized as racial. In this formulation, race is an issue only for those white people who are self-conscious white supremacists. The social erasure of whiteness as a racial location—the erasure from consciousness and from articulation—has been a rather recent phenomenon. Prior to the 1960s, the racial locations of whiteness, especially in the South, were often self-consciously held and expressly articulated within a white supremacist context. The white supremacy that prevailed in the United States before that time has been competently critiqued. However, the post-1960s phenomenon of whiteness as the unself-conscious, unspoken norm in U.S. law and society has not been adequately exposed for the racial inequality and social injustice it produces. So-called racial neutrality, in the arena of law and policy today, holds tremendous weight in that it works to legitimize the status quo. I argue that presumably race-neutral laws, policies, and practices in a post-1960s context are often premised upon a universal notion of whiteness. This way of understanding race is reified in the dominant cultural, economic, political, and legal practices in the United States.

For instance, when an academic syllabus has a section on race, it most often addresses persons who are not white. Similarly, mass media discussions of race focus on persons who are not white. Such a practice has two significant and interrelated functions. First, it reifies a conception of race as meaning nonwhite. Second, it assumes that race was not an issue when white scholars or groups were read or discussed.[10] As a result, whiteness as a racial position, constituting particular racialized cultures, is unseen and submerged, perpetuating the idea of whiteness as racial neutrality.

Another common approach within academia and the media is to talk about whiteness only in terms of self-conscious white supremacist groups or individuals. This perception of whiteness as a racial category only in its most extreme and obvious forms misses the everyday social and structural practices that presume certain meanings about whiteness. In other words, it continues to submerge whiteness as a racial and cultural identity of its own.

Several problematic attitudes underlie such a conception of race. These attitudes include: (1) that from a white person's perspective, race is about "them" (nonwhites); (2) that white racial identity has little meaning for the majority of white people in their sociopolitical and personal lives; (3) that being white fails to connote particular cultural groups; and (4) that whiteness is disconnected from the organization of social structures.

Racializing whiteness is important for numerous reasons. The reasons are social and political but fundamentally ethical. The ethic of which I speak is rooted in the ideals that "we the people" find in our major forming documents: liberty, justice, equality, and freedom.

When the meanings assigned to whiteness go unexamined, whiteness, as a racial perspective, is not seen and "race" connotes only nonwhite groups. As long as whiteness is not seen as racial, many, if not most, social and legal rules and practices will continue to be perceived and viewed as racially "point-of-view-less" or neutral. This is, in part, why whiteness has sustained privilege and power over a century after the abolition of slavery in the United States and decades after the civil rights movement. A significant sustaining force of many such rules and practices is the presumption of their neutrality. As whiteness becomes consciously racialized from a critical race perspective, such rules and practices often are revealed not as neutral, but rather as reflecting the perspectives of those racialized white. "Neutrality" is the product of the perceptual trick that keeps whiteness from being seen.

There is potentially much at stake in revealing that these social and legal rules and practices are not neutral. When they can no longer lay claim to neutrality, in other words, when the perspectives from which they were derived are brought to the surface, the social force granted to these rules and practices is checked. When their biases are exposed, the questions change, and authority is fought for on grounds other than claims to neutrality. Racializing whiteness has the potential to have a dramatic impact on U.S. society. It could reduce the presumption of racial neutrality and drastically alter discourse as well as claims to authority or legitimacy.

Naming the locations and meanings of whiteness subverts the idea of a predetermined racial destiny. A consideration of the constructions of whiteness disrupts and dismantles essentialist racial thinking. In other words, it exposes the meanings attached to light skin as being the product of social forces rather than biology/genetics. Whiteness takes shape as the institutionalization of mediated language and ideas.

Studies that explicitly racialize whiteness from a critical race perspective can offer a reorientation to issues of race. This reorientation is captured in Frankenberg's words, slightly altered here: "Race is not centrally about me—I am not white."[11] This reorientation to race, which racializes whiteness, does not allow white people to miss or ignore the racialness of their own experience. White racial cognizance enables white people to see how their whiteness shapes their identity, experiences, and opportunities. Furthermore, this reorientation to issues of race helps to shift a view of racism as individual acts and prejudices to include the less visible systems and institutions that confer power and privilege. Awareness of whiteness functions in this way simply by exposing the white mystique of legal and social rules and practices. White racial cognizance assigns everyone a place within the larger system of race relations and diminishes the authority of the rules and practices premised on claims to racial neutrality.

Meanings Attached to Whiteness

A useful way to begin to understand the meanings that attach to whiteness in contemporary U.S. culture and society is through a consideration of the statements below.[12] The statements presume the perspective of a person racialized white.

1. Mass media representations of God and godliness (such as Jesus, Mary, Moses, and God) are of persons who have my skin color.
2. I can be sure that curriculum materials in high school and college testify to the existence of my race.
3. I can be sure that the variety and diversity that characterize the people of my color will be represented in course material, workplace material, and the media.
4. When I date someone from a different racial group, I can be sure that this person is not perceived as declining in social status because of my race.
5. I can be pretty sure that a single image of my race does not predominate in course and workplace materials and in the media.
6. I am never asked to speak for all the people of my racial group.*
7. It is an option for me to learn the traditions and norms of other racial groups, but it is not culturally necessary that I do so.
8. If I do not learn the traditions and norms of other racial groups, I face little penalty or cost in terms of my success.
9. I can perform well in a challenging situation without being called a credit to my race.
10. When flagging down a cab and an available cab fails to stop, I can be fairly certain that I was not denied service because of my race.
11. I can be lazy, walk slowly across the street, dress in second-hand clothes, or not return phone calls without people attributing these choices to my race.
12. I can apply for a bank loan and be sure that my skin color will not work against the appearance of being a good credit risk.
13. I know that my presence in a neighborhood does not reduce the value of property in that neighborhood because of my race.
14. I can be pretty sure that studies of diseases and disorders and of their medical treatments include a significant percentage of people from my racial group.
15. If I am pulled over in my car by a police officer, I can be pretty sure that I have not been singled out because of my race.
16. If I am denied rental housing, I can be pretty sure that I was not denied because of my skin color.
17. I can select "nude"-colored pantyhose or "flesh"-colored Band-Aids and have them fairly closely match my skin color.*
18. I regularly see standards of intelligence, beauty, and sophistication defined by men and women with my skin color.
19. When I attend a black-tie dinner, I can be fairly certain that no one will presume that I am a waiter or a server.

These statements are helpful for a number of reasons. First, they highlight the fact that whiteness is the submerged norm. For instance, whiteness dictates the product shades "nude" and "flesh." These labels simply presume that racial position and, in so doing, function to normalize whiteness as the American standard. There is no need to state "white flesh"; simply "flesh" suffices. These statements also expose some of the privilege that is afforded the white racial classification. For instance, access to neighborhoods and schools is not generally restricted for white people because of race, while studies repeatedly reveal that nonwhite people, especially black and Hispanic people, are blocked from access through redlining practices within the real estate and rental industries.[13]

The general cultural assumption that whiteness reflects a superior racial status is evident in both legal and social practices today. The examples are numerous. In 1998 parents racialized white in Riverside, California, fought against naming a new school for Martin Luther King Jr., arguing that the school would be "branded" black and this would hurt the students' chances of getting into college.[14] Here some white parents exposed, and helped perpetuate, the assumption that whites are widely perceived as having greater intelligence than blacks. These familiar assumptions are apparent in courtrooms as well. For instance, a study by the administration of New York governor George Pataki concluded that "black and Hispanic people sentenced for minor felonies or misdemeanors in New York were treated more harshly than whites in similar circumstances."[15] Disparities in the treatment of differently racialized bodies in law is heightened when sex is a factor. Rape case studies continue to reveal that white complainants are more likely to be viewed as rape victims when the attackers are black. On the other side of the same coin, a nonwhite male accused of rape is far more likely than his white male counterpart to be seen by jurors and judges as a rapist.[16]

As a result of the benefits that white people share, albeit to varying degrees, it is possible, indeed necessary, to talk about whiteness as an overarching culture that exists concurrently with ethnic and/or religious subcultures among white people. These benefits based on whiteness vary, however, depending most significantly on one's gender, class, religion, and sexuality. I refer to these as "fiercely enforced social categories," because one's movement in and through U.S. culture and society—from bathrooms to sporting events to clothing to such legal and religious institutions as marriage—demands that one location within any given category be selected or imposed, even if only temporarily. These are the labels that U.S. society demands of anyone in order to move about, lay claim to resources, and take advantage of the benefits of the rule of law. Gender, race, class, sexuality, and religion are some examples of fiercely enforced social categories. Any given person holds a "package of identities" that reflects that person's locations (such as white, male, middle-class, gay, Baptist) within these fiercely enforced categories.

White people in the United States, to varying degrees, are afforded unearned advantages that go unnoticed, particularly by white people themselves, and that shape a cultural framework. The list of statements above reveals some such advantages. What is needed is a shift on the part of white people: an ethical stand in opposition to dominance and in the name of social justice. One necessary dimension of the tremendous work of dismantling a racial social hierarchy premised on domination is the development of a critical white racial ethic. The full development of such an ethic, with its conceptual layers and philosophical grounding, is a study unto itself and beyond the scope of this chapter. Below, however, I provide a sketch of what such an ethic entails and argue for what I believe to be the initial steps toward a critical white racial ethic.

Critical White Racial Ethics

Many ethicists have called for the rejection of a culture of dominance that prevails in the United States and across much of the planet. Critical white racial ethics makes a very specific, very practical contribution to the call to dismantle dominant social structures and replace them with a paradigm of plurality, equality, and mutuality. It addresses prevailing practices of dominance based on a racial hierarchy that presumes the superiority of whiteness.

This presumption, whether conscious or not, is what produces and reproduces privileges conferred upon those racialized white. Academics are more comfortable talking about "white privilege" in relation to racial practices that pervade U.S. culture and society. It is necessary, however, not to lose sight of the fact that white privilege is the outcome of a pervasive presumption of the racial superiority of whiteness. In other words, white superiority is the presumption and white privilege is the material consequence.

From an ethical perspective, it is critical to name the values that underlie behavioral and social structural patterns. It is not surprising that the right to dominance surfaces as the value that supports the belief in white racial superiority. Rosemary Radford Ruether argues that modern industrial western European cultures drew upon and inherited patriarchal, hierarchical, and militaristic models from past worlds and social movements.[17] In developing a broad historical understanding of this culture of dominance, Ruether points to the destructive results of its cumulative force in a contemporary global context and advocates for an "ecological culture and society."[18] According to Ruether, an ecological culture and society demands: (1) the fundamental reconstruction of communities such that people can comprehend and be responsible for the ecosystem, (2) the egalitarian distribution of the means of subsistence, and (3) the replacement of a culture of "competitive alienation and domination" with compassionate solidarity.[19] Critical white racial ethics is one necessary response to the culture of domination that those concerned with issues of social justice seek to transform. An egalitarian distribution of resources must include symbolic, spiritual, psychological resources, as well as material resources. If dominance-seeking is not a desired value in human relations, and if the people, institutions, and government of the United States aim to realize such ideals as freedom, liberty, and equality in law,[20] then the pervasive presumption of the superiority of whiteness, even if largely held unconsciously and enacted in seemingly innocuous daily activities and discourse, must be shattered.

Critical white racial ethics, a process of self-conscious racial re-formation, guided by a commitment to the dismantling of racial hierarchy, is in order. Critical white racial ethics is informed both by a sense of historical context and an understanding of our many "fiercely enforced social categories." One aim of critical white racial ethics is that "we the people" must continually renegotiate our own liberty and justice by making whiteness visible and shaping a racial re-formation that extends well beyond national borders.

Critical white racial ethics works toward a culture and society within which racial constructs—in their various gendered, classed, and sexualized packages—do not legitimately impose hardships and advantages depending on which categories one falls within. It accomplishes this through a process of (1) being continuously and vigilantly conscious of the perceptual framework through which bodies are viewed or interpreted; (2) consciously choosing the principal values that guide an individual or institution's behavior and experience, rejecting dominance and aiming toward plurality and mutuality; (3) discerning whether the assumptions and presuppositions through which bodies are viewed are consistent with those values; and (4) entering into a process of aligning desired values with perception and with behavior, action, and emotion.

"Fiercely enforced social categories" are best understood as conceptually interactive and contextually bound. In the process of seeing and identifying whiteness as a racial location, it is important not to reduce race to a social category that stands alone, but rather to understand race in dynamic interaction with gender, sexuality, and class, among other variables.

Ironically, what is necessary in order for race to become irrelevant in the social world, at least in terms of attaching advantages or disadvantages along racial lines, is for race to be acknowledged as relevant, even as we work to collapse racial constructs. Race must be acknowledged, not from an essentialist or biological/genetic viewpoint, but as having been assigned such tremendous significance, both historically and today, that it provides unearned advantages to those racialized white, albeit to varying degrees.

It is particularly important that the racialness of white experience be explicitly addressed. In other words, the ways in which being classified racially as white has shaped one's experiences, identity, opportunities, and barriers must be articulated and explored. In the process, the symbolic mechanisms (such as representations of God and nature) and institutions (such as law, banking, the real estate industry, and academia) that maintain white privilege need to be explored for the ways in which they function as such. Furthermore, they must be considered for the ways in which they contribute to a general obliviousness to how light skin shapes white experience. In other words, how do these mechanisms, institutions, and behaviors help hide the racial position of whiteness and promote the myth of racial point-of-view-less-ness? A critical white racial ethic demands that whiteness be explicitly named and addressed in everyday social interaction and policy considerations. As Frankenberg has argued, it is necessary to speak of whiteness, because to do so assigns everyone a place within the system of race relations in U.S. society.[21]

It is through the process of coming to see the social locations of whiteness that fears rooted in racial constructions can be confronted. It is through the confrontation of these deeply embedded racialized assumptions, about bodies and the fears that they generate, that the full humanity of a body in any race-gender-class-sexuality-package becomes a greater possibility. As whiteness becomes visible within a larger racial system, the presumption of racial neutrality that privileges a white racial stance is rendered suspect. The "color-blind" approach in law and policy reveals the failure of attempts to go around, rather than through, racial categories.[22] When racial point-of-view-less-ness is revealed instead as a white racial position, legitimacy must be argued for from an explicit racial stance, as opposed to racial neutrality, thus creating the potential to radically alter the terms of discourse. Removing the myth of racial neutrality dramatically alters the formula for legitimacy-building.

It is the entrenched presumption of white racial superiority, interacting with gender, sexuality, and class, that undermines attempts to individualize responses to racial privilege. Those who claim to approach each person on an individual basis and treat that person on the basis of how she or he behaves do not adequately address the facts of racial privilege and disadvantage. Reducing racial privilege and disadvantage to a personal framework, such that individual acts and prejudices provide the measure of the individual, erases the institutional and structural dimensions of race. Attempts to individualize "race" are ultimately inadequate because they are too simplistic. They fail to take into account our society's embedded symbolic systems and its everyday practices in such institutions as law, religion, government, education, banking, and real estate.

Recall the game of Monopoly. Assume one player, symbolized by the shoe, begins to play, going around the board, perhaps visiting jail, but certainly earning money and purchasing property. Now suppose that after the shoe has played for a significant amount of time the thimble and even later the wheelbarrow are permitted to play. The shoe, representative of propertied white men and to a limited extent their wives and offspring, would possess the vast majority of the board's property, while the thimble, representative of non-property-owning white men and to some extent their wives and offspring, would frequently have to pay the shoe for landing on its holdings, making movement risky, the accumulation of capital difficult, and purchasing power quite limited. The wheelbarrow, representing men and women who are understood as not white, would be in an even more difficult position, being susceptible to the properties of both the shoe and the thimble, due to the fact that the vast majority of the properties have already been purchased.

This analogy is limited because the game of Monopoly only partly reflects America's race, class, and gender hierarchies. Furthermore, the analogy fails to account for the fact that the land and natural resources that became compartmentalized into a capitalist structure were the sustenance of American Indians, mestizos, and Hawaiians.

Still, despite its limitations, the analogy is useful. In U.S. society one accumulates symbolic power along with economic power. Symbolic power includes the power to label certain groups of people, including one's self. Symbolic power includes the ability to represent persons and spiritual beings of great cultural importance as white. Nowhere is this more obvious than in current mass-media representations of God and significant religious figures—Moses, Mary, and Jesus—as racialized white.[23]

Exclusive access to the game permits the accumulation of both economic and symbolic advantages. These advantages are not erased when access to the game is broadened, but rather are made visible as the newer players struggle to survive and succeed in an exclusionary environment. It is naïve to assume that when legal barriers to citizenship are toppled through pronounced formal equality (that is, when access to the game is granted), deeply entrenched tenets about who counts as a real citizen, as fully human and as godlike, will likewise be overcome.

The point is that privileges accumulate and get entrenched in social structures such as law, religious institutions, schools, banks, neighborhoods, and the home and are enacted there on a daily basis. While the expression of racial hierarchy differs today from that at other moments during U.S. history, a familiar pattern emerges: Those racialized white are understood generally as more socially valuable and derive advantages as a result. Such constructions of whiteness continue to function on the contemporary Monopoly board by dividing bodies along racial lines.

Explicitly identifying and articulating whiteness opens many avenues. It allows for engagement in a process of seeing bodies, institutions, policies, experience, histories, behaviors, and symbols in new ways through a lens that captures white racial locations. The practice of identifying and articulating whiteness works to reshape one's perceptual framework. Coming to see whiteness is not a one-time event but a practice and a process that allows for more thorough identification and clearer articulation of white racial locations with practice and experience. A critical white racial ethics is a process that has many dimensions and many possibilities of expression. Such expressions are linked by a common goal: overcoming supremacist meanings of whiteness within U.S. culture and society.

Before something can be addressed, it must first be acknowledged, and before it can be acknowledged, it must be made visible. Critical white racial ethics calls first and foremost for a reconceptualization of race such that whiteness is explicitly racialized. Today European

American people, in particular, do not see the social dimensions of being racialized white and therefore cannot identify the meanings attached to whiteness. Communication patterns play a significant role in the submergence of whiteness. The absence of the word *white* from common cultural descriptive practices, such as in the media, schools, workplaces, and so forth, is neither trivial nor inconsequential. The absence is evidence of its function as unquestioned norm, as the taken-for-granted "way that it is." This broad-based cultural assumption works to separate whiteness from the world and its own conceptualization, granting it the status of the default for humankind.

Many people view the history of race-based disadvantage and privilege as irrelevant to today. This tendency reflects, in part, a historical memory that stops at specific junctures (that is, the abolition of slavery and the civil rights movement in regard to black Americans, the assignment of plots of land in relation to American Indians, and civil rights legislation generally) and presumes a fair playing field thereafter.[24] Such historical memories are inadequate because they dismiss decades of exclusionary practices within employment, housing, voting, banking, education, and so on.[25] The Monopoly analogy above reveals some of the failures of such narrow vision. The ways in which we talk about the past can contribute to the broad-based cultural denial of its relevance to our behaviors, practices, rules, and perceptions today. The language we use to describe the past shapes how we make sense of the past and, in turn, presents a framework for viewing the present.

Identifying and articulating whiteness is no small feat. There is tremendous resistance to such efforts, particularly from those racialized white. Even when one is committed to entering the process of critical white racial ethics, one must see through the constant smoke and mirrors of past messages, present representations, and modes of communicating, relating, and behaving that continually work to render whiteness invisible while constructing it as superior. The reformulation of perception and conceptions that capture the racial locations of whiteness in everyday behaviors and interactions is a monumental task. It requires personal honesty and exploration, historical knowledge, an understanding of institutions and social structures, and ultimately a commitment to personal and societal elimination of the disbursement of privilege and disadvantage on the basis of racial categorization, in concert with factors such as gender, class, and sexuality.

Resistance to seeing white privilege comes in many forms. For some people racialized white, resistance stems from a one-dimensional, race-based analysis of privilege and disadvantage that ignores other fiercely enforced social categories such as gender, sexuality, and class. Fiercely enforced social categories must be understood as interconnected and interactive, shaping quite different bundles of privilege and disadvantage for variously situated bodies within the category white. Some white people seek to distance themselves from the idea that whiteness confers benefits because they do not want to see themselves as members of an oppressor group. Conceptualizing race as always interconnected with gender, class, and sexuality results in a complex analysis that allows for anyone to be viewed as a package of both privileges and disadvantages. Such a framework avoids reductionist tendencies and better reflects our complicated world.

Some resist acknowledging white privilege by arguing that they did not ask for such privilege; some claim that they do not want it. Supremacist meanings of whiteness have been and continue to be imposed upon perceptions of both nonwhite and white bodies. It is important to note that whites engaged in intimate relationships with persons who are not racialized white often do not experience the meaning of whiteness as conferring privilege within their relational context. In relationships with non-whites, whites are not completely stripped of the many forms of white privilege expressed within the larger social context, such as access to housing or credit.

The fact is that white privilege is not the result of something that any given white person requests. The presumption of the superiority of whiteness is for most white people largely not self-conscious, but rather is the product of taken-for-granted ways of seeing and behaving that are learned and perpetuated through everyday behaviors. It is the cultural density of such learned patterns that translates into the social structural dimensions of white privilege. Regardless of whether a person racialized white asks for racial privileges or wants the presumption of racial superiority, supremacist meanings of whiteness are imposed whether welcome or not. Such privilege accrues from living in a racialized social context over which each individual has limited control.

Resistance also rises from the discomfort that often accompanies acknowledging white racial privilege. This discomfort may come from any variety of conscious and/or unconscious sources. Acknowledging white privilege necessitates, for those racialized white, a reassessment of one's success and accomplishment and ultimately of one's identity. This does not mean that those racialized white cannot claim success and accomplishment, but these claims and experiences are transformed somewhat by adding white privilege as a factor. For instance, having access to a neighborhood with quality schools does not necessarily translate into receiving a good education. One still has to do some work to pass classes and to receive good grades. Access to certain neighborhoods and schools is often the result of white privilege. Putting forth the effort to grasp what is offered is an accomplishment.

Some people interpret acknowledging white privilege as demanding that one operate out of guilt, sometimes called "white guilt." Feelings of guilt are a common and perhaps a natural response to the awareness of the historical and contemporary disbursement of privilege and disadvantage along racial lines. If not channeled into transformative action, however, feelings of guilt function in the same way resistance does. Guilt often creates the impulse to apologize rather than to work to change how one perceives and behaves. While guilt may be common, it is not a useful place to stay, because it is debilitating and, as such, only facilitates the perpetuation of the racial status quo. There is a huge difference between being ashamed of being white and taking responsibility for white privilege. A white racial ethic aims to dismantle racial hierarchy and therefore demands vigilant work on individual, interpersonal, and institutional levels. Guilt and shame, therefore, must be explored and utilized as tools for self-awareness and for learning about racial meanings and the social values they enforce. Both must ultimately be transformed, however, into critical awareness of whiteness and action that works to dismantle its supremacist meanings.

A national tradition of individualism contributes to the resistance of many. There is a tendency to want to reduce one's thinking about race exclusively to the behavior or prejudices of an individual. As discussed above, personalized conceptions of race and racial privilege and disadvantage fail to capture systems that confer privilege and power to those racialized white.

Lack of knowledge of U.S. history also generates resistance. Many believe that the abolition of slavery, and then the civil rights movement, brought an end to racial privilege for those racialized white. Such a claim could only be sustained by the erasure of the unjust social practices that have preserved a presumption of the superiority of whiteness and confer privileges to those racialized white. The means and the form of its preservation are different in contemporary contexts than in the past. However, the presumption remains embedded deep within social structures, as revealed, for example, by contemporary studies of punishment allocation within the criminal justice system, and of housing and lending practices.

Conclusion

Some people experience the proposition of a critical white racial ethics as posing a tremendous threat. The threat is derived from a perceived loss of power or social privilege if the racial status quo is altered. There is only a loss of power when power is held and claimed by means of domination. Those who benefit from the current racial structure, presuming as it does the superiority of whiteness, can only be understood as losing power as measured by a social paradigm based on dominance. While such a paradigm has prevailed in modern Western history, it no longer works, if it ever has.[26] Such a paradigm threatens the survival of planet Earth and blocks the realization of freedom, liberty, and justice. These ideals have no static definition but take shape through a highly contextual process of balancing competing perceptions of reality and a variety of interests and viewpoints. The paradigm of dominance can no longer pretend to reflect or shape human dignity.[27]

Critical white racial ethics can only mean loss within a paradigm of dominance for those who conceive of power as control over others. So conceived, power is necessarily a limited commodity. Those who perceive of critical white racial ethics as effecting tremendous loss, especially for those racialized white, fail to recognize that there is no greater drain on human energy than fear. Holding and sustaining supremacist meanings of whiteness is ultimately premised upon fear. There is power to be gained by freeing one's self from such fear.

Critical white racial ethics utilizes perceptual frameworks as a tool for evaluating individual beliefs and behavior as well as institutional practices, policies, and rules. Identifying perceptual frameworks allows the principal operating values to be revealed. Critical white racial ethics works to keep assumptions and presuppositions about variously racialized, sexualized, gendered, and classed bodies at the forefront of consciousness, and to reveal the guiding values of a person or institution. It does not necessarily demand that the individual or institution will reject dominance, but it helps make values a conscious choice rather than a taken-for-granted practice.

This ethic presents a challenge to fundamental values within U.S. law and society. Most significantly it challenges the value of dominance, specifically dominance premised on white racial superiority. Critical white racial ethics may begin with racial identification and awareness, but it does not stop here. Racial categorization must be explored in combination with gender, class, sexuality, and other significant factors that are more or less enforced depending upon context. When one grasps the interplay of these social categories, persons are understood as holding various packages of privileges and disadvantages within any given context.[28] White racial ethics fosters an awareness of one's own package of privilege and disadvantage and those packages held by variously situated others.

A critical white racial ethics explicitly names the racial locations of whiteness and identifies values to bring about a perceptual shift that allows for bodies to be seen with less distortion due to social hierarchy. The values of interdependence, equality, and mutuality are the foundation of critical white racial ethics. These values take shape in any given context through a balancing process of perceptions, interests, histories, and viewpoints. Ultimately, the success of critical white racial ethics will be its own demise, the abolition of the supremacist meanings of whiteness.

Notes

1. Borrowing from and critiquing intellectual traditions including liberalism, Marxism, the law and society movement, critical legal studies, feminism, poststructuralism/postmodernism, and neopragmatism, these theorists examine the process of making or naming reality and the relationship of knowledge and power to a liberal-capitalist ideology and the racial status quo. These scholars write from their own context within academia, thus inviting critique of their positions and perspectives vis-à-vis movements within marginalized communities. Mari J. Matsuda, Charles R. Lawrence III, Richard Delgado, Kimberlé Williams Crenshaw, eds., *Words That Wound: Critical Race Theory, Assaultive Speech, and the First Amendment* (Boulder, Colo.: Westview, 1993), 3–10. Numerous critical race scholars in various disciplines have discussed race and racism in the arena of law. Texts concerned with race and the U.S. legal system are numerous and include Richard Delgado, *The Coming Race War? And Other Apocalyptic Tales of America after Affirmative Action and Welfare* (New York: New York University Press, 1997); Derrick Bell, *And We Are Not Saved* (New York: Basic Books, 1987); A. Leon Higginbotham, *Shades of Freedom: Racial Politics and Presumptions of the American Legal Process* (New York: Oxford University Press, 1997); Matsuda et al., *Words That Wound*; and Patricia Williams, *The Alchemy of Race and Rights: The Diary of a Law Professor* (Cambridge, Mass.: Harvard University Press, 1991).

2. The link between whiteness and citizenship rights and privileges has been firmly entrenched since the establishment of the United States. For instance, in Cheryl Harris's study of property law and race, Harris argues that people classified as white in the United States share a range of access to

resources and opportunities that are restricted or denied to certain racial "others," but have become the "vested interest" of white people. Another exploration of the advantages afforded white people in U.S. law is Haney Lopez's study of racial prerequisite cases. Lopez begins in 1790, when the U.S. Congress limited those who could become naturalized citizens to "white persons." The racial requirement of whiteness remained a part of U.S. naturalization law until 1952. Lopez traces the rationales relied upon by federal courts to justify who was white and who was not, revealing some disturbing and fascinating contours of the social architecture of race and race consciousness in the United States. State law, like federal law, reflects the constructed character of racial categories. Throughout much of U.S. history, state laws codified different definitions of black, Indian, mulatto, mongrel, and so on. Laws rarely set out explicit definitions of white. Rather, those considered white by federal or state law varied, depending on who was categorized as not white. That a person could be white one moment and then, upon crossing a state line, not white the next— or could be not white in one federal court and white in another—attests to the social construction of race. Cheryl I. Harris, "Whiteness as Property," *Harvard Law Review* 106 (1993): 1707; Barbara Flagg, "'Was Blind, but Now I See': White Race Consciousness and the Requirement of Discriminatory Intent," *Michigan Law Review* 91 (1994): 953; Ian F. Haney Lopez, *White by Law: The Legal Construction of Race* (New York: New York University, 1996); Martha Mahoney, "Whiteness and Women," *Yale Journal of Law & Feminism* 5 (1993): 217.

3. There exists no sound scientific evidence to support the claim that racial markers such as "white" and "black" reflect a genetic/biological race. See Nancy Stephen, *The Idea of Race in Science: Great Britain, 1800–1960* (London: Macmillan, 1982); Stephen Jay Gould, *The Mismeasure of Man* (New York: Norton, 1981); Martin Barker, "Biology and the New Racism," in *Anatomy of Racism,* ed. David Goldberg (Minneapolis: University of Minnesota Press, 1990); and Ethel Tobach and Betty Rosoff, eds., *Challenging Racism and Sexism: Alternatives to Genetic Explanations* (New York: Feminist Press, 1994). Richard Herrnstein and Charles Murray, in their work *The Bell Curve* (New York: Free Press, 1994), suggest that racial inequality is a hereditary condition or biologically/genetically based. For a thorough analysis that invalidates the data relied upon by Herrnstein and Murray, see Claud Fischer et al., *Inequality by Design* (Princeton: Princeton University Press, 1996).

4. It has been argued that the circulation of the categories race, sex, class, and gender in critical discourse might actually work to inhibit the "interrogation of differences as well as the possibilities of the political self." Robyn Wiegman, "Introduction: Mapping the Lesbian Postmodern," in *The Lesbian Postmodern,* ed. Laura Doan (New York: Columbia University Press, 1994). These categories must provide an analytical framework, even if incomplete, until such categories no longer so dramatically shape one's experiences in society. Confronting these categories and critiquing their enforcement are crucial to the collapse or reconfiguration of the meanings of these categories.

5. Clifford J. Levy, "Minority Defendants Handed Harsher Sentences, Study Says," *New York Times,* 10 April 1996; Samuel Walker, Cassia Spohn, and Miriam DeLone, *The Color of Justice: Race, Ethnicity, and Crime in America* (Belmont, California: Wadsworth, 1996); Susan Brownmiller, *Against Our Will: Men, Women, and Rape* (New York: Bantam, 1975); Susan Estrich, *Real Rape: How the Legal System Victimizes Women Who Say No* (Cambridge: Harvard University Press, 1987), esp. 6, 32–38, 107 n.2, 110 n.9, 115; Jennifer Wriggins, "Rape, Racism, and the Law" in *Rape and Society,* ed. Patricia Searles and Ronald J. Berger (Boulder, Colo.: Westview, 1995).

6. Mike Leachman, Phil Nyden, Bill Peterman, and Darnell Coleman, "Black, White, and Shades of Brown: Fair Housing and Economic Opportunity in the Chicago Region" (Chicago: Leadership Council for Metropolitan Open Communities, 1998).

7. Kathryn Tholin, ed., "Tools for Promoting Community Reinvestment: Using Data to Analyze Lending Patterns in Your Community" (Chicago: Woodstock Institute, 1996).

8. See Ruth Frankenberg, *White Women Race Matters: The Social Construction of Whiteness* (Minneapolis: University of Minnesota Press, 1993), 136–42 and 6–7. Frankenberg's study of thirty women reveals that for most of the white women the term *race* signified being non-white.

9. Ibid., 6.

10. This pattern plays out concerning gender as well. Only during that section of a course in which women are read and discussed is gender explicitly made an issue. Again, such practices present gender as if it were not an issue when reading and studying the works of men. Through such practices "gender" becomes a signifier of women.

11. Frankenberg, *White Women Race Matters,* 6. I have altered Frankenberg's statement by adding the word *centrally.*

12. The asterisked statements are derived from Peggy McIntosh, "White Privilege: Unpacking the Invisible Knapsack," *Peace and Freedom* (July/August 1989). The rest are derived from my work with Pamela Bradwein, Associate Professor of Sociology and Political Economy, School of Social Sciences, University of Texas at Dallas, as we worked to articulate and teach the meanings of whiteness in a contemporary context.

13. See Leachman et al., "Black, White, and Shades of Brown," and Tholin, "Tools for Promoting Community Reinvestment."

14. "Some Parents Fear Stigma of King High," *Chicago Tribune,* 5 January 1998.

15. Levy, "Minority Defendants Handed Harsher Sentences." See also Walker et. al, *The Color of Justice.*

16. See, for example, Brownmiller, *Against Our Will,* 237; Estrich, *Real Rape,* 6, 32–38, 107 n.2, 110 n.9, 115; and Wriggins, "Rape, Racism, and the Law."

17. Ruether explores patterns of domination and the cultural resources deployed to justify them, from the Mesopotamian, Hebrew, and Greeks

worlds. She considers how these patterns were reshaped and articulated through the synthesis of asceticism, apocalypticism, and Christianity during the Middle Ages and then by Calvinism, the scientific revolution, colonialism, and industrialization, and how they constitute our present global context. Rosemary Radford Ruether, *Gaia and God: An Ecofeminist Theology of Earth Healing* (San Francisco: Harper, 1992), 173–99.

18. Ruether details the destruction generated by a culture of domination, including dramatic population increase, decreases in food supplies, climate alterations, soil erosion and drought, expanding gaps between concentrations of wealth and of poverty, expanding militaries, and toxic waste, among other effects. Ruether, *Gaia and God*, 85–111.

19. Ruether argues that two lines of Christian tradition (the covenantal and the sacramental) are reclaimable and instructive for the development of the ecological culture and society she claims is necessary. *Gaia & God*, 201, 205–53.

20. I do not presume a transcendent meaning of "liberty," "justice," "freedom," or "equality in law." The realization of any one of these concepts requires a highly contextual balancing of histories, perceptions, interests, and commitments.

21. Frankenberg, *White Women Race Matters*, 132–34, 242–43.

22. For a critique of "color blindness" or the application of "race-neutrality" in law, see Patricia Williams, "Metro Broadcasting, Inc. v. FCC: Regrouping in Singular Times," *Harvard Law Review* 104 (1990), 525.

23. Charlton Heston played Moses in the film by the same name, and Willem Dafoe acted the part of Jesus in *The Last Temptation of Christ*, while Mary was played by Barbara Hershey. George Burns performed the role of God in the film *Oh, God!*

24. It also reflects a lack of knowledge about U.S. racial history, such as employment patterns, worker-organized exclusion and inclusion efforts, government policies and practices, real-estate and lending practices, and the workings of criminal justice system that have continued to perpetuate white racial privilege.

25. For historical accounts of exclusion from employment and other resources, see Teresa Amott and Julie Matthaie, *Race, Gender and Work: A Multicultural Economic History of Women in the U.S.* (Boston: South End Press, 1991); Jacqueline Jones, *Labor of Love, Labor of Sorrow: Black Women, Work and the Family* (New York: Vintage, 1985); and Manning Marable, *How Capitalism Underdeveloped Black America* (Boston: South End Press, 1983).

26. Ruether, in *Gaia and God*, discusses patterns of domination and the means of their justification within ancient Mesopotamian, Hebrew, and Greek societies. Ruether explores how these patterns were reshaped during the Middle Ages and then again by Calvinism, the scientific revolution, colonialism, and industrialization. She argues that the patterns of domination are the result of cultural practices "whereby male elites in power deny their inter-

dependency with women, exploiting human labor and the biotic community around them. They seek to exalt their own power infinitely by draining the lives of these other humans and nonhuman resources of life on which they depend. They create cultures of deceit that justify this exploitation by negating the value of those they use, while denying their own dependence on them" (*Gaia and God*, 173–201, quote on 200).

27. See, for example, Ruether, *Gaia and God*, 85–111.

28. I derive the concept of a "package" as one's personal combination of privileges and disadvantages from Peggy McIntosh's similar metaphor, that of a knapsack, in "White Privilege: Unpacking the Invisible Knapsack," *Peace and Freedom* (July/August 1989).

2.
Climbing Jacob's Ladder
Alma Lillie Hubbard's Musical Career in New Orleans, 1900–1932

ROSALIND F. HINTON

▨▨▨

Alma Lillie Hubbard was born on February 16, 1895, to Miss Lizzie Willis in Crystal Springs, Mississippi. Lizzie Willis was twenty years old and unmarried. Deciding that she could not provide for Alma as a single mother, she wrapped the baby in a blanket, placed her in a wicker basket, carried her to the New Orleans home of her half-sister, Maggie Smith Howard, and left her on the doorstep. From this humble beginning, Alma Lillie Hubbard would carve out a career as a concert artist, creating a path that eventually led to New York City and the Broadway theater. By the age of thirty she had fashioned herself into a black middle-class professional and entertainment entrepreneur and eventually resided at 409 Edgecombe Avenue in Harlem's Sugar Hill district—an apartment building claimed by such American luminaries as Walter White, Thurgood Marshall, and notable musical talent Noble Sissle.[1]

Hubbard was never a self-made millionaire like black cosmetic entrepreneur Madame C. J. Walker or insurance mogul Lena Walker of Richmond, Virginia. But their stories are aberrations rather than norms. Hubbard's success is part of the more routine, though no less amazing, story of many African American female professionals in the 1920s and 1930s in that she negotiated an economic environment that allowed for modest opportunity and advancement but not for financial stability or independence. As part of the first generation to make it into the middle class, Hubbard had no inherited wealth and few resources to fall back on in times of trouble. Her hold on the middle class was always fragile. For her and for others, gender restrictions and Jim Crow policies constantly undermined their options. Highly valued positions in the dominant economy were often hard to find and even harder to keep. It therefore took more than individual effort for Hubbard to pull herself out of poverty.[2]

This chapter explores the resources that aided Hubbard in her rise to the middle class. Hubbard's success was not an accident or a stroke of good luck, but a fruit of a conscious strategy of uplift by the communities that nurtured her. Stephanie Shaw comments that African American communities "threw up highways" for their sons and daughters. This reality was certainly true for Hubbard. People who were illiterate, who would never enter the middle class, and who had few material resources of their own pooled what little they had in order to advance themselves and their children. Hubbard's communities gave her the space to explore her talent, the motivation to succeed, and the strategies that helped her transcend the circumscribed roles expected of African American women in the Jim Crow South.[3]

Four resources were critical to Hubbard's success. These were family, church, college, and travel. Hubbard's life offers unique insights into how these contexts became resources for middle-class standing. Family and church members pooled resources that created stability and allowed children room to explore their talents. A strong performance tradition at church and college imparted communal values that helped combine personal achievement with community advancement. Travel not only exposed the educational barriers black women encountered at home, it also offered opportunities that could be leveraged both personally and communally. Ultimately, Hubbard's use of these resources sheds light on that illusive and permeable category called the black middle class, so this chapter will conclude with a discussion of the black middle class.

The first resource in Hubbard's rise to the middle class was her family network. Hubbard's mother initiated the first strategy of advancement from within this network by getting her from Crystal Springs to New Orleans. Lizzie Willis was an orphan who had few options in rural Mississippi other than sharecropping and domestic work. She therefore took a calculated risk that her daughter would be better off in New Orleans. Maggie's husband, Leonard Howard, a deacon and trustee in his church, had all the signs of an ambitious man who could provide a stable home life and an education for a young girl. In fact, Leonard eventually became an accountant and Maggie, spared the dirty work of a domestic, oversaw Hubbard's moral and musical education at home and through her church.

As an adult, Hubbard often felt an acute sense of abandonment traceable to her mother's actions, but her mother's decision reflected a complex response to the difficulties of being young, single, penniless, and black in the Jim Crow South. As a matter of fact, the hostile rural environment caused many African American mothers and fathers to make the difficult decision to part with their children and send them to relatives and friends in the city. In this way, parents tapped their extended-family networks to get their children to places with more resources.

Willis, with only a few cousins, one half-brother, and one half-sister, created an enduring network that enriched many lives even into succeeding generations. For instance, after Lizzie Willis eventually married and moved from domestic work to a stable position running a boarding house for a Jewish landlord, she adopted a boy whose mother could not care for him. Hubbard, who was twenty at the time, treated the adopted boy as a brother and sent money and clothing to him throughout his life. In another instance, Alma Lillie's guardian, Maggie Howard, also took care of a girl, Lorenzo Jones, until the child's mother had a more stable home environment. Jones became Hubbard's lifelong confidant and friend. The ties between the various groups remained strong throughout Hubbard's life. After her step-brother married and refused to educate his own daughters, Hubbard sent her nieces books and instilled in them the desire for a good education. Hubbard also sent her mother money in times of trouble. Hubbard visited Jones on her way to Crystal Springs every other year, corresponded regularly with her mother, and was at her mother's deathbed.[4]

Historian Jacqueline Jones, in her study of black female laborers, *Labor of Love, Labor of Sorrow,* commented that whites looked down on this reciprocal care and thought that it encouraged laziness in African Americans. But Hubbard's life shows that an ethic of care and mutual responsibility was deeply woven into the fabric of African American communal life. The reciprocal give-and-take manifested in this ethic enriched family support systems and provided an intricate safety net that allowed members to move beyond mere necessities and play with life's possibilities. Family members had many honorary aunts, uncles, and cousins to rely on in times of trouble. If economic setbacks occurred, economic devastation did not necessarily follow, because family members offered multiple avenues around problems. Through these networks, families supported each other as they worked toward a better future for themselves and their children.[5]

Living in New Orleans exposed Alma Lillie to the cosmopolitan atmosphere of the black urban church, another resource in her rise to the middle class. Maggie and Leonard Howard attended Wesley Methodist Episcopal Church, known as Mother Wesley. Wesley was primarily a church of laborers, domestic servants, and laundresses. Many of its members were, like Alma Lillie, born in a rural setting. These church members, offered little opportunity in the general economy, poured their considerable energies into influencing what was often their only collectively owned territory, the black church. In some cases church offered a substitute for, and in other cases an extension of, one's power and influence in family life, a place where opinions mattered and contributions were noticed.

Individual members influenced church affairs through the collective power of the church's smaller social units, its classes. Wesley's six hundred members were divided into seventeen classes with an average size of thirty members. Classes met faithfully at eight o'clock on Tuesday nights. As a child, Alma Lillie Hubbard and her guardian, Maggie Howard, belonged to class number fourteen. It is interesting to note that class attendance was dropped as a requirement in white Southern Methodist churches by 1866. African Americans, however, kept the class format for many reasons. For one thing, regular attendance and individual accountability could be monitored in the more intimate class setting. It also diluted the power of the minister and ensured a democratic process in which every voice mattered. In African American churches, classes offered the primary vehicle for both individual development and communal responsibility.

These intergenerational classes were the primary units of socialization into the life of the church. They nurtured leadership as class members developed their own intimate weekly worship rituals, planned programs, raised money, prayed together, and shared in the problems and the celebrations of the larger community. As children matured, they took on more and more responsibility for the class functions and became more comfortable in leadership roles.[6]

Hubbard's earliest musical training must have been around the weekly concerts and friendly competitions staged by classes, benevolent associations, choirs, and church musical soloists. It was also here that Hubbard was first introduced to the collective power of women. While men dominated the list of church officials as class leaders, deacons, stewards, and trustees, women absolutely dominated the performance roster. In a historically aural culture wherein literacy had been illegal for three hundred years, and limited access to education was only a thirty-year tradition, the power women wielded through performance should not be underestimated. Music and performance was the method and the means of passing on the traditions and aesthetic values of African American culture.

Through performance, women socialized children into the collective values, traditions, and history of their African American slave heritage through a pedagogy that was also part of the African American tradition of musical performance. While this training did not ensure the success of every child, success did not come without it. Children were instilled with a communal ethic that countered the "each man for himself" strategy and the lack of purposeful direction that church people characterized as "street life."

The Ladies Prayer Meeting minutes at Wesley demonstrate how women claimed authority as leaders, shaped the cultural life of the community, and at the same time took responsibility for the financial life of the church. Announcements created a sense of anticipation, if not sheer joy, around the upcoming events. One announcement read, "There will be a grand entertainment at the residence of Sister Ophelia Talbert under the auspices of the Steward's Sisters." A concert by church soloist and Sunday school director Nellie Williams raised $4.75 for the Wesley trustees. The women of the church sponsored a trolley ride excursion that was so successful the trustees had their own trolley ride fund-raiser a few months later. In 1905, the sisters of the church instituted Silver Dollar Day. The minutes read, "The sisters will on the second Sunday in July have this day known as Silver Dollar Day and they [will] all pay one dollar each." This amount reflects an enormous commitment of resources, because it was nearly half of a week's salary for a female domestic. A week did not go by without inter-class competitions, benevolent association anniversaries, and class rallies or church festivals.[7]

Each performance was critical to the material stability of the church community. The week's financial coffers often began with not much over a dollar on the books. The total weekly receipts often amounted to no more than forty-five dollars. Out of this sum, the pastor, the recording steward, sexton, and the organist had to be paid. The number of groups and individuals "in need of temporal relief" also grew weekly. Wesley made monthly contributions to New Orleans University, the Freedman's Aid Society of the Methodist Church, and the local home for the aged. The church met requests for contributions from other religious denominations and paid Sunday school fees for children without means. There were also the utility bills and notes that came due on church property. None of these obligations could have been met without women-led performances.

It flows from the nature and number of performances, and the transparency of the intergenerational class organization, that children shared in a communal ethic of responsibility and social uplift. Children gained musical skills and explored their talents in a communal setting where each performance was vital to the survival and stability of the church community. This is quite different from learning an instrument at home and performing in rarefied semi-annual recitals that are ornamental rather than vital to community life. The fact that their talents were always expressed through these community performances also reinforced the three-way dialectic between God, individuals, and the community. Children learned the purpose of developing their own gifts and talents. Talents were gifts from God that became gifts to the larger community.

Performances also socialized children into an alternative historical memory. For instance, Hubbard's first written review came when she was ten years old, in the 1905 edition of the *Southwestern Christian Advocate,* the Methodist regional newspaper. The event was a Lincoln's Day ceremony. Pageants such as the Lincoln's Day ceremonies put black students at the center of their own history. They were rituals of memory and public recollections of oral traditions. The stories, even when they were embellished, created a counter-memory that propelled church members into a constructive future. Wesley members recalled the interracial founding of the church, when both black and white members overcame illiteracy by reading side by side. They retold the story of how slave ancestors built the church by lamplight in the middle of the night, and how the women of the church carried bricks to the church site in their skirt pockets. Another story passed down through the membership was that the Emancipation Proclamation was first read aloud in the city of New Orleans from the Wesley pulpit. Wesley members told and retold many stories that carried a moral imperative of excellence and equality for its members. These stories taught children of Alma Lillie's era that they could overcome their own difficulties as others had before them. They also instilled in children the idea that full equality under the law was not a privilege granted by whites, but a birthright earned by their ancestors.[8]

As a child, Hubbard also learned to embrace a wide array of traditions and musical tastes even as she learned that some music was not appropriate for church or for ladies. Although church members separated themselves from street life, material culture has a way of breaking through rigid ideological boundaries. The underlying rhythms and sounds of African American music moved between church and secular settings as vocal quartets, spasm bands pieced together with homemade instruments, and brass brands crossed between both worlds. At times it seems that the only difference between the music performed on the street and at church was the intention of dedication to the Lord. Church members embraced popular songs of the day in their vaudeville acts, Japanese teas, and lawn parties. They preserved the "stirring exhortations and the singing of our hymns and the weird songs so familiar in the olden times." Wesley members also embraced the European stylings developed by the Jubilee choirs situated in historically black colleges. In fact, as early as 1877, Wesley Church sponsored the New Orleans Jubilee Club, a group made up of Wesley Church members and New Orleans University students, in "A Grand Concert, Dialogue and Tableaux Exhibition."[9]

In many ways Hubbard's church life prepared her for the musical stage. The numerous events on Wesley's calendar give us a hint as to how black performers acquired a natural ease. They simply performed so often that they were comfortable onstage in front of crowds. Performance helped children embody a sense of their own individual talents. Musical competitions in church, like the "cutting contests" between jazz musicians on the streets of New Orleans, pushed children to ever-higher levels of personal achievement. Church provided Hubbard with a wide musical vocabulary, performance ease, and historical self-understanding that focused her ambition and musical talents. Like many musicians, she was able to move to more popular musical venues when the doors to classical performance were shut to African Americans.

Church performances also instituted a set of bodily practices associated with strategies of respectability. Speaking, singing, and acting helped children develop poise under pressure and other life skills necessary for survival in the hostile world of Jim Crow. These bodily practices negated the community's forced relationship with servitude both in the slave past and in the prevailing politics of Jim Crow. Respectability also included responsibility. Because resources were so scarce, individual and communal survival were deeply intertwined. Therefore early socialization patterns encouraged children to develop and use their talents for the betterment of the community. But more than material concerns were on the minds of church members. Creative talent was deeply appreciated in the community. Respectability can imply exclusivity, but Hubbard's community was surprisingly open to the world, eagerly absorbing the surrounding culture. Church members not only embraced but mastered a variety of styles and expressions and made them their own. In this way performance cultivated a sense of self-righteous belonging and inclusion in the mainstream of American life.

Other types of public performance at Wesley sculpted respectability in a more exclusive manner. Trials that monitored members' sexual misconduct were part of the routine of church life. The fact that Hubbard's guardian, Leonard Howard, was recording secretary for these trials put Hubbard close to these events. Hubbard's adult Victorian sensibilities concerning moral rectitude and appropriate public behavior were certainly influenced by these trials. For instance, Sister Francis West was accused of "living in adultery [and] giving birth to a child with no lawful husband." At her trial, Ms. West stated that she was living with the father of the child and that they were not married. She also said, "the child was born in April and is now dead." The committee found her guilty as charged and she was expelled. In another case, Sister Georgiana Pines pleaded guilty to adultery and asked for the prayers of the committee but was pronounced expelled by the pastor.[10]

Church members used trials as a way of distinguishing themselves from "street women." The area that the church occupied was in a section of Storyville, New Orleans's legal prostitution district, which was not policed. The poorest of the black prostitutes lived and worked in close proximity to the church. All black women walking to and from work were subject to harassment or worse and were considered fair game for exploitation. Therefore anything that resembled occasional prostitution, such as out-of-wedlock arrangements, was not considered a viable survival strategy in an environment where women defined their own virtue on a daily basis against the backdrop of explicit prostitution.

These trials also show how communal needs often supplanted individual interests, especially for women. If anything, they taught a young girl like Hubbard the importance of reputation and public image. Hubbard learned the lessons of these trials and, as an adult, she carefully crafted her image as a well-educated, elegant, and respectable married woman, despite difficulties in her marriage. These trials also showed that stable family situations and marriage were very important to the African American community: an understanding that Hubbard's mother already conveyed through the paradox of her own unwed status and her search for a stable family situation in New Orleans for her daughter.

Family and church provided a moral and musical foundation for Hubbard that was refined in the next important context on the way to adulthood, college. College quite literally propelled Hubbard into a black educational aristocracy. A Department of the Interior survey published in 1917 noted that of the 161,969 elementary school-age children in Louisiana, only 38 percent, or 60,650, attended school. Only 443 black students continued beyond elementary school. This fact meant that Alma Lillie was not simply in the elite group that W.E.B. Du Bois referred to as the "talented tenth," but among the top 2.7 percent of African Americans of the era. This aristocracy was created as much from structured barriers to resources as from African American class consciousness. But by the same token, African Americans were not afraid of climbing into the middle of American life and in fact asserted their right to do so.[11]

Hubbard attended Straight College, a freedman university chartered after the Civil War by the Congregational Church and the American Missionary Association. It is ironic that so few could go to college, because the colleges countered the exclusive race-based logic of the white majority with an ideology of radical democratic freedom. In fact, the freedman universities may very well have been one of the few institutions in America that carried forth a vision of inclusion and equal opportunity after the Civil War. An early history of the American Missionary Association expressed this sentiment. "However great has been the contribution made by the Association to education, it is far less significant than the witness it has borne everywhere to the equality of men at whatever race or color."[12]

The collective consciousness that was instilled in children at church became a responsibility for "social uplift" in college. "Social uplift" was a practical political strategy for African American inclusion. It balanced the demand for full inclusion against the reality of its denial. Although the policy did not do away with race or class prejudice, it provided a framework for addressing the exclusionary practices of the white majority. Teaching was an important way of extending the educational opportunities of the few to the vast majority. A classmate of Alma Lillie's at Straight, Lucille Hutton, explained, "We had to pass on what we got to others and the best way to do that was teaching."[13]

Certainly the importance of higher education in the direct economic uplift of black women cannot be underestimated. Hubbard finished the teacher training program at Straight in 1915. Her $400-a-year salary as an elementary school teacher put her among the elite of both white and black women in terms of wages. Hubbard's school salary was better than that of most white women in the clothing industry, who made nine dollars a week only if they were "excellent at piece work." Her teaching salary was double that of white female department store clerks or factory workers, who made around five dollars a week working twelve-hour days. And of course it greatly outstripped the weekly wage of two to five dollars for domestic work.[14]

But college gave Hubbard resources beyond vocational training. Besides her education courses, she took voice, advanced piano, ear training, and harmony at Straight College. She also studied with two graduates of Fisk University who organized the first Jubilee clubs at Straight College. Jubilee choirs embraced a diverse vocal repertoire that included Italian opera and popular song, but they were most closely associated with the anthemic, concertized spiritual. Black composers and performers of the concertized spiritual were, for the most part, college-educated, classically trained, and experts in Western musical forms. They also understood the harmonic and rhythmic structures in African-derived music such as spirituals, hymns, work songs, and jazz. Hubbard's training as a Jubilee singer—a valuable commodity—placed her in this prestigious group of musicians and opened doors for commercial success across the color line. As a performer, a Jubilee singer coming out of college also carried a social legitimacy that blues and vaudeville musicians did not have. As a Jubilee singer, Hubbard embodied the moral character, good taste, and educational aspirations of the African American community. Command of the genre gave her spokesperson status both inside and outside of the community.[15]

Hubbard's musical training at Straight allowed her to push her career in multiple directions. Along with teaching, she lost no time in forming the New Orleans Ladies Quartette with three of her Straight College classmates. In the summers, when Hubbard was not teaching in the public schools, she toured with the quartet in the New England states. While her performance venues for these trips are unknown, it is likely they were black and white Congregational and Methodist churches. Hubbard also secured a job as organist and choir director at her own church, Mother Wesley.

The three positions together—teacher, performer, and church choir director—gave Hubbard financial independence, legitimacy as a performer, and a musical platform, housed in her church, from which to launch her own career and influence the musical life of the city. These combined roles gave her the status and financial security that no single position could offer. She was not just a schoolteacher but also an accomplished performer. She was not a common performer, but an educator and the only female music director of a major black church in the city. Hubbard had come full circle in her church. At the age of twenty she was now responsible for developing the resources that were so vital in her own rise to the middle class.

In many ways, women like Hubbard held within themselves the multiple options of an entire family network. Difficulties along one path allowed them to fall back on—or actually fall forward into—other career networks. For instance, Hubbard married just three short years after she began teaching. Since married women could not teach in the public schools, she lost her job. The loss of her primary source of income was not devastating, however. Hubbard activated friendship networks established at Straight, and she and her husband tested their fortunes in Detroit where a member of Hubbard's quartet lived. Thus, in June of 1920, the women of Wesley presented Hubbard with "a handsome amount" of money that deferred the cost of her forced adventure.[16]

Certainly Hubbard recognized that travel out of the South was almost a necessity for those who wanted to advance within the South. For instance, Hubbard received the best formal education that an African American women could get in the South, but it was still inadequate. Straight College's academic dean, Ludwig Larson, said of Hubbard's college experience, "It may be well to state that the Normal Department, so-called, was really a high school course with a little pedagogy in the twelfth grade." While young white women in the South had the same educational background, most had more local opportunities to better their situation. African American women, on the other hand, were barred from white colleges and discouraged from going beyond teacher's or nurse's training in black colleges. These conditions made getting a four-year degree, much less a master's degree, an arduous task that required travel to other parts of the country. Black women who wanted advanced degrees or special training took unpaid sabbaticals and studied in the summers in more racially receptive cities such as Philadelphia, Chicago, Detroit, and Los Angeles.[17]

Travel, first to Detroit and later to Chicago, propelled Hubbard to ever-higher levels of musical achievement and placed her amid many experienced and emerging African American artists, entrepreneurs, and entertainers. In truth, the convergence of African Americans studying in northern cities in the summers created an African American version of the east-coast summer Chautauqua. New music was created and older traditions were passed along during these summer exchanges. African American musicians studied in conservatories, cut records, and networked with composers and artists from around the country. For instance, while in Detroit between 1920 and 1923, Hubbard performed with Albert Greenlaw, an original Fisk Jubilee singer who was known as the "Canadian Basso Cantante." She also worked with Pauline J. Lee, a contralto and pianist who founded a school for

African American musicians, the National Conservatory of Music in Chicago. Hubbard parlayed these prestigious contacts into a better paying job in New Orleans. By 1924 she was music director at New Orleans University, a Methodist-affiliated freedman university started by members of Wesley after the Civil War. She also reclaimed her position as musical director at Wesley.[18]

In 1926, Hubbard initiated a second round of study trips, this time to Chicago. During these summers Hubbard worked toward a four-year degree in music. She also gained expertise as a concert artist and expanded her reputation as an expert performer and teacher of concertized spirituals. She studied at the American Conservatory of Music and recorded spirituals with both Gennett and Paramount Recording Studios. Thus, in 1929 she parlayed her expertise in the genre into the white world when she took a job as Marc Connelly's New Orleans music consultant for his Pulitzer Prize–winning Broadway production *The Green Pastures*. Hubbard introduced Connelly to the black churches in New Orleans and picked the spirituals that would become the musical book for his award-winning play. A 1930 newspaper article reveals how much ground a woman could cover in one summer. The *Louisiana Weekly* welcomed Hubbard home from "summer vacation," commenting that she performed at the Royal Theatre in Chicago, recorded for Paramount, and was a special guest in New York at a performance of *The Green Pastures*.[19]

But Hubbard's personal success also carried a community obligation. Formal concerts in New Orleans were a way the entire community marked the progress of its children and, by extension, its own stature. Photos of returning artists, many of whom were women, were often featured on the front page of the *Louisiana Weekly* newspaper. That newspaper's reviews show that Hubbard consistently performed to capacity crowds. A 1926 review stated, "Large audience welcomes popular soprano." A 1927 review reported that "a colorful audience taxed the capacity of the auditorium of New Orleans University." A 1929 review stated that a "capacity crowd greeted her." But nothing topped the hyperbole preceding her 1926 concert, her first major performance after her extended stay in Detroit. The newspaper proclaimed, "All society should be out in full numbers to pay homage to our own Queen of Song."[20]

Because African Americans were barred from white concert halls and restricted by law to little more than a sixth-grade public education, women like Hubbard became major conduits of learning for the black community. Like their mothers before them, these women crafted cultural memory, supported community causes, and created opportunity for a new generation of children. On the practical side, they extended and elaborated on the infrastructure their mothers had built so that they could sustain their own musical careers.

Hubbard's performances show how the women who traveled in the summer and took sabbaticals for study helped craft a cosmopolitan community despite racial discrimination. Hubbard not only performed Verdi and Mozart masterfully, she introduced her community to popular white American composers such as Carey Jacobs Bond and John Cademan, and African American composers such as R. Nathaniel Dett, William Grant Still, and Richard Dawson. Readings, a part of most programs, were also varied. Selections were taken from Western literary canon classics such as *The Odyssey*, from the American transcendentalist Henry David Thoreau, and from African American poets, activists, and writers such as Frederick Douglass, Paul Laurence Dunbar, Countee Cullen, and Claude McKay.

In performance Hubbard also extended and elaborated on the terms of respectability for a new generation. She projected an image of a thoroughly modern woman of the 1920s. In stage appearance and in life, she pushed the boundaries of Victorian womanhood, while she maintained a strict standard of femininity. For instance, her 1926 concert review led with a description of her clothing, a "creation of white georgette designed in one piece with a bodice which fell to the bottom of the skirt and trimmed in rhinestones." A 1928 review commented that "her dainty costume brought gurgles of delight from the young ladies." Cultural critic Albert Murray explains that style "is an assimilation in terms of which a given community, folk or communion of faith embodies its basic attitudes toward experience." Hubbard's style reflects a community that felt they deserved the best, could achieve the best, and also knew what to do with the best when they got it.[21]

While these concerts reveal a decidedly middle-class sensibility, Hubbard exposed her community to the rich classical Western tradition on her own terms. African American artists were treated as equals to other classical artists in the Western canon. African Americans compared and contrasted the best of their own with the best Western civilization had to offer and internally assessed their own contributions to society. And, if reviews of Hubbard give us insight, the local community was pleased with its local heroes. The *Louisiana Weekly* stated in one review, "The Negro spirituals and folk song are founded on true religious principles and so will stand the test. . . . America must concede that the Negro has given America its only real music. . . . Mrs. Hubbard, our own, has shown us how to sing them."[22]

Travel to large population centers such as Chicago also deepened Hubbard's self- understanding both as an American artist and as a black artist in America who had unique contributions to make because of her African American heritage and musical background. Hubbard shared these insights as she introduced the New Orleans community to the classical treasures of the Harlem Renaissance. For instance, Hubbard produced "A Night of Negro Music Featuring Alma Lillie Hubbard in Pantomime and Song" at the New Orleans University auditorium. The title of the concert played on an African American association with minstrelsy and, at the same time, refuted it for the more elegant style of pantomime. In this concert, she devoted the entire evening to African American composers.[23]

Like the generation before her, Hubbard used her connections and expertise to build an infrastructure of performance that helped shape the cultural life of New Orleans. Her productions also gave financial support to important community projects and expanded opportunities for young people. For instance, in 1927 Hubbard instituted a city-wide Methodist choir competition to fund the community home for the aged. Seventeen choirs participated in the first contest, and the contests continued through 1933. The admission, at twenty-five cents, promised receipts of nearly four hundred dollars, yielding far more than the taffy pulls and church fund-raisers of Hubbard's childhood—days when the Daughters of the St. Catherine Benevolent Society brought in $8.97 on their anniversary Sunday, or when the senior choir concert netted $3.07 for the church. While the money was important, the competitions pushed church members to higher levels of achievement and transmitted the dress style, discipline, and decorum of Hubbard's university jubilee choirs. The contests were another platform for Hubbard's set of bodily practices that negated servitude, despite the fact that many of the choir members were the servants of white people.[24]

In a persistent theme that had begun with her first professional job as organist at Mother Wesley, Hubbard was responsible not only for netting the funds for her own salary, but also for raising money for university organizations. For instance, in March of 1927, Victor Recording Studios made New Orleans a stop on its recording swing through the South in search of new talent. Hubbard and the groups cut two sides of a Victor record. Alma Lillie sang "Reign, Massa Jesus, Reign" as a solo, and the Glee Club sang "Climbing Jacob's Ladder." In an alliance that seems strange by today's standards, Hubbard marketed the record to alumni groups in support of the football club. A letter from the New Orleans College Club in Chicago responded favorably, "The Club was delighted with your effort and the consideration which you have shown in helping the Foot Ball Club." The group promised to help sell the records in December at their second Sunday meeting.[25]

Hubbard's growing reputation as a Jubilee singer allowed her to break through racial barriers and broker African American culture to the white world. In this capacity, she integrated the local radio airwaves with her University Glee Club in 1927. She also took her university choirs to white churches and drew "many white friends" to the university. Her roll as "goodwill ambassador of spiritual songs to the opposite group" helped rapport with sympathetic whites who had access to philanthropic dollars. In 1931 a concert she produced, performed in, and directed with a city-wide chorus of five hundred was the first event African Americans held in the city's brand-new municipal auditorium. Inroads such as these were important because they licensed the transgression of racial borders at a time when residential segregation restricted where African Americans could work, live, and play.[26]

Hubbard won a Rosenwald Fellowship in 1932 for study in Chicago. While she was on sabbatical, she was fired from New Orleans University when it merged in 1933 with Straight College to form Dillard University. Hubbard's teaching job was lost in the transition because both schools implemented cost-cutting measures as their funding sources dried up. Despite her vast experience, she still did not have the four-year music degree that Dillard would require. Once again Hubbard was faced with potential economic devastation. But once again the fruits of her earlier talent, ambition, and networking paid off. She joined the touring company of *The Green Pastures,* by now a Pulitzer Prize–winning play and the most talked-about show on Broadway. From this point, she made the professional move to New York. She returned to New Orleans for a few concert appearances and biannual visits to her mother, Lizzie Willis, in Crystal Springs, Mississippi.

One potential resource was conspicuously ineffective in Hubbard's rise to the middle class: her marriage to Berry Hubbard, a Methodist minister's son and aspiring professional baseball player whom she met at Straight. The marriage held promise in the early years. Berry was a talented tenor who understood and to some degree supported Alma Lillie Hubbard's musical aspirations. He performed on one of her quartet recordings with Paramount. He also sang in one of her New Orleans recitals. Alma Lillie also gained status from her marriage; not only was she making formal appearances at Wesley and New Orleans University, she also built a respectable public image around her role as a married woman. Mrs. Hubbard made the social pages when she entertained at home. She went to other women's homes for games of whist, an early form of bridge. One entry in the social pages, headlined "Mrs. Alma Hubbard Entertains," extolled her hospitality: "One of the many brilliant affairs of the past week was a lovely whist complimentary to the Red Circle Club, in the very cozy and attractive home of Mrs. Alma Hubbard in Telemachus Street. Many fashionably dressed ladies vied with one another for the pretty as well as attractive prizes."[27]

But the romantic notion of a marriage in which two people join together and shape a common destiny was not to be for Alma Lillie Hubbard. Her own experience may explain why many black women creatively expanded their family, friendship, and business networks in ways other than marriage. It also illustrates the double burden women bore because of their husbands' limited job opportunities. Her marriage was basically an emotional and economic drain. Marriage cost Alma Lillie Hubbard her financial independence, because she lost her teaching job. While Berry's baseball career floundered, Hubbard traveled between Detroit and New Orleans, performing and teaching. It was her full-time job that brought them back to New Orleans. Berry's best job was as an insurance adjuster, and this came to him through Alma Lillie Hubbard's guardian, Leonard Howard. This job did not last, however. The financial obligations invariably fell to Alma Lillie. Berry also gave her a sexually transmitted disease that left her sterile. The final word on Berry Hubbard came from Lizzie Willis, Alma Lillie's biological mother, in 1942: "Well you say you haven't seen Berry. Oh well, he's no good no way, so don't bother which I know you won't." Berry and Alma Lillie divorced, and Alma Lillie remarried a number of years after moving to New York. It was with Joseph Sherrill, a younger man who respected Hubbard's independence and career, that she eventually shared the prestigious Edgecombe address.[28]

Alma Lillie Hubbard had traveled a long way from the humble circumstances of her birth in Crystal Springs, Mississippi. But what were the features of Hubbard's ultimate destination, the black middle class? On a very practical level, definitions of the middle class must address the relationship between individuals and financial capital. Members of the middle class exercise some control over other workers but are themselves subordinate to capital. The middle class also exercises varying degrees of economic, political, and ideological control over their own and others' destinies.[29]

As a classically trained musician, Hubbard had unique skills that were highly valued in the newly emerging entertainment industry. She therefore climbed into the middle class and occupied a white-collar rather than a manual position in this growing economy. Hubbard's skills as a musical performer, and her talent at community building, also gave her standing in the black sub-economy of the day. African American women often moved between the two economies to maintain standing in the middle class. They could seldom cut themselves loose from the black community and depend solely on their positioning in the white community.[30]

Hubbard's own leveraging of resources helps us understand how African Americans staked a claim in the American middle class. Her life also shows how this claim remained hampered by the social and economic realities of segregation. Hubbard gained a certain level of control over her financial destiny, but her financial independence was never total and always tenuous. Economic stability could be quickly lost because of racist or sexist policies that limited education and job opportunities. Hubbard softened the blow of such obstacles because she had multiple career options. Like her mother, she had the capacity to make options out of little more than aspirations. She used family, friendship, church, and school networks and built on each new travel experience.

Hubbard exercised control over people and ideas in a much different manner than, for example, a middle manager who coaxes workers into complying with prevailing ideology and work patterns. Like other black women, Hubbard was more likely to liberate and motivate those under her care than to control them. Her students performed with her in whatever arena had granted her access. If there was no access, she built the venues from the ground up so that she and her students could perform. She also brought the fruits of her education and her travel back into the community. She garnered resources and multiplied opportunities for those directly under her supervision and also for the larger African American community in New Orleans. She gave entrée into public spaces that had previously been barred to blacks.[31]

Hubbard was suspicious of racial ideologies that marginalized African Americans. Like the generation before her, she constructed a "counter-memory" of African American achievement through performance. Her relationship to class and gender ideologies was more ambivalent. Hubbard wiggled between notions of the feminine and feminism. She used traditional notions of the feminine such as her marriage, her church affiliation, her dress, and her education to establish her legitimacy. She then used this hard-won respectability to break out of the race, gender, and class stereotypes that confined women like her mother to domestic work and sharecropping. Hubbard also supported and subverted traditional class ideologies as she transmitted the attitudes, dress, and intellectual content of an emerging middle class.

But asserting her right to study and perform Western classics in an age when African Americans were relegated to industrial education held other meanings. Hubbard's musical virtuosity negated the prevailing ideologies of African American ignorance and devolution. Like the women of Wesley before her, she transmitted the poise, moral righteousness, and human virtuosity necessary for survival in a hostile world. She also offered an alternative model of capitalism, rooted in communal values in which individual and collective aspirations were complimentary rather than mutually exclusive.

Hubbard's climb shows that when material goods are few, the creation of networks and the reconfiguration of resources are crucial. Because of the collective nature of black life and the lack of private resources, family, church, and college networks, as well as travel, were crucial factors in the rise to the middle class. Family networks extended resources and opportunities for children. Church and college multiplied those opportunities. The early socialization that instilled children with a collective consciousness, and at the same time encouraged the exploration of their individual talents, were also important to middle-class success. Focused ambition, personal mastery, and poise helped make children into self-reliant adults. Self-reliance was critical to Hubbard and other black women because they had to literally build the infrastructure that sustained their middle-class standing. Following in the footsteps of the women before her, Hubbard assembled her own resources into such an infrastructure and expanded opportunities for a new generation.

Notes

1. Instead of changing Alma Lillie Hubbard's name as her life story progresses, I have used the stage name she took after marrying her first husband, Berry Hubbard. Hubbard kept this name professionally throughout her career. Her surname therefore differs from her mother's. Her birth date appears in a Record of Baptism, 16 February 1896, Wesley Methodist Church Records 1864–1951, Amistad Research Center, New Orleans (microfilm, United Methodist Church archives, Lake Junaluska, North Carolina).

2. The two Walkers were the first female black millionaires of the Progressive Era. As capitalists, part of the bourgeoisie as opposed to the middle class, they controlled their own ventures. Madame C. J. Walker owned the factories and beauty shops that made and distributed her hair care products. Lena

Walker controlled her insurance company's manual and intellectual labor force whose skills were for hire, for instance her sales force and accountants. In the late 1890s, southern states introduced a series of Jim Crow laws that guaranteed white supremacy through the time of the civil rights movement in the 1960s. The laws created racial separation in transportation and public facilities and disenfranchised black voters. Law and custom also limited African American access to capital, education, and the more highly rewarded market positions in the new economy. See George M. Fredrickson, *The Arrogance of Race* (Hanover, N.H.: Wesleyan University Press, 1988), 260.

3. Stephanie Shaw, *What a Woman Ought to Be and to Do: Black Professional Women Workers during the Jim Crow Era* (Chicago: University of Chicago Press, 1996), 1.

4. Lootie Neal, interview by author, tape recording, 15 July 1988, Crystal Springs, Mississippi.

5. Jacqueline Jones, *Labor of Love, Labor of Sorrow: Black Women, Work, and the Family, from Slavery to the Present* (New York: Basic Books, 1985). I do not want to underplay the patriarchal or hierarchical nature of black church life, but the democratic processes that were also institutionalized in black churches should not be ignored. Many men and women gained leadership skills through these processes.

6. Wesley Methodist Church Records (1864–1951).

7. Minutes, Ladies Prayer Meeting, 26 September 1904, 26 June 1904, 27 July 1904, 13 November 1904, 25 October 1906, 27 July 1904, 25 June 1905, 18 March 1906, Wesley Methodist Church Records.

8. *Southwest Christian Advocate* stated, 16 February 1905. See Elsa Barkley Brown, "Mapping the Terrain of Black Richmond," in *The New African American Urban History,* ed. Kenneth W. Goings, Raymond A. Mohl (Thousand Oaks, Calif.: Sage, 1996), 85, for further discussion of story in the African American community.

9. Lynn Abbott, "'Do Thyself a' no Harm': The Jubilee Singing Phenomenon and the 'Only Original New Orleans University Singers,'" *American Music Research Center Journal* 6 (1996): 13, 29.

10. Wesley trials were overseen by the church trustees and class leaders, but women served as jurors and targeted violators for trial. Leaders and Stewards' minutes, 28 April 1905, 29 October 1902, Wesley Methodist Church Records.

11. Department of the Interior, Bureau of Education, *Negro Education: A Study of the Private and Higher Schools for Colored People in the United States Bulletin, 1917* (Washington, D.C.: Government Printing Office, 1917), 2.283.

12. W. N. Hartshorn and George W. Penniman, eds., *An Era of Progress and Promise 1863–1910: The Religious, Moral and Educational Development of the American Negro Since His Emancipation* (Boston: Priscilla, 1910), 145; Robert W. Woodruff Library, Atlanta University; American Missionary Association History (photostat excerpt) 1924, 11.

13. Lucille Levi Hutton, interview by Florence Borders, tape recording, 5 February 1988, Lucille Levi Hutton Papers, Amistad Research Center.

14. *Sixteenth Biennial Report of the Department of Commissioner of Labor and Industrial Statistics of the State of Louisiana, 1931–1932. Circular of Information for Girls in New Orleans.* Educational Committee of the YWCA, Louisiana Collection, Tulane University, New Orleans.

15. The First Jubilee choirs were formed at Fisk University in the 1880s. The concertized spiritual was an artistic development of the slave spiritual that was the result of the first slaves attending college. It wedded Western vocal technique to African American traditional spirituals, creating a uniquely American form of classical art song. These songs held in tension the slave past and the aspirations of African Americans after slavery. Harry T. Burleigh was the first composer to arrange spirituals in solo form; Roland Hayes and Marian Anderson made his arrangements popular. Carl Diton was a composer-pianist and organist who was the first to create pipe organ transcriptions of these spirituals. His famous variations on "Swing Low, Sweet Chariot" were composed on the organ at the Mormon Tabernacle in Salt Lake City, Utah. Violin virtuoso Fritz Kriesler played Clarence Cameron White's violin and orchestral arrangements. Nathaniel Dett created instrumental and orchestral pieces based on themes gleaned from African American culture. Reverend Daniel Lyman, "Deeper Meaning of Negro Spirituals," *The Christian Educator* 29 (February 1929); Eileen Southern, *Biographical Dictionary of African American and African Musicians,* s.v. "Carl Diton" (Westport, Conn.: Greenwood, 1982); Fritz Kreisler, *Nobody Knows De Trouble I See,* comp. Clarence Cameron White (Victor 64824).

16. *Southwestern Christian Advocate,* 1 July 1920.

17. L. T. Larson to George R. Arthur, 5 June 1929, Rosenwald Correspondence, Amistad Research Center, New Orleans.

18. Obituary Index, s.v. "Albert Greenlaw," *Detroit (Michigan) Contender,* n.d., Detroit Public Library, Detroit, Mich.; Maude Roberts George, "The Negro in Illinois: Women in Music," s.v. "Pauline James Lee," Illinois Writers Project Papers, Vivian G. Harsh Collection, Chicago Public Library, Chicago, Illinois.

19. Lynn Abbot, liner notes, "Religious Recordings from Black New Orleans 1924–1931," *Louisiana Weekly,* 4 January 1930.

20. *Louisiana Weekly,* 16 April 1927, 9 November 1929, 26 December 1925.

21. Albert Murray, *The Omni-Americans: Black Experience and American Culture* (New York: Da Capo, 1970), 54.

22. *Louisiana Weekly,* 30 April 1927.

23. Ibid., 14 January 1928.

24. Ibid., 30 April 1927; "Benevolent Collection for the Year 1905," Wesley Methodist Church Records.

25. Robert M. Dixon, John Godrich, Howard Rye, *Blues and Gospel Records 1890–1943* (Oxford: Clarendon, 1997), 677; Alcee A. Boyd to Alma Lillie Hubbard, n.d., Alma Lillie Hubbard Papers, Schomburg Center for Research on Black Culture, New York Public Library, New York City, New York.

26. New Orleans University Catalogs 1874–1926/27, Amistad Research Center, New Orleans; *Louisiana Weekly,* 25 December 1925, 12 May 1931, 8 August 1931.

27. *Louisiana Weekly,* 6 March 1926, 17 March 1928.

28. Lootie Neal, interview by author, Lizzie Neal to Alma Lillie Hubbard ("to My darling Baby"), November 27, 1942, Alma Lillie Hubbard Papers.

29. Patricia Hill Collins, *Black Feminist Thought: Knowledge, Consciousness, and the Politics of Empowerment* (New York: Routledge, 2000), 60.

30. Hubbard was part of the middle class, that group of propertyless workers whose skills were for hire by industrialists. Class reflects the differing "life chances" that flow from one's market position, affecting factors such as access to education and health care, life expectancy, and consumption levels. Hubbard's skills gave her a better economic position than many black women. This fact improved her opportunities or life chances. See L. Bart Landry, "The Social and Economic Adequacy of the Black Middle Class" in *Dilemmas of the New Black Middle Class,* ed. Joseph R. Washington Jr. (Symposium, University of Pennsylvania Afro-American Studies Program, 1980).

31. Collins has also noted the liberating effect of black women's power. See *Black Feminist Thought.*

3.

The Poetry of Pauli Murray,
African American
Civil Rights Lawyer and Priest

ELAINE CALDBECK

The Reverend Dr. Pauli Murray lived a life engaged in struggles for liberation.[1] She embraced with passion the roles of poet, labor activist, feminist, civil rights lawyer, African American studies professor, and Episcopal priest. Her poetry provides a strong expression of her beliefs and feelings, revealing the foundation for her life. Thus, exploration of her ideas in verse provides a point of entry to understanding this woman, her intellectual products, and her activism. From her youth, Pauli Murray wanted to be a writer.[2] She rose to significance as an activist and intellectual not through any spotlight-grabbing leadership positions, but through her published words. Beyond legal, political, and theological treatises, she authored a family memoir and an autobiography as well as prose articles and poetry on racism and sexism.[3]

Born in 1910 in Baltimore and orphaned by age three, Murray grew up with her maternal aunt and grandparents in Durham, North Carolina.[4] Her ancestors included three generations of highly educated free Blacks and also the offspring of an attractive slave raped by her white master. She grew up embedded in the complexities of race, class, and gender. Her family emphasized education, mutual support, giving back to the community, deep faith, and active membership in the Episcopal church. After high school, Murray moved to the North to escape the oppression of southern segregation and to attend college.

During the late 1930s she joined the Workers Defense League in its efforts to spare Black sharecropper Odell Waller from the death penalty.[5] In response to his execution, she enrolled in law school at Howard University. As students, Murray and her friends honed methods of nonviolent protest at lunch counters and on buses.[6] At Howard she also contributed a reframed refutation of the "separate but equal" doctrine, and her new argument made possible the success of *Brown v.*

Board of Education.[7] For a group of Methodist women, she completed *States Laws on Race and Color*, a guide to all segregation legislation in the United States, which became the bible of the civil rights movement.[8]

In the 1960s Murray applied her civil rights knowledge to the "woman question" and aided President Kennedy's Commission on Women, later writing memos used for lobbying in support of including the word "sex" in the 1964 civil rights anti-discrimination legislation. With others, she founded the National Organization for Women to enforce that law. While engaged in these activities, she was also the first African American woman to earn a doctorate from Yale Law School. Her dissertation, "The Roots of the Racial Crisis: Prologue to Policy," traced the historical causes of the marches and riots in the 1950s and 1960s to colonial America.[9] She used her degree as a pioneering woman professor of law, politics, and Afro-American history at Brandeis University and of law at Boston University. After retirement, she attended seminary, graduating in time to be the first Black woman ordained to the Episcopal priesthood. Her sermons and theological articles were among the earliest to challenge both Black and feminist theologians for ignoring the multiple oppressions of African American women.

The poetry produced by Murray's life experience leaps off the page with emotional intensity. Her autobiography and memoir are documented in careful detail; the prose is clear and easy to read. But it is her verse compositions that reveal her most passionate explorations of race, gender, and identity. Murray wrote most of her poetry during the 1930s and 1940s, much of it while living in Harlem. She found many mentors in the city: Countee Cullen, Langston Hughes, Jean Starr Untermeyer, Leonora Speyer, Robert Hayden, Waring Cuney, Isabel Taylor, and Sterling Brown.[10] African American publications including *The Crisis* and *Opportunity* printed her poems; for two decades, verse was a significant part of her public voice. In the 1950s, she received grants to polish her writing at the MacDowell Colony in rural New Hampshire; she worked there contemporaneously with James Baldwin. Eventually, the public use of her epic poem "Dark Testament" to mourn the death of the Reverend Dr. Martin Luther King Jr. created acclaim for Murray's poems. This interest brought about the publication of her book *Dark Testament and Other Poems* in 1970.[11]

The content of her poems is at once personal, particular, universal, global, and arresting. The emphasis of her work varied even within any given year, depending on her experiences. In the 1930s and 1940s, she wrote to reflect on failed love affairs, strong friendships, race riots, and society's inherent inequalities. One poem chronicles the pain and humiliation of facing a government employee to file for general assistance.[12] She knew this trauma firsthand from her starving years during the Great Depression. Murray also produced love poems, sometimes in the style of a previous generation, using Greek mythological allusions to carry the meaning.

Still, the central theme of the majority of her published pieces was race. She unflinchingly explored Black history and the Black experience in America. In the 1950s, Murray celebrated the bravery of schoolchildren integrating southern schools and mourned the horrors of lynching.[13] Further, she wove class issues through the content of many pieces; the poet never underestimated the complexity of oppression.

The only theme that seemed to change over time was that of her racial identity. Early poems explored developing, maintaining, or asserting African American identity against the dominant culture. The subtle growth of her self-definition, acceptance, and integration can be traced as she slowly incorporated all the ethnic and historical elements of herself.

Although she embraced feminism by the 1940s, her poetry rarely mentions gender issues. Murray published one poem that compares women and men, focusing on the difference as biological.[14] She lifted up the woman as superior based on her ability to give birth, an interesting choice for a woman with no children. Murray primarily explored gender questions later in her life and in prose. However, one poem from the 1930s or 1940s, which celebrates a Black woman who builds ships, reads as a feminist statement. Other poems explore religion and life in general. Many of her compositions, no matter the theme, reveal an assumed theology, a version of Christian religion that informed, guided, and strengthened a people amid the worst of racism and poverty. In general, she followed the customs of the era, writing as if male language were inclusive and universal. Her love poems are the exception; in these she avoided gendered language.

Murray divided her book of poetry into four sections that reflect her foci. The first consists of her epic "Dark Testament." The second chapter focuses on race issues. The third takes as a title a Walt Whitman line, "I . . . am not contain'd between my hat and my boots," and addresses philosophical themes. The last chapter, "No Greener Spring," offers no explanation of its title; primarily its content considers love, loss, and faith.[15] I focus here on a sample of her poems with often overlapping themes of identity, race, gender, class, and religion.

Despite any attempt at orderly discussion, Murray's poetry does not fall neatly into categories. Most of her poems combine these subjects; a blend of experiences based on race, gender, class, and religion inseparably shaped her worldview. She wrote the majority of her published poems between her college graduation in' 1933 and her admission to law school in 1941.[16] Given her ardor for words and revision, she likely tinkered with her works over the years, so assigning precise dates may not be possible.

Identity

Murray's poems with themes related to identity suggest the human, personal dimensions of the author, beyond activism or professionalism, the inner conflicts exorcised by writing poems. (The examples selected here do not mention race; those follow in the next sections.) While somewhat universalizing, these works offer insight into the mind-set and view of human nature that underlie all her work.

The anguished poem below might be about a relationship between a parent and child, two friends, or lovers. It may be about her former husband, a friend or relative who chose to pass for white, or some other love.[17] The author's view of the other person and his or her affinity implies an appreciation for and reflection on the identity of the other.

> *Tears*
> Three times have I known tears—
> When I loved you,
> When I lost you,
> When you lost yourself.[18]

Conversely, misunderstanding causes a similar outcome. If the author misunderstood who the beloved was, perhaps he or she was not so much "lost" as never understood. The work indicates, however, that the other person gave in to some external pressure undermining a valued identity.

The next piece might be about making love, or arguing, or any intense interaction between two individuals or within a psyche. Given its placement in the book and the connotations of its words, Murray seems to be describing a sexual encounter, maybe even a one-night stand. However, the very ambiguity and availability of alternate meanings make the work intriguing.

Conquest
Last night you were a river
Swollen with March thaws,
Ruthlessly tearing my roots
Until, rudderless, I was borne,
A fragment in your flood.
When you are once more self-contained
In your swift channel
Shall I find reassuring earth
Beneath me and, restored,
Let dancing shadow mark your passage?[19]

Murray does not reject passion, be it libido or wrath; still she asks what follows. After the blending of the two, she wonders if she will find the ground of her own self again. Moreover, she asks whether the ebb of passion means that the once intense storm will become playful, insubstantial, and pass away. From title to final phrase, the poem suggests images of a loss of control, loss of self, and an unsure future. The author does not unambiguously celebrate the experience; after all, she has been conquered. An equally likely interpretation is that the flooding river is another element within her psyche. Possibly, a quiet part of the self is querying about an overwhelming expression of anger, despair, joy, sexual passion, or fear. Most of us have known a time when outside events shake our sense of identity, leaving us temporarily feeling fragmented, swept off solid ground by an intense inner reaction. Many interpretations make sense; thus, the poem could connect with the experience and humanity of many readers.

In the next poem, the author explicitly explored an internal clash she knew well.

Conflict
Some day the poet and warrior
Who grapple in my brain
Shall lock in final contest
And I will be ground under.
For I must sing, and yet
I wield a sword whose point
Shall find my breast when all is done.[20]

Murray's self-descriptions in her autobiography and memoir affirm she had both a temper and a gentle, sensitive side. Her methods of activism seemed to put both to use. Sensitivity allowed her to see the complexities and multiple sides of issues with empathy. Anger provided energy to act for change. Apparently, at least some of the time, her two natures warred internally, feeling to her as if they endangered her existence. Finding a balance between gladiator and muse left her aware that her aggressive side brought her into danger. Though she described no clear integration of the elements, owning and naming them may have made the internal conflict less overwhelming.

A short, clever poem dated November 1937 uses metaphor to suggest looking at the larger whole beyond an argument or societal flaw, instead of rushing to rejection and destruction. The author placed individual human differences in a global perspective, without resorting to overused, familiar images.

> *Quarrel*
> Two ants at bay
> On the curved stem of an apple
> Are insufficient cause
> To fell the tree.[21]

These lines reveal Murray's gentle humor and optimism as well as her passion. One does wonder which "quarrels" she imagines between two ants. The author could be poking fun at foolish disagreements, or perhaps conflicts between two people of color, those who need to be allies. Given Murray's passion for justice, the issue to be kept in perspective was not likely to be racial oppression itself. Nonetheless, the message could be that despite its racist flaws, our democratic, constitutional society has enough value that we should keep it. This pithy piece affirms the value of the whole without considering how or whether to resolve the quarrel. The open, universal nature of this nonspecific poetry prompts thought and allows readers their own interpretations.

Race

Section two of *Dark Testament and Other Poems* focuses on issues of color and race and begins with a quote from Langston Hughes's "I am the American heartbreak"—words that recall Du Bois's frustration with being "the problem."[22] Dated February 1938, this epigrammatic piece epitomizes her themes.

> *Color Trouble*
> If you dislike me just because
> My face has more of sun than yours,

Then, when you see me, turn and run
But do not try to bar the sun.[23]

In his foreword to the book, Morris Milgram, fellow member of the
Workers Defense League, asserts that this poem is humorous.[24] Possibly it is, for the effect is highly ironic, a reversal, the assertion of
strength against rejection. Her words aver that the person who dis-
likes and needs to run is the one with the difficulty, not the person
whose face has color. Thus the person with the problem should go
away and leave the poet alone.

In another poem of strength, Murray uses the winemaking process
and its by-products as metaphors to describe Black life in America.

> *To the Oppressors*
> Now you are strong
> And we are but grapes aching with ripeness.
> Crush us!
> Squeeze from us all the brave life
> Contained in these full skins.
> But ours is a subtle strength
> Potent with centuries of yearning.
> Of being kegged and shut away
> In dark forgotten places.
>
> We shall endure
> To steal your senses
> In that lonely twilight
> Of your winter's grief.[25]

Here Murray observes that fermentation, potentially explosive, is a
reasonable outcome to expect from tightly capped oppression. Life
and hope may be crushed but are not ended forever, only transformed. The loss of power is not permanent. Darkness and night are
potent, positive images here, but Murray does not explicitly mention
race. She implies that being bottled and contained creates a different
kind of strength, one that will explode. If Murray stood in solidarity
with eruptions of rioters, still she asserts that endurance would overcome. The last sentence suggests some quiet resolution slipped in during the night. While this might suggest the methodology of looters, it
also might imply more subtle mutations of persons or culture, intellectual or emotional changes. In this poem, the author writes for a
people in first person plural without gender-specific language. Clearly,
racism is not the small quarrel to be ignored.

In the next poem, Murray explores skin color in the personal repercussions of racism. In the two previous poems, she shows no chink in her armor and admits no pain. Here, "Mulatto's Dilemma" expresses strong feelings about the consequences of mixed racial heritage like her own. As in "Color Trouble," she faults the sun for erasing the safe ambiguity of lighter hues. Even this assignment of blame suggests the vulnerability of color: one must always be aware of the danger; one cannot relax or let down her guard and enjoy being outside on a sunny day.

> *Mulatto's Dilemma*
> I curse the summer sun
> That burned me thus to fateful recognition.
> Should such a thought strike terror to my frame
> More than another? I am the strongest of this lot
> And fit to do the work for two. Were I but paler
> By a single tone they would not see me tremble;
> Or if in shackles here, they'd buy my strength
> And let another starve—but being free,
> (If being dark is freedom),—they stare
> At me; they note the curl below my hat;
> They trace the darker line below my chin.
>
> Oh God! My face has slipped them but my soul
> Cries with the fear of brownness before a bar
> Where brown's already judged by sight. Can I
> Endure the killing weight of time it takes them
> To be sure?
>
> If I could lay my quivering brain
> Before them, they'd see a brain is but a brain
> And know that brown men think and feel, are hurt
> And broken even as they.
>
> Oh for the pride
> Of Blackness! To stand unmasked before them,
> Nor moved by inquisition. Accepted or refused—
> Not crucified.[26]

Murray's words express the pain of rejection for unchangeable features of skin and hair. Discovery may mean life-threatening danger, not just outcast status; terror is appropriate. She stresses the paradox of strength and vulnerability, ability and rejection rooted in the experience of slavery. By questioning the possibility of freedom, she emphasizes the continuing burden of the history of bondage in present oppressions. In the face of these evils, the poet does not reject the other. Instead, she seeks understanding and affirms the human commonalties beneath the skin. Her desire for pride in Blackness seems to be a hope and a cry, concluding with religious language. She names the possibility of pride, of asserting worth, although it is tinged by pain. Her closing implies the question, "Will the painful death and daily torture of racial oppression never be ended by an empty tomb and resurrection?"

In her autobiography Murray recounts a few particular painful incidents when friends or relatives excluded her or regretted her presence because she looked more "Black" than they did. In these situations, her presence brought discrimination upon her even lighter-skinned companions who might have otherwise been thought white. The gulf between the races, especially under segregation, means ordinary people view the world and each person's place in it by making such conclusions. Reading this poem reminds one that Murray lived this experience of being examined and judged daily by every stranger who looked at her. The lightness of her skin probably deepened the scrutiny, due to the ambiguity of her appearance; with its constant inspection, society never granted her freedom. Written in the first person, this 1938 poem reveals great pain. However, one cannot assume that these were the author's only feelings or experiences around her racial identity at this time. "Color Trouble," dated February 1938, and the undated "To the Oppressor" both assert strong instincts to defend the vulnerabilities revealed in "Mulatto's Dilemma."

Murray spent years polishing her epic poem "Dark Testament." She worked under the tutelage of Stephen Vincent Benét; it was her response to a verse in his *John Brown's Body* that called for an African America epic poet.[27] Begun in 1939 and frequently revised, her final version published in 1970 is excerpted here. Her words weave an American story of immigrants, slavery, hopes, dreams, pain, and survival. Her vision does not celebrate separatism, ignore hateful institutions, or imagine romantic solutions. Grounded in a spirit of inclusiveness and honesty, Murray named differences and commonalities among and between peoples. She insisted on hope to feed the human spirit. Two excerpts from "Dark Testament's" twelve stanzas illustrate her skill with words and her intent.

> *Dark Testament*
> (stanza 1)
> Freedom is a dream
> Haunting as amber wine

Or worlds remembered out of time.
Not Eden's gate, but freedom
Lures us down a trail of skulls
Where men forever crush the dreamers—
Never the dream.

I was an Israelite walking in a sea bottom,
I was a Negro slave following the North Star,
I was an immigrant huddled in ship's belly,
I was a Mormon searching for a temple,
I was a refugee clogging roads to nowhere—
Always the dream was the same—
Always the dream was freedom.[28]

(stanza 8)
Hope is a crushed stalk
Between clenched fingers.
Hope is a bird's wing
Broken by a stone.
Hope is a word in a tuneless ditty—
A word whispered with the wind,
A dream of forty acres and a mule,
A cabin of one's own and a moment to rest,
A name and place for one's children
And children's children at last . . .
Hope is a song in a weary throat.[29]

In "Dark Testament" her words embodied endurance against the impossible and hope for the fulfillment of seemingly ordinary human needs. Her allusions to Israelite, Eden, and Mormon stress the religious dimensions of peoplehood and faith in the future. She describes the intense anguish of racism and oppression, where "freedom / Lures us down a trail of skulls / Where men forever crush the dreamers. . . ." Her words hint that racism is permanent, or at least that hope and freedom are dreams that will be crushed. Even so, the poem seems to reflect her own iron courage as she fought societal barriers to gain access to the simple things that privileged folk never had to question.

She completed this assertion of resilient hope and constancy in struggle amid the 1943 Harlem riots of exploding hopelessness. She demanded parity, asking not for gifts but for freedom and the same minimum opportunity given other immigrants.[30] For example, early generations of generally white pioneers claimed land by settling and cultivating it. Generations of African Americans labored without pay or freedom; their post–Civil War request had been for forty acres and a mule, the minimal assets for survival.[31] Despite the confiscation of rebel officers' plantations, no restitution was provided to the newly freed.[32]

Possibly Murray's fragile mantra of hope was as much for herself as for the reader, claiming the necessity and value of dreams. James McBride avers that having hope in a desperate situation is a survival skill, a method for keeping moving.[33] He suggests that when a person, a community, or a people lapse into hopeless despair they are immobilized, no longer able to act to attack or transform oppression. Murray never stated this idea directly, yet it reflects the values she lived. Moreover, the themes of "Dark Testament" recur throughout her life and writing. Murray's 1965 Yale dissertation, "Roots of the Racial Crisis: Prologue to Policy," was a richly researched scholarly prose exposition on the same content.[34]

"Dark Testament" contains innumerable profound and pithy insights. This historical epic was very important to Murray. She took *Song in a Weary Throat*, the title for her autobiography, from the final line of stanza eight.[35] These words emphasize hope as the driving force that kept her going despite weariness or discouragement. Murray kept on challenging racism and sexism because she *hoped* for a better life for the next generation. Her belief in better dreams lay firmly in her own family history. She knew that the struggles of her ancestors, both slave and free, had created some opportunities for herself and for others. In writing *Proud Shoes: The Story of an American Family*, she found strength to continue her journey in the concrete evidence she collected to document family stories.[36] Her book affirms a family that defied and disproved stereotypes about African Americans' lives. However, *Proud Shoes* also supports Derrick Bell's claim: "Even those Herculean efforts we hail as successful will produce no more than temporary 'peaks of progress,' short-lived victories that slide into irrelevance as racial patterns adapt in ways that maintain white dominance. This is a hard-to-accept fact that all history verifies."[37] Murray's life experience and written works suggest that she understood the "both/and" of assuming unending racism while continuing to act against it. She did not have utopian hopes that one achievement or effort would correct all of society's failings.

Gender, Identity, and Race

In her 1938 "Mulatto's Dilemma," Murray's first-person singular voice seems to sing from the raw, weary throat of "Dark Testament," and it seems to hold less hope. In her poem "Ruth," she depicts a woman working in a shipyard. Such opportunities were primarily available to women during World War II; thus the piece may date from a little later in her life. In it she affirms the beauty and battle strength of an African American woman.

Ruth
Brown girl chanting Te Deums on Sunday
Rust-colored peasant with strength of granite,
Bronze girl welding ship hulls on Monday,
Let nothing smirch you, let no one crush you.

Queen of ghetto, sturdy hill-climber,
Walk with the lilt of a ballet dancer,
Walk like a strong down-East wind blowing,
Walk with the majesty of the First Woman.

Gallant challenger, millioned-hope bearer,
The stars are your beacons, earth your inheritance,
Meet blaze and cannon with your heart's passion,
Surrender to none the fire of your soul.[38]

Murray includes images from the Anglo-Catholic worship of an Episcopal church she attended.[39] She begins with the bit of church Latin juxtaposed with a strong woman of "metal and rock." The contrasts continue: peasant, Queen, ghetto, welder, dancer; by combining them the poet contradicts all the typical categories. Reality often defies categories. In addition, Murray lauds the challenge, the heavenly hope, and the depth of passion firing this woman's soul. Most of all, Ruth is proud; she is brown, bronze, or rust. Throughout this poem, Murray lionizes the variety of skin shades among people of color, like this woman; all are awe-inspiring. In her family and self, Murray knew that being African American embraced much more variety than the single word "Black" suggests. She preferred to represent that diversity. Murray sees Queen Ruth as heroic and encourages her in her battles.

In her autobiography, Murray mentions seven different friends named Ruth. One wonders if the poem's title refers to an individual. Alternatively, the name could point to the faithful daughter-in-law of the biblical story, meaning a woman of faith. The choice may have been metaphorical rather than literal.[40] The poem's content does not reveal the exact relationship between author and subject. Murray might simply be creating an imaginary persona to meet the need described in "Mulatto's Dilemma." Despite the celebratory tone of "Ruth," this poem is not in the first person; the author may not personally own the strength and pride of color she celebrates. "Ruth" may show Murray's evolution from "Mulatto's Dilemma," or it may simply be another attempt to imagine that desired "pride of Blackness." Yet such pride may be the other side of the vulnerability: possibly the pain of the dilemma could only be voiced if this pride also existed.

Similar to authors of a more recent generation, such as bell hooks and Victor Anderson, Pauli Murray cultivated her own growth; the longer she lived the more wholeness she encompassed. Probably she was in her late twenties when she wrote the painful "Mulatto's Dilemma," naming the trauma of living with immutable, unwelcome physical characteristics in a racist society.[41] She seemed somewhat more at ease with her racial identity by her early thirties when she most likely wrote "Ruth." Even if her poems do not document a straight line of progress in her self-image, the later poems show the strong identity of color she possessed or to which she aspired.

As Murray neared age sixty, she apparently was still growing; her poetry celebrated her inner life as well as her genealogy. Written in Cambridge, Massachusetts, while Murray was a professor at Brandeis, her 1969 "Prophecy" alludes to family stories of a Fitzgerald ancestor who may have been Irish royalty. She celebrates a soul she believes to be freed of limits.

> *Prophecy*
> I sing of a new American
> Separate from all others,
> Yet enlarged and diminished by all others.
> I am the child of kings and serfs, freemen and slaves,
> Having neither superiors nor inferiors,
> Progeny of all colors, all cultures, all systems, all beliefs.
> I have been enslaved, yet my spirit is unbound.
> I have been cast aside, but I sparkle in the darkness.
> I have been slain but live on in the rivers of history.
> I seek no conquest, no wealth, no power, no revenge;
> I seek only discovery
> Of the illimitable heights and depths of my own being.[42]

This time she wrote in the first-person singular; however, her imagery holds that person in tension with all peoples. Her words triumphantly claim universalism, as if saying the past can be healed and solved; we are each unique and yet all alike though diverse; we must value both these realities. She balances each negative phrase with a positive counter-phrase. The poem's overall emotional tone leans more toward the sparkle than the trauma in the depths of self. She does not mention darkness or shades of bronze or brown, only the inclusive "color." This is Murray's only published poem from 1969. Thus it is impossible to know whether this celebration of herself and her role as prophet represents the whole of an integrated self. With hindsight, her sense of prophecy is a clue to her growing, even if still unconscious, move toward ordination. At the least, this poem shows the self she wanted to present to the world. By now she had achieved success, and society had changed dramatically since the depression and war eras. She had good reason to be less frightened, less angry, less hopeless, and less bitter. The triumphs of the civil rights movement provided a buoyant sense of hope. Moreover, this poem resonated with Howard Thurman's ideas.[43] She had known him and depended on his chaplaincy and support while a law student during World War II. Likewise, her valuing of race did not affirm ontological Blackness; she would likely have agreed with Victor Anderson's recent call to move beyond it.[44]

Race and Class

Murray never forgot the trauma of graduating from college into economic chaos. She knew how race overshadowed class in treatment of African Americans by the New Deal during the Great Depression. Her poem "Psalm of Deliverance (To the Lost Class of 1959 from one of the Lost Class of 1933)" drew on this knowledge.[45] While emphasizing the achievements of 1950s schoolchildren, she noted that her own lost generation had found redemption in this new fight for integration. Several sections of this "psalm" address the painful history of the intersecting oppressions of race and class. One stanza in particular reveals the humiliation of filing for public aid. Yet it closes with a refrain of hope, an assertion that recovery and reclamation will occur.

> *Psalm of Deliverance*
> *(To the Lost Class of 1959 from one of the Lost Class of 1933)*
> Name: Henry Jones (or James Smith or Lucy Brown)
> Place of Birth: U.S.A.—Any town or hamlet south of
>   Washington, D.C.
> Age: Twenty-three
> Education: A.B., Graduate of City College, Class of '33

Occupation:	Unemployed.
Race:	Negro (circled as practically unemployable)
Residence:	Formerly YMCA, but vague as to last six months. Probably sleeps in subway or park.
Skills:	Majored in Social Science and History. No professional experience; has held part-time jobs as clerical worker, handyman, dishwasher, elevator operator, porter, janitor.
Reason for leaving last job:	Reduction in personnel (last hired, first fired).
Disposition:	Certified to W.P.A. at $23.86 per week, where in time he will be identified as a boondoggler! Case closed in Home Relief Files with the following notation: "In his twenty-fourth year, his youth died!"

We have remembered, and remembering,
We rise from the shadows and stand beside you!

We have returned from a place beyond hope;
We have returned from wastelands of despair;
We have come to reclaim our heritage;
We have come to redeem our honor![46]

Here, writing at the MacDowell Colony in 1959, twenty-six years after her own college graduation, she remembered the shame of poor relief. She affirmed the overcoming of despair as deserving of honor alongside the courage of the new generation. Perhaps presaging Derrick Bell's framing of the heroic, Murray deemed the very act of surviving the awful years of her youth a triumphant accomplishment. She named this as an achievement of her entire generation.

Likewise, stanzas within "Dark Testament" intensely portray the effect of racial caste, the ever-shifting methods that adjust to maintain oppression and keep African Americans at the bottom.

> Dark Testament
> (stanza 10)
> The drivers are dead now
> But the drivers have sons.
> The slaves are dead too
> But the slaves have sons,
> And when sons of drivers meet sons of slaves
> The hate, the old hate, keeps grinding on.
> Traders still trade in double-talk

> Though they've swapped the selling-block
> For ghetto and gun!
>
> This is our portion, this is our testament,
> This is America, dual-brained creature,
> One hand thrusting us out to the stars,
> One hand shoving us down in the gutter.[47]

These powerful words again aver that life, especially in America, offers both the best and the worst. The nation is at best an ambiguous home for people of color; still, they are indisputably Americans. The good may consist only of hopes and dreams; the reality is the evil of slavery, reinvented with each generation. For Murray's friend Morris Milgram, these words were life-changing. In his introduction to *Dark Testament and Other Poems,* Milgram wrote that Murray's parallel between ghetto and slavery pushed him to become a housing developer, building thousands of integrated units.[48] He could not forget the truth of her images or cease to fight that oppression; she "radically altered the course of my life."[49]

Religion

Murray also found transformative ways to write her life experiences into the seemingly narrow Episcopal liturgy. She expanded the white pseudo-universal words to address the prayer needs of Black Episcopalians. Written in New York in 1959, this poem is one of several that deal with the trauma of lynching; its language is liturgical.

> *Collect for Poplarville* (Adapted from the Book of Common Prayer)
> Lighten our darkness, we beseech thee, O Lord;
>   Teach us no longer to dread
>   hounds yelping in the distance,
>   the footfall at the door,
>   the rifle butt on the window pane.
> And by thy great mercy defend us from all perils and dangers of this night;
>   Give us fearlessness to face
>   the bomb thrown from the darkness,
>   the gloved hand on the pistol,
>   the savage intention.
>   Give us courage to stand firm against
>   our tormentors without rancor—
>   Teach us that most difficult of tasks—

to pray for them,
to follow, not burn, thy cross![50]

The original text was a simple family prayer for bedtime; she omitted only a Trinitarian closing.[51] Without her words, the prayer is universal and comforting. The prayer, with her poetic additions, created a statement for oppressed people. Murray reclaimed this prayer for the truth of being a Black American from Reconstruction through the 1950s. She writes of a faith of prayerful resistance instead of revenge, a theology of naming and rejecting evil and calling the self to rise above the actions of those who hate. This is not an easy, assimilative theology, but a trumpet decrying a twisted, cross-burning Christian culture.

As modeled by her adoptive mother and aunt, Pauline Dame, Murray faced hard issues directly and fought to follow her faith. Her poetry shows that when normative cultural images or institutions made no sense to her or excluded her, she used poetic words to create a reality that did make sense and include her. Over a decade before Murray's formal theological training, her theology resembled that behind the nonviolent vision and integrity of the Reverend Dr. Martin Luther King Jr. By 1959 King, with training from the Fellowship of Reconciliation (F.O.R.), had been involved in protests in some Southern cities. However, Murray's acquaintance with protest, white violence, and the F.O.R., preceded King's by a decade. Her theology here most likely developed out of her own experience and reading.

Murray's poem offers both strength for resistance and incitement for change, shaming the oppressors by naming their evil within a familiar prayer. She does not offer an explicit extended agenda beyond being better Christians then white brethren are. She simply forces the reader to face the horrors of lynching and other racial violence.

Another poem, likely an early one, affirmed a theology that might be seen as otherworldly yet, like the poem above, acknowledges painful realities. In it, she raises the issue of race through the word *slave*, and suggests liberation, hope, or otherworldly solutions in the word *dream*. Likewise, she states that pain is a consequence of love, and that love provides the strength to bear the pain. Similar to some liberation theologians, Pauli Murray celebrated a God who suffered and loved.

Nazarene
Some say that he was legend,
The dream of slaves and beggars,

Or hippy poet so charged
With music of the spheres
That stones sang beneath his naked feet.
I care not if he lived
Or uttered any word
Or healed a single leper.
I know only that his name
Reveals that gift of pain
That only love can bear
And having borne still cry
"I love."[52]

Affirmations ring strong from this complex poem. Faith does not need to provide a name for the Holy, nor insist on literal historical truth. Faith holds as its center the love that bore pain and still loves. Thus Pauli Murray envisioned God and faith, and embodied them herself. Perhaps her ideas will resonate with the yet-to-come theologies of a God who suffers with the poor and the marginalized.

Murray, although modest about her skill as a poet, created powerful, moving verse compositions. She used the written word to work through her own pain and joy, as well as to express the strength and dignity of her oppressed people. Fully human, and fully aware of her humanity, she stood alone in life while part of a supportive, struggling community that she sought to uplift and challenge with her words and images.

This quiet, intelligent, sensitive, woman with quick wit and gentle humor spent her life standing firmly for her people, community, identity, and values. She skillfully used the languages of theology, law, and poetry to improve the world and redress wrong. Her poetry explicates her favorite issues and her development of self. The most pervasive themes in Murray's poetry are ambiguity and complexity. Acknowledging that racism was painful, crushing, and overwhelming, she insisted it could be withstood. Discrimination and rejection could be faced by detailing those traumas. She asserted Christianity's promise of strength to endure oppression, as well as the hope that activism and righteousness would overcome evil so that future generations could have a better life. She fought despair with hope and with the belief that ongoing struggle would yield gradual change. She affirmed the selfhood and rights of all peoples, particularly her own, as well as universality to bring all together. Murray insisted on interracial efforts and reconciliation to regain and sustain awareness of the full humanity of each person. Furthermore, it is in her poetry that she shows the passion that existed before, and beneath, the activism that drove her to challenge every barrier, to try to do her part in the "relay race" to effect social change.

Notes

1. Pauli Murray, *Song in a Weary Throat: An American Pilgrimage* (New York: Harper & Row, 1987).

2. Ibid., 85–86. In this autobiography Murray never mentioned a specific type of writing as a goal.

3. An abbreviated list of her books and articles appears at the end of this chapter.

4. Murray, *Song in a Weary Throat,* 2–3, 5–6, 13.

5. Ibid., 150–76.

6. Ibid., 198–209.

7. Ibid., 255.

8. Pauli Murray, *States' Laws on Race and Color: And Appendices Containing International Documents, Federal Laws and Regulations, Local Ordinances and Charts* (Cincinnati, Ohio: Woman's Division of Christian Service, Board of Missions and Church Extension, Methodist Church, 1950), 746.

9. Pauli Murray, "Roots of the Racial Crisis: Prologue to Policy" (Ph.D. diss., Yale Law School, 1965), 1304.

10. Pauli Murray, *Dark Testament and Other Poems* (Norwalk, Conn.: Silvermine, 1970), 9.

11. Ibid., 116.

12. Ibid., 41.

13. Murray, *Dark Testament,* 41.

14. Ibid., 67.

15. Ibid., 74–100.

16. Ibid., 9.

17. For example, she mentions her own brief annulled marriage, undertaken during the depths of the Great Depression. Murray, *Song in a Weary Throat,* 76–77.

18. Murray, *Dark Testament,* 75.

19. Ibid., 98.

20. Ibid., 70.

21. Ibid., 57.

22. W. E. B. Du Bois, *The Souls of Black Folk* (New York: Bantam Classic, 1989, originally 1903), 133–45.

23. Ibid., 30.

24. Ibid., 10. He had also been part of the team that fought for Odell Waller's life.

25. Ibid., 31.

26. Murray, *Dark Testament,* 32–33.

27. Murray, *Song in a Weary Throat,* 131–33. Stephen Vincent Benét, *John Brown's Body* (Chicago: Elephant, 1927, 1990).

28. Murray, *Dark Testament,* 106.

29. Ibid.

30. Despite perceptions of the self-sufficiency of America's pioneers, almost all gained their livelihoods from land they settled on and did not pay for, a seldom-identified government subsidy to their enterprise.

31. Eric Foner, *Nothing but Freedom: Emancipation and Its Legacy* (Baton Rouge: Louisiana State University Press, 1983).

32. Ibid.

33. James McBride, *The Color of Water: A Black Man's Tribute to His White Mother* (New York: Riverhead, 1996), 262.

34. Murray, "Roots of the Racial Crisis," 1304.

35. Murray, *Song in a Weary Throat.*

36. Murray, *Proud Shoes,* vii–xvii.

37. Derrick Bell, *Faces at the Bottom of the Well: The Permanence of Racism* (New York: Basic, 1992), 12.

38. Murray, *Dark Testament,* 40.

39. Of course, the use of church Latin could also imply that the Ruth she writes of is Roman Catholic. I am merely guessing, since Murray wrote of discovering Anglo-Catholic worship when she moved north, that this poem relates to that experience.

40. For example, Adelene MacBean was a close, supportive friend who traveled through Virginia with Murray and shared her arrest on a segregated bus. Murray, *Song in a Weary Throat,* 138–49.

41. Murray, *Dark Testament,* 32.

42. Ibid., 71.

43. Howard Thurman, *The Search for Common Ground: An Inquiry into the Basis of Man's Experience of Community* (Richmond, Ind.: Friends United, 1973, 1986), 104.

44. Victor Anderson, *Beyond Ontological Blackness: An Essay on African American Religious and Cultural Criticism* (New York: Continuum, 1995).

45. Murray, *Dark Testament,* 41–48.

46. Ibid., 48.

47. Ibid., 28.

48. Ibid., 7.

49. Ibid., 6.

50. Ibid., 38.

51. According to the Use of the Protestant Episcopal Church, *The Book of Common Prayer* (New York: Church Pension Fund, 1977), 912, Lectionary Year C, the Sixth Sunday After Epiphany.

52. Murray, *Dark Testament,* 68.

Bibliography

Archival Source

Murray, Pauli. Collection MC 412. Schlesinger Library of Radcliffe Institute, Cambridge, Mass.

Published Works by Pauli Murray

"All for Mr. Davis": The Story of Sharecropper Odell Waller. New York: Workers Defense League, 1940.

"Why Negro Girls Stay Single: Negro Males Expose Women to Jane Crow as Well as Jim Crow." *Negro Digest,* July 1947, 5–9.

States' Laws on Race and Color: and Appendices Containing International Documents, Federal Laws and Regulations, Local Ordinances and Charts. Cincinnati, Ohio: Women's Division of Christian Service, Board of Missions and Church Extension, Methodist Church, 1950.

Proud Shoes: The Story of An American Family. 1956. Reprint, New York: Harper & Row, 1978.

"Roots of the Racial Crisis: Prologue to Policy." Ph.D. diss., Yale Law School, 1965.

Dark Testament and Other Poems. Norwalk, Conn.: Silvermine, 1970.

Song in a Weary Throat: An American Pilgrimage. New York: Harper & Row, 1987. Reissued as *Pauli Murray: The Autobiography of a Black Activist, Feminist, Lawyer, Priest and Poet,* Knoxville: University of Tennessee Press, 1989.

4.
The Lunch Counter Struggle, 1960–1963
Women Remapping Boundaries of Race, Gender, and Vocation

BARBARA R. I. ISAACS

□□□

This chapter explores how the socially constructed boundaries of gender and public discourse were challenged when Black and white female students "sat down" at the segregated white lunch counters in the South. To illustrate how some of these students were empowered and "desilenced" even as others were silenced, I have chosen to contrast the experiences of female students at two Methodist Church–related institutions of higher education: Bennett College, a single-sex, historically Black institution of higher education in Greensboro, North Carolina; and Randolph-Macon Woman's College in Lynchburg, Virginia. I will focus on the students' relationships with the presidential leadership of these two campuses. My primary resources for this study include these presidents' addresses and statements; campus, local, and national newspaper articles; and personal interviews with women from these campuses who participated in the sit-ins.

Bennett College

When a Black female walked into white Southern public space in the 1950s, the Hebrew Scriptures' figure of Jezebel was never far behind her. "The creation of Jezebel, the image of the sexually denigrated Black woman," notes Patricia Hill Collins, "has been vital in sustaining a system of interlocking race, gender, and class oppression."[1] The raped bodies of slave and non-slave females also lingered in the long shadow of the Black female standing before the white Southern male. In 1960 the courageous leadership of Dr. Willa Player and the prophetic witness of Bennett students would dramatically change Greensboro's white Southern public space.[2]

In 1955 Player became the ninth president of Bennett College and the first Black woman college president in the United States since Dr. Mary McLeod Bethune assumed the presidency of Bethune-Cookman College in 1923. In the 1940s the Bennett community had reaped a bountiful academic harvest through the strategic curriculum evaluations initiated by Player as director of admissions and coordinator of instructions. Her 1948 dissertation, *Improving College Education for Women at Bennett College,* was "the first study of a black college's alumnae that attempted to evaluate the influence of the college's curriculum and environment in the lives of its graduates."[3] Player's conclusions led to Bennett College's increased emphasis on students' addressing the complex social problems in the larger community. The moral bases for this evolution of the student's daily journey were Christian thought and Methodist emphasis on "good works," united hand in hand with faith.

In her inaugural address, Player told the overflow audience of students, faculty, administration, trustees, Greensboro citizens, and leaders of the Methodist Episcopal Church:

> Ours will be the task of sending out graduates equipped in every respect to help release from bondage a region enslaved with the chains of hate and segregation, and lead forth a people into the full understanding and realization of their rights, their privileges and responsibilities as citizens in America's envisioned democracy. At this point, there can be no standing still, no compromise, no equivocation.[4]

Player's presidency carried the marks of a bold spirit and a secure vision. Her very presence on the campus in the role of president broke open new vistas for the women at Bennett. Under her leadership in 1957, Bennett College gained membership in the Southern Association of Colleges and Schools.

On September 22, 1957, Roslyn Smith, class of 1961, submitted the obligatory Bennett College freshman essay on one's vision of self. In her own words, Smith describes her values, revealing the young mind that would soon absorb the words of Player, Dr. Martin Luther King Jr., Dr. Howard Thurman, and Dr. Benjamin Mays, spoken from the Bennett Chapel pulpit.

> Intellectual independence is my first requisition in life; to learn to think and to meet all complex problems with faith. The goal of

my achievement is to better educate myself and prepare to find position in the society and world in which I live. I believe that spiritual guidance is the basis of all foundations, and it has a definite place. The beliefs of concerns for the improvement of one's neighbor are a product of civilization. Fairness, honesty, truth, and respecting the rights of others are principles that create in an individual favorable opportunities and surroundings. . . . This is as I am.[5]

Player understood that these obligatory freshman essays revealed the callings, not only of their authors, but also of the institutions of higher education that admitted these students. In her February 8, 1958, keynote address before the National Council of United Negro College Fund Alumni, Player's words set the stage for her own "This is as I am" stand in Greensboro:

One of the tragedies of human experience is the failure in our southern region to recognize that no [individual] can reach his optimum potential unless every [individual] is free to grasp the opportunity, as he sees it, to explore his full range of abilities in the best possible environment, with the best possible resources at his disposal. . . .

We wish desperately to see our 33 colleges survive because they nourish the idea of Christian leadership inherent in our founding. Over the years our colleges have provided a leadership of a peculiar quality in that the service motive and the notion of brotherhood are outstanding. Our first leaders were predominately ministers and teachers. They gave and gave of their physical and spiritual strength and their knowledge without ever counting the cost.

In our world today we have a great need for many people who can help resolve the problems created by new recognitions, new challenges and new responsibilities. . . . Our leadership must be skilled in *creative thinking, problem-solving, scientific and technical know-how,* and in *organizational techniques and procedures.* . . .

The task for today is to work tirelessly, to possess the vision necessary to create from the very fabric of our historic past a concept of dignity, liberty, and leadership which will respond to the imperatives of our day and relieve the tensions which inevitably come with social change and social progress.[6]

Upon her return to the Bennett campus, Player publicly took her stand in Greensboro. When the Reverend Martin Luther King Jr. was slated to address the local school integration fight in Greensboro on February 11, 1958, neither North Carolina Agricultural and Technical

College, a public co-educational Black college known as A & T, nor the Greensboro Black public schools would accommodate the event within their public space.[7] Only Bennett College stepped forward to take the risk in hosting this event. Player set the college on a prophetic mountaintop when she proclaimed to the Greensboro and the campus communities that Bennett was "a liberal arts college where freedom rings."[8] Her leadership would not be silenced.

King's address in the Bennett Chapel challenged the students to be maladjusted[9] to the old order:

> The buses in Montgomery are desegregated but I'm not sure they are integrated. They will only be integrated when people sit side by side because they want to, not because it is the law. We can't win bitterness—fighting hate with hate, violence with violence. It can only be done with love. We must say to our white brother I will meet your capacity to inflict pain with love and win you over in the process. . . .
>
> I never intend to adjust myself to mob rule, segregation, discrimination and the self-defeating effects of physical violence. It may be that the salvation of the world lies in the hands of the maladjusted. . . .
>
> This is a great hour in America and for all people all over the world. There will be problems. Some may have to face losing their jobs. Some may face bombings and some even physical death—but it will be worth it.[10]

On February 1, 1960, four Black male freshmen from North Carolina Agricultural and Technical College walked into Greensboro's downtown Woolworth's store, bought a few items, and then sat down at the "white only" lunch counter to purchase something to drink. Though they remained at the lunch counter for several hours, the students were not served. When Woolworth's national office advised the Greensboro store to continue following local custom, that is, segregated service, women at Bennett College and dozens of male students at A & T joined the passive-resistance protest at the Woolworth's sit-down lunch counter on February 2. This act of solidarity with the four freshmen "ignited the student phase of the civil rights revolution."[11] In a February 2 letter to the president of the F. W. Woolworth's Corporation, the men declared the intent of their passive-resistance protest and sought resolution to the situation.

Interviews of Bennett participants in the lunch counter sit-ins reveal the deeply rooted determination of these students to participate in the public discourse of segregation. Bettye Davis, class of 1963, made the commitment to join the four A & T freshmen at the "white only" lunch counter on February 2 and to remain at the lunch counter until it was integrated:

> I came from a small town in Georgia, thirty miles south of Augusta, where all the pains of being Black had been a part of my experience: sitting at the back of the bus; going to the grocery store with my mother and watching some white woman pull my mother's buggy full of groceries out of line and put hers in front of us. I just knew it was time for a change, and something needed to happen.[12]

Soon after the sit-in movement began in Greensboro, Player convened the Bennett faculty and staff and announced her full support of the students and her decision "to throw the full weight of the college behind the students," as one Bennett administrator, Charlotte Alston, recalled.[13] The specific purpose of this assembly was to invite faculty and staff to work with the students during these difficult times.[14]

On the fourth day of the sit-ins, the Greensboro police arrested and detained overnight nearly one dozen Bennett women. "The only thing the jailers said to us was," noted Davis McCain, "'We thought you girls had'—yes they call us girls—'a lot of culture, but you don't, because you don't know your place.'"[15] The point is that the women did know their places: at the sit-down lunch counter, on the first floor of the movie houses, behind department store counters, in the best classrooms the state provided, on the voter registration books, and at the front of the bus.

Within the first week of the Greensboro student sit-ins, the mayor warned the city that the students' "unswerving determination to achieve their purpose"[16] had caught the interest of the nation. By the beginning of the second week of these sit-ins, the student civil rights movement had spread to Winston-Salem, Charlotte, Fayetteville, and Durham,[17] and a field secretary of the Congress of Racial Equality (CORE) had announced a picketing of F. W. Woolworth stores in New York City. "The purpose of the picketing," noted the CORE field secretary, "would be to persuade as many people as possible not to patronize them and thus pressure chain officials into integrating the lunch counters in North Carolina and other parts of the South."[18]

During the second week of the 1960 February sit-ins, students from Bennett and A & T formed a student coalition for civil rights. The group met in Bennett's science hall and elected Bettye Davis secretary, who later recalled that night's conversations.

We talked about what it would mean for our parents and our children. . . . We talked about little things that were big to us: our parents being able to go on a vacation and not to have to worry about staying with an Aunt Susie who lived in New York, traveling in a car with a chicken box and a loaf of bread all the way, and carrying some kind of urn or jar because we couldn't use a public bathroom. Many of us cried, because we couldn't really see in our minds that it was going to happen, but we knew that it had to.[19]

At the beginning of the lunch counter sit-ins, "downtown" hoped Player would urge the Bennett students to go back to the campus and stay away from the protests at Woolworth's. Player's niece, Linda Brown, who lived in the president's house during the first semester of the sit-ins and also participated in them, recalled that her aunt stated instead, "They are acting out of their conscience. They will take their exams in jail if they have to, and we will make that possible."[20] Player was the gatekeeper of a campus where, in her own words, "no person [was] the object of contempt . . . where the human spirit [was] released to find its highest and most creative expression."[21] She witnessed to the Bennett students the power in choosing to identify and name herself by assuming "an active role in making her meaning, establishing her identity [and the identity of the campus]."[22]

In 1960 Bennett students understood the significant support the college's administration and the faculty offered them. Bettye Davis would years later trace her decision to participate in the sit-in protests to Player's addresses before the packed chapel services: "It takes guts to be an individual, and that's what I want you to be. It doesn't take a lot of guts to go with the group. Be an individual; be you. If you believe in something strongly, do it, and be willing to pay the consequences."[23] Player's dignified leadership model brought a sense of empowerment to the whole student body. She instilled a sense of purpose in the Bennett students. As Bettye Davis McCain put it, "She thought that every young lady on that campus was competent, intelligent, and going to make a contribution to society."[24] Their contribution did not have to wait until they stepped off the campus with their diplomas.

Bennett's chapel was the life-giving center of the campus for students, faculty, and administration. The weekly chapel preaching, for Roslyn Smith, punctuated her vocational vision. Dr. Martin Luther King Jr. was the most memorable chapel speaker during her college years. "When we learned Dr. King was coming to our campus to speak at chapel, we immediately wrote our relatives," Smith remembered.

"He had a measured way of speaking, so profound . . . it was as if we were sitting there almost holding our breath."[25] She filtered this preaching through the image of her own mother's sacrifices under harsh economic circumstances in West Virginia. She heard a call to corrective action: Black students had to address the injustices surrounding them. In February of 1960 she took her place at the segregated lunch counters in Greensboro.

The voice of Howard Thurman from the Bennett pulpit set before students like Smith the lines along which they would write their life narratives.[26] Thurman's challenge was to continually expand the breadth of one's own life narrative. He took the life of the historical Jesus and set before the students prophetic questions for their lives: What are the lines along which you will choose to live your life in our society today? How will you relate your steps and your voices to the critical social issues of your world? How will you prepare for the questions you will have to answer?

Like the Bennett faculty who first established the obligatory freshman essay, Thurman believed in the need for individuals to face themselves before they face the greater community. He challenged the student to emerge "articulate, and particular" against the background of anonymity. He guided students to the measure of a prophet named Jesus, and challenged them to imagine their own eternal witness to truth and love.

Once students made the personal commitment to participate in the sit-ins, they attended an orientation session led by experienced A & T students, who knew the Bennett students were about to encounter angry white men and women surrounding them at the lunch counters and along the streets. The potential consequences of their decisions, the potential cracks in their design, and the unexpected reactions were always on the minds of the first students who joined these sit-ins. These uncertainties included: Would someone always break away and call for help if things got out of control? Could taking part in the sit-ins jeopardize their standing at Bennett or A & T? Would bail be secured for those persons arrested? Would their families be hurt in any way by their participation in these sit-ins? Could they handle the verbal and physical abuse by keeping the purpose of their acts of civil disobedience always before them?

On April 21, 1960, forty-five A & T and Bennett students were arrested on charges that they were trespassing at the S. H. Kress & Co. lunch counter. The next day the *Daily News* broke the story with front-page headlines and a picture of a well-dressed female student awkwardly entering the back of a paddy wagon without assistance from the police officers surrounding it. The news of the arrests, the first for which warrants had been issued, peeled off Greensboro's genteel mask. The lines of the struggle were now definitely drawn. The front page informed the public that "all 45 students were photographed and fingerprinted at the city jail and released for trial in Municipal County Court."[27] The article listed the names and home addresses of the local students arrested. Among them was Gwendolyn Mackel, Bennett College's senior class president:

> I remember some fear, but also a great deal of courage. It was something we knew we had to do. . . . I had grown up in a family where "this is the order of the day." Before I was born, my parents fought for improved classrooms for the Black students in Monroe, Louisiana. This was a part of our life. We didn't ride in the back of the bus. We had to walk or wait until someone could drive us where we needed to go. We did not say, "Yes, Sir" and "Yes, Ma'am" and "No, Sir" to white people. We were taught not to.[28]

The public discourse of the Bennett College women participating in the lunch counter sit-ins and the Greensboro community was layered with self-referential questions: "Does a [Black] woman have the right to contribute directly to public discourse in a way that reflects badly on [white] male behavior? That is, does a [Black] woman have the right to make public meaning, to which we all as a culture must subscribe?"[29] Certainly, in 1960, this was an instance of racial and gender trespass in the eyes of local custom. Bennett women were revealing the racial sin of the South, its Jim Crow laws, to an appalled global community. And not only the sin, but the ugly spirit of the sin. The female students' bold spirits caught the community off guard. They dared to name themselves as citizens with civil rights and privileges. These women would not be distracted by the racial epithets shouted at them as they sat at segregated lunch counters and picketed downtown movie theaters. They would not be silenced.

When Bennett students were arrested, Player brought them sandwiches and jail kits filled with personal necessities. They knew she would stand by her promise to pass out their graduation diplomas in jail if necessary. "You could 'take it to the bank,' as they say, because that was the kind of person she was," remembered Yvonne Jeffries Johnson, class of 1964.[30]

The witness of the Bennett students who chose to sit down at the segregated Woolworth's lunch counter in 1960 became a call for other acts of social transformation by students like Yvonne Jeffries, who arrived at Bennett the following fall. The seeds of her vocational vision had been nurtured by a savvy extended family. Her uncle, the first African American to receive a Ph.D. in dairy science in the United States and a professor at North Carolina A & T, directed her to the passionate discourse on Bennett's campus in August of 1960. Her aunt's participation in the 1963 Greensboro mass sit-in movement with other elementary school teachers, many of them Bennett alumnae, had directed Yvonne Jeffries's attention to active participation in the desegregation of Greensboro's downtown.[31] In a 1996 interview, Yvonne Jeffries Johnson recalled,

> It wasn't about whether you were going to go to school. It was about *where* you were going to go to school. It wasn't about whether you were going to be a contributing member of society. It was about *how* you were going to be a contributing member of society. For me, it was never, "Will I make a contribution?" It was, "*What* contribution will I make?" That definitely was a family pattern.[32]

Jeffries recalled an event from her childhood involving a family friend she knew as Mrs. McGroom.

> My mother and Mrs. McGroom would often go downtown on the bus. . . . When we were eight or nine they would take us with them. . . . You were always with someone, so they would guide you, or keep you out of harm's way. . . . We were really, really protected. . . . It was sort of a rule that you go to the back of the bus, but, if the back of the bus is filled and there are a few seats in the front, you can sit in them. My mother and Mrs. McGroom had been riding so long, they knew the bus driver. It was crowded and we were standing up. We were sort of to the front, standing. Two seats became available right up front. I said, "Mrs. McGroom, do you want to sit down?" She said, "No," and my mother said, "No." Mrs. McGroom said, "You sit down." It was a two-seater. There was a white man sitting in one of the seats. When I got ready to sit down, he put his foot up in the chair. Mrs. McGroom took her umbrella and she went "pow" right on his leg. She always carried an umbrella. The bus driver pulled over. My heart was in my mouth. He put that man off the bus. It was like nobody said anything. I was going to get up. Mrs. McGroom said, "No, you sit there." I will never forget that woman's absolute bravery, and the kind of focus she had on me. . . . "Maybe I can't do it, but damn it, you're going to do it, and you're going to sit there."[33]

Supported by Player, the Bennett students resisted Greensboro's efforts to silence them. They met the expectations that Player had set before the campus and herself in her 1956 inaugural statement. In their disclosure of how they meant to be in this world, there could be "no standing still, no compromise, no equivocation."[34]

In April 1960 well-dressed Bennett women wore placards hung over their shoulders that demanded "Jim Crow Got To Go" and "What's Right Can Be Done." There would be no standing still as long as injustice ruled the day in Greensboro. The silence had been shattered. The Bennett women were declaring their certain way of being in the world. Linda Brown identifies the personal history of the Bennett women that compelled them to remap these socially constructed boundaries:

> You get the courage for prophetic witness because it's in your history. Your father and your mother worked themselves to death, and you understand why. Nobody has to tell you why. Nobody has to tell you why you had to go to college. And that story is repeated and repeated and repeated. Or, like I did, you come from a privileged Black family, where you are told from the day that you are born that you have a responsibility because you're privileged. People are depending on you. You've got your brothers and sisters struggling in this country and you need to do something; to witness, to make change. You have a politicized family. I didn't need the civil rights movement to politicize me. I was political from birth. I sat at the dining room table and heard my father, who was working with the Urban League, talk about how Black men could not get jobs. I didn't need the civil rights movement to teach me about that.[35]

The Bennett women did not settle for desegregated lunch counters. As soon as the lunch counters were opened to all, the Bennett women announced to the managers of S. H. Kress & Co. and Belk department stores that from now on if they wanted their business, they would have to employ Blacks on the sales floor, not just down on the floor scrubbing. Their demands brought results.[36] The Bennett women continued to claim their places in the Southern public space.

Randolph-Macon Woman's College

Rebecca Owen and Mary Edith Bentley would become leaders of the student movement at their school, Randolph-Macon Woman's College (R-MWC) in Lynchburg, Virginia. In an interview Owen spoke of an early childhood memory:

My whole relationship with the Christian faith and my relationship with Black people were very intimately tied together from my
earliest memories. I remember it was my fourth birthday. Estelle,
the African-American woman who took care of me, made me a
beautiful cake and cooked the dinner. I said that I wanted her to
stay for dinner and my birthday party. . . . It's so vivid. I remember I was standing by the ironing board in the kitchen. Estelle was
there, my mother was there, and my sister was there. And there
was dead silence. My mother said that Estelle wouldn't be comfortable having dinner with us. Later my sister gave me hell
because I didn't know how to talk to Estelle. I felt shamed by it,
but I knew something was wrong. . . . I remember then thinking—
it's kind of vague—that it was unfair and that this wasn't the way
Jesus would want it.[37]

When she was fifteen, Rebecca Owen attended the national Methodist youth gathering at Purdue University where, for the first time, she
would experience meeting with Black students apart from the racist
shadows of rural tidewater Virginia. The experience was a theological
watershed for her:

From this time, I was not able to escape the feeling that there
should be some relationship between what I heard in my church
and the injustices I knew in the community. I returned home
deeply puzzled and talked with my minister and other persons
whom I respected. I was rebuffed. But it was suggested I might
give some clothes to a Negro family. I felt a resentment to my
church and I was unable to resolve in my mind why people said
one thing and did another. I quickly became silent, yet my thinking and reading continued.[38]

During her senior year in high school, Owen attended a Methodist
missionary conference for youth at Lake Junaluska, North Carolina. It
was here that she met the director of the Henderson Settlement in
Frakes, Kentucky, and accepted the invitation to spend the summer
after her high school graduation in mission at the settlement.[39]

Owen entered Randolph-Macon Woman's College in the fall of
1957. The college had first opened its doors in 1893 with the commitment to provide a higher education for women equivalent to that
offered the men at Randolph-Macon College in Ashland, Virginia. It
was the first women's college admitted to the Southern Association of
Colleges and Schools and the first in the South to receive a charter for
a Phi Beta Kappa chapter. The Methodist founders' vision was set
before each student annually in the student handbook:

We wish to establish in Virginia a college where our young women may obtain an education equal to that given in our best colleges for young men, and under environments in harmony with the highest ideals of womanhood; where the dignity and strength of fully developed faculties and the charm of the highest literary culture may be acquired by our daughters without loss to woman's crowning glory—her gentleness and grace.[40]

The current bearer of this torch, Dr. William F. Quillian Jr., was beginning his sixth year as president of Randolph-Macon Woman's College in 1957. He was the first ordained minister in the Methodist Church to serve as president of the college.[41]

In the fall of her sophomore year there, Owen became involved in the activities of the Virginia Methodist Student Movement (MSM) and "met students who were concerned with the same questions and problems."[42] In 1959, her junior year, Owen was elected president of the Virginia MSM and an officer of the national MSM. The publication of this national movement, *motive* magazine, was now the mainstay of Owen's pilgrimage. Its high-caliber theological articles raised important ethical questions for Owen and challenged her to understand vocation as a calling in the present rather than the future.

A few months after a *motive* magazine article challenged students to root out sinful structures and to call forth virtuous deeds from all citizens so that all might experience justice within the community,[43] a moral battle cry went up on the Randolph-Macon campus. In the final issue of the Randolph-Macon student newspaper for the 1959–1960 academic year, Christie McCoy presented her fellow students with the challenge to respond to an immediate truth that could no longer be ignored if their culture was going to awaken to the injustice it had created for so many of its citizens:

At R-M the whole subject of segregation vs. integration is carefully avoided. The role of white Southern students is of vital importance in this movement. Why, then, are they silent? Why are we at R-M silent? . . . We are plagued by a deep conflict within ourselves on the subject. We realize that integration is morally right—fewer Southerners every day claim to reconcile segregation and Christianity—but it is difficult with our psychological-sociological conditioning to picture integration put into effect. To many of us the prospect seems disastrous. The moral argument has won us over in principle, but we still have trouble acting accordingly. . . . As a leading white Southern school, it is our responsibility to know what is happening, to take a stand, if not as a student body, then at least as individuals.[44]

In September 1960, Owen attended the annual General Assembly of the National Student Christian Federation in Denver, Colorado. In this setting, the call for action came from the stories of Black brothers and sisters in Christ who had "sat down" at lunch counters in Greensboro and across the South on behalf of just racial relationships and the dignity of all God's children. For students like Owen, that call could not be denied. They discovered the courage and the ability to respond. Reporting on the assembly for *motive* magazine, Tom Lord wrote:

> A new spirit was evident in the Assembly's deliberations on the nonviolent movement. Previously, ecumenical meetings have been permeated with theological formulations about the nature and unity of the church. This meeting, however, spoke of action. Allen Burry, president of the NSCF, stated, "We have discovered our life together in our involvement in the nonviolent protests." And "the time has come for us to quit talking only—let's act." The courageous stand taken by those in the sit-ins seems to have given many students a new enthusiasm to "do" something in their own campus communities.[45]

Owen was elected to the national leadership team of the National Student Christian Federation. During her senior year, she carried both state and national leadership roles in the ecumenical Christian student federations.

Upon her return to Randolph-Macon for her final year, Owen initiated discussion groups between students at her own school and three other church-related institutions of higher education in the Lynchburg area: Lynchburg College, Sweet Briar College, and Virginia Theological Seminary. The Black students opened the eyes of the white students to the daily Jim Crow humiliations of their lives. Owen was reminded of Estelle's humiliation on Owen's fourth birthday.

Randolph-Macon senior Mary Edith Bentley was a participant at this discussion table. During her first two years there, from the fall of 1957 through the spring of 1959, Bentley attended the Virginia MSM conferences at the University of Virginia, Blacksburg. These state-level MSM conferences, along with *motive* magazine, kept students connected with the national voice of the MSM. Though a music major, Bentley by her own admission had her "left foot sort of over in the religion department."[46]

During her junior year, Bentley joined a group of religion majors and their department's chair who were reading together Reinhold

Niebuhr's *The Children of Light, the Children of Darkness*. The chapter "Democratic Toleration and the Groups of the Community," though meant to address in particular the horrors of the global community in the early and mid-1940s, surely sparked discussion regarding the sin of racism within the Jim Crow laws of the South:

> A democratic society must use every stratagem of education and every resource of religion to generate appreciation of the virtues and good intentions of minority groups, which diverge from the type of the majority, and to prompt humility and charity in the life of the majority. It must seek to establish contacts between the groups and prevent the aggravation of prejudice through segregation. It must uncover the peculiar hazards to right judgment, which reveal themselves in inter-group relations. A democratic society must, in other words, seek proximate solutions for this problem in indeterminate creative ventures.[47]

Through her contact with these religion majors, Bentley's calling began to take clearer shape. Bentley was elected president of the Randolph-Macon MSM chapter. She was an excellent example of the potential for Christian leadership seen in college students such as herself who were awarded the National Methodist Scholarship.

On December 14, 1960, these two white Southern women at Randolph-Macon chose to break the recently passed 1960 Virginia trespass law, together with four other students representing the Black and white institutions of higher education in the greater Lynchburg area. They participated in a sit-in at Patterson's Drugstore in Lynchburg in the name of just racial relationships and the dignity of all God's children. Because the owner, Mr. Patterson, had refused to respond to their questions regarding the store's discrimination policies, the students felt that they had to press the issue further. They were arrested.

Rebecca Owen and Mary Edith Bentley stood in solidarity with the Black community in Lynchburg and the Black students who were beaten and arrested in the lunch counter sit-ins across the South. They chose to trespass upon, and thereby unmask, the dehumanizing principalities and powers in the Southern culture surrounding them. They were well aware of the historical Christian testimonies to the likelihood of persecution for such actions. However, they were not prepared for the lack of support from the very Christian institutions that had empowered them to search for new truths. Now, when they courageously risked acting upon these truths, those institutions tried to silence them.

After consulting the dean of students at Randolph-Macon and the student chair of its judiciary committee, Quillian decided to bring Owen and Bentley before that committee, although Owen was actually one of its members, representing the senior class. In Quillian's eyes, they had broken one of the school's tenets, stated in its handbook: "In all other circumstances, whether at home or elsewhere, it is expected that Randolph-Macon students will conduct themselves in such a way as never to bring criticism upon themselves or upon their college."[48] Some students and alumnae felt the breaking of this rule would justify expelling Owen and Bentley. As Frances Mayes, who attended Randolph-Macon in the late 1950s, reveals in her article *10,000 Rules to Live By*, "Anyone's broken rule was tied to your 'honor.'"[49] Honor was defined within the Southern custom of the day for young women: "We were kept in place by the appeal to a higher sense, morality; the rule was the thing, not the personal judgment of the act behind the rule."[50]

The judiciary committee chose no punitive action, after assurance from both Owen and Bentley that neither would participate in an act of civil disobedience during the remaining half of their senior year. At the winter assembly on January 3, 1961, the committee's statement to the student body echoed the Randolph-Macon code of honor understood by all students: "The Judiciary Committee has great respect for a person's freedom of thought and action as long as it is within the law, but believes that action taken not in accordance with the law is harmful to both community and the college."[51] Prophetic Christian witness could not be translated within the Randolph-Macon code of honor.

Quillian also chose this assembly for his formal statement to the student body and the two women who participated in the December 14 sit-in. (The next day Randolph-Macon students had staged a second sit-in; they were not arrested.) The heart of Quillian's message is found in these lines:

> I am sure that the students who have participated in these two "sit-in" demonstrations have done so because of deep religious convictions. I feel sure that these convictions have resulted from careful study and discussion over a period of many years of the meaning and implications of the Christian faith. I imagine that they have prayed over this question, seeking God's guidance, more than most of us have. The concerns which they share are concerns which have been clearly expressed by most of the major church bodies or denominations to which you and I belong. Not

everyone will agree with a particular interpretation of the Christian faith and its meaning for our daily lives, but it is important for all of us to respect the person of deep conviction who is earnestly and honestly seeking God's will. To say that we respect the convictions of those who have participated in the sit-in demonstrations does not mean, however, that we agree with or approve of these particular actions. It is my belief that these were unwise. . . .[52]

His reasons, which sounded almost brutal to Owen and Bentley's ears, suggested their insensitivity to the consequences of their actions. His remarks even included the charge that the sit-in had undermined the sense of goodwill in Lynchburg established by its Bi-Racial Committee. Quillian chose to bring Owen and Bentley under his control, reminding them, through the Judiciary Committee, of the rules under which they could remain on campus.

In his eyes, they were not sensible regarding what they were capable of accomplishing, despite the strength of their deep convictions. Now he would have to take charge and clean up not only the damage to the Randolph-Macon code of honor, but also the damage to Black and white relationships within the Lynchburg community itself. In his eyes, Owen, in spite of scholastic achievements that included a Phi Beta Kappa key and a Woodrow Wilson fellowship, had failed to grasp the historical and cultural bases of racial tensions.[53] Owen and Bentley were presented to the whole student body as arrogant and incompetent.

Quillian's words at the winter assembly shamed Owen and Bentley in front of the entire student body, faculty, and administration. In a 1993 interview with graduate student Theresa Carroll, Mary Edith Bentley Abu-Saba shared these reflections on that gathering in 1961:

> What I remember him saying was, "Don't you dare think about doing this again," in a very stern voice. My father [a Methodist minister] was there; all the seniors were wearing their caps and gowns. Nothing was said celebrating our actions. I guess he [Quillian] felt he needed to do that. He wasn't going around saying, "Oh, what a wonderful thing you've done." I left that public occasion feeling humiliated.[54]

Owen recalled, "I might have felt chastised, but I don't think I felt repentant."[55] In a 1994 interview, she recalled her anger with the administration's refusal to personally sit down with her and Bentley and to honestly discuss the position it found itself in with its trustees, alumnae, community, and present students because of their actions:

> . . . It wasn't about my changing the whole college. I think there was a way that Dr. Quillian [and other names] . . . I think if they had put their heads together they could have spoken to me in a way that I would have understood. I mean, I was not stupid. I certainly had the overall feeling that they thought that I had done a terrible thing to the college. They did not want any publicity about it. They did not want me even to speak to the students at the college. They did not want to listen to me. . . . They did not want other college students to know about it. . . . I think they could have found a way to have said to me, look, these are the political realities, I'm sorry. . . .[56]

Quillian also failed, from Owen's perspective, to help the campus as a whole struggle healthily with the tensions raised by the sit-in, because of his unwillingness to engage in open discussion with the student body. In her eyes, he kept his distance by delivering only a terse statement that would serve to cover the positions of the administration.

Quillian spoke as a Southern gentleman who sought changes through quiet evolution, respectful conversation. Passionate engagement in implicit acts of faith was not in his repertoire. His was a "wise voice," in touch with the larger community and its consternation. It was a "savvy voice," placing the final action of the institution in regard to the two students' "unwise" actions in the hands of a student-faculty judiciary committee rather than the board of trustees. One might also describe it as a "conflicted" voice. In his October 24, 1958, annual report to the college's board of trustees, Quillian had proclaimed a particular affirmation of individual dignity:

> This is the task to which Randolph-Macon is dedicated, that of encouraging the optimum development of each person as a unique, creative being. Such a task we believe has meaning and significance only as it is grounded in deeply rooted convictions. From its foundation Randolph-Macon has been committed to that belief in the dignity and worth of the individual which is at the heart of the Hebrew-Christian tradition. Thence comes the ultimate meaning and significance of our life as teachers and students.[57]

Criticism of Quillian arose from trustees, alumnae, and the community because Owen and Bentley were not expelled by the college. Quillian responded formally in writing to questions raised by twelve

Lynchburg alumnae: ". . . The whole approach of the Judiciary Committee is to concern itself with the total situation, including particularly the attitude of the student, rather than with the nature of a specific offense."[58]

There was clearly a sense that the Judiciary Committee had, in truth, handled this particular offense "in a different way from the other cases."[59] It is probable that Quillian was the catalyst that encouraged as deep an understanding of the total situation as possible before determining a penalty. His leadership style in addressing the clamor brought on by the students' arrest, though not prophetic, can be seen as pastoral, especially compared to the rulings of other presidents of Southern institutions of higher education. It was not uncommon for students in the South to be expelled for participation in the lunch counter sit-in movement. The two white male students from Lynchburg College arrested on December 14 with Owen and Bentley were "strongly censured by Lynchburg College officials (the president and the Board of Trustees) for their part in the sit-in demonstration."[60]

A powerful example of the faculty's unanimous support of Quillian's leadership choices can be found in a letter written by a faculty member of Randolph-Macon's Department of Greek the day after the students' sentencing:

> It seems to me that many people might benefit from reading more Greek tragedy. First they might come to recognize that one is sometimes faced with a problem, like Orestes' for instance, to which there is no "right" answer—and one must choose a solution, which seems to be the least of possible evils. Secondly, they would realize that the solution which might be right enough for a person with *simple* responsibility would be utterly wrong for a person with *multiple* responsibilities—i.e. is answerable to many different groups outside himself. It is easy enough to say, "I would have done so-and-so," when it's a matter of one's own conscience—but tragedy puts a man in a bad place, orients him against several different responsibilities and then asks not "How do you feel about this?" but, "What needs to be done?" . . . You're batting 1000 in my book.[61]

Owen and Bentley were never given a public opportunity to address the student body as a whole; in fact, Owen was even denied permission to accept invitations from Yale University and Smith College to speak to their student groups regarding the December 14 sit-in. The dean of students at Randolph-Macon insisted Owen could not afford the time away from her studies after already spending eighteen days in jail that winter. Owen chose to go anyway. ". . . I didn't need to keep up my schoolwork. I think I had one B at Randolph-Macon, and that was my freshman year."[62] She spoke to Yale's Christian groups at William Sloane Coffin's request and addressed students at Smith on a broader scale. Owen recalled that Coffin, then Yale's chaplain, had hoped to be invited to Randolph-Macon to participate in discussion groups on the campus. The invitation was never extended by the administration.

On February 6 1961, Owen and Bentley deliberately accepted, with the other four Lynchburg students, their thirty-day jail sentence: "We are now seeking to fulfill the first witness by accepting the consequences of our protest—by going to jail—for we believe that if social justice is to be righted, we who speak against it must be willing to accept personal discomfort and hardship."[63] The image of two Randolph-Macon women walking the block to jail after their sentencing shocked the community.

Owen and Bentley became the first white women in the modern student civil rights movement to join the "jail, no bail" strategy of the movement that had formally begun on February 1, 1961 in Rock Hill, South Carolina, under the leadership of Congress of Racial Equality field secretary Tom Gaither. On the same day that Owen and Bentley walked to the Lynchburg jail, Ed King, executive secretary for the Student Nonviolent Coordinating Committee, called for greater sacrificial participation in the lunch counter sit-ins:

> . . . Join them [Gaither, nine black students in Rock Hill, and four new volunteers—Diane Nash, Charles Jones, Ruby Doris Smith, and Charles Sherrod] at the lunch counters and in jail. Only by this type of action can we show that the non-violent movement against segregation is not a local issue for just the individual community, but rather a united movement of all those who believe in equality.[64]

The *Washington Post*'s front-page coverage included the eye-catching picture of two Lynchburg policemen forcibly ejecting from the court a white Episcopalian priest who had refused to obey the segregated seating enforcement of the courtroom. It also included a courageous challenge from the students who were sentenced to begin thirty days in jail: "We have confidence that no person of good conscience will stand idly by—will remain silent—while we students who sought to speak against the destruction of human potential which results from racial discrimination are punished for implementing our faith in Christian-democratic principles."[65]

The story of the students' sentencing became the centerpiece of the Reverend Duncan Howlett's sermon on February 12, 1961, at Washington's All Souls Unitarian Church. He concluded with these remarks:

> After the six Lynchburg students had been led into the Lynchburg jail, their fellow students formed a double line on the other side of the street. Most of them were Negroes, but many white students also joined in the demonstration. They had been told that if they conducted themselves with dignity and remained stretched out in a line they could not be dispersed as a mob. Together they sang hymns and Negro spirituals. Then they said the Lord's Prayer.[66]

Owen and Bentley were invited by the Randolph-Macon student newspaper's staff to express their reasons for taking part in the lunch counter sit-in. The following is an excerpt from their response:

> . . . It is the logical outcome of a number of years of thought and development. . . . We see inherent in this faith (the Judeo-Christian heritage) the central question of what is our active response to God's love. This is the question that each individual must answer. This question must be answered not on the basis of the expedient, the prudent, the lucrative, the conventional, but rather from one's own desire to participate in God's will for His creation. . . . We do not see the sit-in movement as an end in itself but rather as an implement for breaking down superficial barriers that obstruct reconciliation of man to man.[67]

Bentley planned to be married on the day after her graduation from Randolph-Macon. After serving the jail sentence, Bentley was informed that the Centenary Methodist Church would not permit her to hold her wedding there if she invited Black guests. Bentley, determined to find a place where she could be wed under conditions that "set right with her conscience,"[68] immediately sought Quillian's permission to use the college's chapel.[69]

> I didn't know what to do. I went to his house and knocked on his front door. He let me in the front door. We stood there in the corridor. He didn't even ask me to come in and sit down. I remember that. We talked for five minutes, maybe. . . . You just see the person who is supposed to be doing the right thing. I just kept wanting him to do the right thing by me. Please? I think that is what I

wanted. To join with me and say, "Oh yeah, golly, that's not the right thing to do, is it—having your wedding and not being able to invite the Black folk that have been so important to you?" I mean, couldn't somebody say that? No. No. No, they couldn't say that. They couldn't see it. They couldn't say it. It was not important. But it was to me. It is still one of those things—I don't feel proud of it. I don't feel proud of how I did it. I was the one who blinked. I said, "Okay, I'll still have it at the Methodist church that will not allow me to have the Black folks, and I will un-invite the Black folk." I did. I un-invited them. I did it myself, with hat in hand, saying, "You kind of understand, don't you?" And the Black folks said, "Well sure, Mary Edith, we understand. We know all about that, honey." Of course they knew all about it. But I was doing it. I was right in there with the white folks doing the same thing, and I knew that I was doing it. I was trying to get them to say that it was all right and that they would forgive me. But, still I did it.[70]

Disillusionment and conflict permeated every layer of her social environment.

But Bentley's social surrender to the white racism of the Christian church in Lynchburg would not be the last word in this particular situation. Don and Perno, two Black cooks from Randolph-Macon's dining hall, had offered to serve at Bentley's wedding reception as their present to her. They had been Bentley's "buddies" since her sophomore days of waiting tables. When the moment came for Bentley to walk down the aisle at Centenary Methodist Church, the first guests she saw were Don and Perno, in their white starched serving chef uniforms, sitting to the right in the back row. It was as if they had sneaked in. Bentley vividly recalled the moment in a 1996 interview: "They're witnessing. They're the witness. I can never talk about that without crying. They were witnessing for the whole Black community. They were there representing the Black community that I un-invited. Then they disappeared after the wedding to go to the reception hall to serve the food."[71]

The conclusion of Niebuhr's chapter "The Individual and the Community" in *The Children of Light, the Children of Darkness* may express the Lynchburg community's dawning awareness in the spring of 1961:

The [person] who searches after both meaning and fulfillments beyond the ambiguous fulfillments and frustrations of history exists in a height of spirit, which no historical process can completely contain. This height is not irrelevant to the life of the community, because new richness and a higher possibility of justice come to the community from this height of awareness. But the height is destroyed by any community, which seeks prematurely to cut off this pinnacle of individuality in the interest of the community's peace and order. The problem of the individual and the community cannot be solved at all if the height is not achieved where the sovereign source and end of both individual and communal existence are discerned, and where the limits are set against the idolatrous self-worship of both individuals and communities.[72]

Rebecca Owen and Mary Edith Bentley's interpretations of their sacred calling caught the attention of the national media (both secular and denominational), the Woodrow Wilson Fellowship Foundation, and national religious and political leaders. The *Washington Post*'s front page reported on the trial of Owen, Bentley, and four students from neighboring institutions of higher education. The denominational publications *Concern* and *World Outlook* covered the sentencing of the two Methodist student leaders. Hans Rosenhaupt, director of the Woodrow Wilson Fellowship Foundation, proposed presenting Owen with her check while she was in jail and lifting her witness before the nation through coverage in *Life* magazine. In Owen's life narrative, Rosenhaupt saw an outstanding example of a woman filled with fire, energy, and courageous conviction, a woman who acted up to her convictions in spite of the threat of cultural backlash. For that foundation, Owen was a symbol of the intellect, character, and personality needed in the faculty ranks of our nation's institutions of higher education.[73] Both Martin Luther King Jr. and Robert Kennedy sent telegrams to Owen and Bentley while they served out their trespassing sentence in the Lynchburg jail.

At the center of Owen's call was her understanding of obedience to the radical discipleship that she heard in the Christian ethics of Dietrich Bonhoeffer and the Methodist Student Movement. In her senior honors paper "What Is Christ for Us Today?" (partially researched during her eighteen days in jail), one reads Owen's passionate dialogue with Bonhoeffer, whose call for civil courage eloquently embodied the call for Christian witness heard at the national Christian student conference the summer before Owen's senior year at Randolph-Macon. Bonhoeffer wrote:

Who stands fast? Only man whose final standard is not his reason, his principles, his conscience, his freedom, or his virtues, but

who is ready to sacrifice all this when he is called to obedient and
responsible action in faith and in exclusive allegiance to God—
the responsible man, who tries to make his whole life an answer
to the question and call of God. Where are these people?[74]

Rebecca Owen and Mary Edith Bentley, along with four other college students on December 14, 1960, answered, ". . . at a segregated
lunch counter in Lynchburg, Virginia." Owen heard Bonhoeffer and
the keynote speakers of the national Christian conference challenging students to "act up" to their deep religious convictions.[75] Owen
summarized in her honors paper her own theological interpretation
of obedience: "Man is called to plunge himself into life, and not to
seek to impose upon it a veneer for religion in order to make its
ungodliness less stark. Man's freedom does not lie in his righteous
ideas or in his piety, but rather in his determination to live responsibly with Christ as the center of his actions."[76] Owen's freedom could
be found not only at the lunch counter sit-in, but also in her passion
to express herself despite her college president's attempt to silence
her.

Conclusion

In Greensboro the humiliation of the Jim Crow laws began to crum-
ble. The children of God stood on their own sacred sense of personal
worth. It was the truth seen over and over again in the faces of the students who sat down for justice in Greensboro. This same truth is
heard in the voice of Yvonne Jeffries Johnson recalling the day in May
1963 when she and hundreds of Bennett students were arrested while
picketing Greensboro's theaters:

> I can remember turning the corner and walking around to the Car-
> olina Theater . . . having hecklers with sticks hit us until the A & T
> football team turned the corner, and that's when it stopped. Then
> you heard some "pow pow" and just kept walking. You didn't look
> back. Certainly there's fear. But when the time comes in each of
> our lifetimes for some profound change, your fear is as small as a
> dot. [Fear] is there, it's real, it exists, but it has very little power in
> terms of the whole event, if you know what I mean. It's like a
> wave, and of course the salt is in the wave, but the salt is just a
> finite part of that wave, and you're riding that wave. You know
> there's no way that you're not going to ride it.[77]

The Bennett College women claimed their right to contribute directly to public discourse in a way that enraged the white Southern community. In the early 1960s Bennett students repeatedly engaged in racial and gender trespass, defying local custom. Their bold spirits caught the community off guard. They took their place in the white southern public space and boldly announced that they would not be moved from it. Their public stand brimmed with the power of naming one's self. These students claimed their dissident and disobedient voices and remapped the social boundaries of gender and race in Greensboro. Their college president's stand and their personal histories affirmed their place at that moment in history.

The Randolph-Macon women also displayed a passionate commitment to remapping those socially constructed boundaries at segregated lunch counters. And in so doing, they also dared to enter into the center of the public discourse and to define themselves. For one, all-too-brief moment in the history of Randolph-Macon Woman's College, they witnessed to an alternative social construction of gender and race.

They stood in good company. In 1955 the voice of Lillian Smith, addressing the issue of segregation in the South, had attracted national attention with the publication of *Now Is the Time*. She confessed for the white Southern Christian, in the hope that there would be for many an awakening to new truth:

> It was not good form to ask questions about our way of life, and we punished those who did so in quiet, subtle ways. If teachers or ministers forgot and discussed these matters in classroom or pulpit, we saw to it that they lost their posts. We were not only segregating Negroes from whites, we were segregating ourselves from our world, shutting minds and hearts away from all that would give us insight and knowledge—still trying, as our great-grandfathers had done, to defend the morally indefensible. During this silent time, the consciences of gentle people went to sleep. They could still be disturbed about evil in many areas of life, and were. But this evil, this injury which segregation inflicts on both the colored and the white groups, they could not bear to look at.[78]

The Randolph-Macon students attracted national attention with their trial and subsequent sentence to jail. Charles Cole and twenty-seven other students at Yale Divinity School sent a letter to the editor of the *Lynchburg News* on January 15, 1961:

> We, the undersigned students at Yale Divinity who are preparing for service in the Christian Church, voice our support of the recent protest against racial injustice which occurred in the form of a "sit-in." . . . We do not speak as detached spectators of the present crisis in human relations, but as persons who are intimately involved in this problem. As Southerners, we protest the pattern of segregation that deny Negro Southerners equality of opportunity and cause destruction of personality and waste of human resources. . . . As Christians, we deplore the gap between official pronouncement of the Christian churches and the moral practices of congregations and individuals who confess the name of Jesus Christ. . . . We rebuke all Americans, Southerners and Northerners, including ourselves, for the way in which we have for so long remained blind to the evil of racial discrimination and silent about the need for immediate change in the laws and customs, which reinforce this injustice.[79]

But then the Randolph-Macon students blinked and said, "Okay, we agree to not trespass upon your insidious construction of social relations within the white Southern culture, as long as we are Randolph-Macon students. We will conduct ourselves in such a way as not to bring criticism upon ourselves or upon our college." Presidential leadership at a Methodist-affiliated college had silenced their voices, unlike the very different leadership of President Willa Player at Bennett College. The sit-ins were a remarkable effort of students at two Methodist women's colleges to put the teachings they had learned in family, church, and college into practice, and the differences in responses to that effort by two college presidents, one a Black woman and the other a white man, are striking.

Notes

1. Patricia Hill Collins, *Black Feminist Thought: Knowledge, Consciousness, and the Politics of Empowerment* (New York: Routledge, 1991), 174.

2. In the introduction to *Hine Sight: Black Women and the Re-Construction of American History* (Bloomington: Indiana University Press, 1994, xxii), Darlene Clark Hine's reflections on editing a historical encyclopedia on Black women's lives in America reminds any historian recovering Black women's history that two of the most important keys to Black women's survival were their well-honed skills of organizing and building communities. They were women who, amid brutal, dehumanizing external circumstances, could internally reimagine themselves. Their battle cries of dignity were testimonies of transcendent truths. Though the dominant culture's social constructions of

race, gender, and class would relentlessly marginalize Black women's voices, exemplary Black women in local and national communities defied those forces and would not be moved from their own sense of being.

3. Jeanne Noble, "The Higher Education of Black Women in the Twentieth Century," in *Women and Higher Education in American History,* eds. John Mack Faragher and Florence Howe (New York: Norton, 1988), 95.

4. 1956 Inauguration book working draft (photocopy), Bennett College Holgate Library archives, 23–24. Excerpts from Player's inaugural address were included in the Women's Division of Christian Service's monthly publication coverage of the Bennett College inauguration activities. Mrs. D. C. Wardlow, "Bennett: A Way of Living," *World Outlook* 17 (December 1956), 41.

5. Roslyn Smith, "This Is As I Am," Bennett College freshman essay (photocopy), personal papers, 1957.

6. Willa Player, "Where There Is Vision...," *Bennett College Bulletin,* vol. 25 (Winter 1958), 7.

7. William H. Chafe, *Civilities and Civil Rights: Greensboro, North Carolina, and the Black Struggle for Freedom* (Oxford: Oxford University Press, 1981), 80.

8. Ibid.

9. In an article published in 1958, King wrote: "There are some things in our social systems to which all of us ought to be maladjusted. . . . I never intend to adjust myself to the inequalities of an economic system which takes necessities from the masses to give luxuries to the classes. I never intend to become adjusted to the madness of militarism and the self-defeating method of physical violence. . . . The challenge to us is to be maladjusted . . ." (from *A Testament of Hope: The Essential Writings and Speeches of Martin Luther King, Jr.,* ed. James M. Washington [San Francisco: HarperCollins, 1991]). It is probable that much of his address in the Bennett College chapel was from this article.

10. Dorothy Ann Benjamin, "'Live as Brothers or Die as Fools,' Negroes Told," *Greensboro Record,* 11 February 1958, 1(B).

11. These words appear on the Greensboro Historical Museum's plaques commemorating the sit-ins, Greensboro, N.C.

12. Bettye Davis McCain, interview by author, notes, Charlotte, N.C., 25 February 1996.

13. Charlotte Alston, interview by author, tape recording, Greensboro, N.C., 22 January 1996.

14. Like the Bennett students' roles in the Greensboro sit-in movement, Player's decisive and courageous handling of this moment in history went all but unnoticed outside the Greensboro community. Her presidency ended in 1966 when she assumed the role of director of the Division of College Support in the United States Office of Education. Darlene Clark Hine's essay "Rape and the Inner Lives of Southern Black Women: Thought of the Culture of Dissemblance" in *Hine Sight* provides an essential framework for me, a white, middle-class feminist historian, to analyze: Black women's politics of silence. Hine argues, "Because of the interplay of racial animosity, class tensions, gender role

differentiation, and regional economic variations, black women as a rule developed a politics of silence, and adhered to a cult of secrecy, a culture of dissemblance, to protect the sanctity of the inner aspects of their lives" (41). She suggests that this veil of secrecy or "invisibility" was well developed by Black women across class lines. Historical documents of Willa Player's leadership at Bennett College point to just such an "undisclosed persona" that sustained her, allowing the assumption of her own agency amid the hostile confrontations that followed when Bennett students stripped away the veneer of Greensboro's civility. Perhaps Player's veil of invisibility contributed to the overlooking of her own pivotal role in nurturing Greensboro's place in the history of the modern student civil rights movement.

15. Bettye Davis McCain, interview by author, tape recording, Charlotte, N.C., 25 February 1996.

16. Julian Morrison, "A & T Students Call Two-Week Recess in Protest Here," *Greensboro Daily News,* 7 February 1960, 1A.

17. "Negroes Splattered with Eggs as Sitdown Spreads to Raleigh," *Greensboro Daily News,* 11 February 1960, 1(A).

18. "Picketing of Stores Planned," *Greensboro Daily News,* 10 February 1960, 1(B).

19. Bettye Davis McCain, interview by author, tape recording, Charlotte, N.C., 25 February 1996. Bettye Davis married Franklin McCain, one of the four A & T freshmen who set off the Greensboro student sit-ins.

20. Linda Brown, interview by author, tape recording, Greensboro, N.C., 19 January 1996.

21. Willa B. Player, "Where There Is Vision," *Bennett College Bulletin* (Winter 1958), 6.

22. Robin Tolmach Lakoff, "Cries and Whispers: The Shattering of the Silences," in *Gender Articulated: Language and the Socially Constructed Self,* ed. Kira Hall and Mary Bucholtz (New York: Routledge, 1995), 32.

23. Bettye Davis McCain, interview by author, tape recording, Charlotte, N.C., 25 February 1996.

24. Ibid.

25. Roslyn Smith, interview by author, tape recording by telephone, Naperville, Ill./New York City, 14 February 1996.

26. Howard Thurman, *Disciplines of the Spirit* (New York: Harper & Row, 1963), 26.

27. Julian Morrison, "Officers Arrest 45 in Demonstration at Store in City," *Greensboro Daily News,* 22 April 1960, 1A.

28. Gwendolyn Mackel Rice, interview by author, tape recording, Chicago, 23 February 1996. Dr. A Maurice Mackel, her father, founded the Natchez, Mississippi, branch of the NAACP in 1940.

29. Lakoff, "Cries and Whispers," 32.

30. Yvonne Jeffries Johnson, interview by author, tape recording, Greensboro, N.C., 20 January 1996.

31. Ibid. The mass movement had erupted when police started arresting Dudley High School student protestors and the college students. "[In 1963] my aunt 'sat in' in the middle of the street," recalled Jeffries Johnson. "It was like, 'Now we can take a lot of things, but you're just not going to mess with our children.'"

32. Yvonne Jeffries Johnson, interview by author, tape recording, Greensboro, N.C., 22 August 1996.

33. Ibid.

34. These are the final words of Player's 1965 inaugural address.

35. Linda Brown, interview by author, tape recording, Greensboro, N.C., 19 January 1996.

36. Bettye Davis McCain, interview by author, tape recording, Charlotte, N.C., 25 February 1996.

37. Rebecca Owen, interview by author, tape recording, New York City, 6 April 1996.

38. Rebecca Owen, application draft to Union Theological Seminary (photocopy), personal papers, 1960.

39. Owen spent the next three summers under the tutelage of Christians who witnessed responsible action in faith to an impoverished community.

40. *Student Handbook* (Lynchburg, Va.: Randolph-Macon Woman's College, 1961), 7.

41. In "Prologue to a President" (*Randolph-Macon Alumnae Bulletin* [spring 1967]: 3), Gillie A. Larew wrote: "One remembers that it was the lay members of the committee who made the point that in a church-related college there was a distinct advantage in choosing for president a member of the denomination with which the college was associated, while it was the clerics in the group who felt that a non-Methodist should be considered if he possessed the prime qualities of scholarship, educational experience, leadership and vision."

42. Owen, application draft to Union Theological Seminary.

43. Arthur Brandenburg, the Methodist chaplain at Duke University, had written an essay, "Toward a Restoration of the Christian Meaning of Vocation," for the January 1960 issue of *motive* magazine.

44. Christie McCoy, "Southern Whites Sidestep Issue of Segregation," *Randolph-Macon Woman's College Sun Dial*, 28 April 1960, 2.

45. Tom Lord, "Current Scene," *motive*, November 1960, 35.

46. Mary Edith Bentley Abu-Saba, interview by the author, tape recording, Greensboro, N.C., 21 August 1996.

47. Reinhold Niebuhr, *The Children of Light, the Children of Darkness* (New York: Scribner's, 1944), 143–44.

48. *Student Handbook* (Lynchburg, Va.: Randolph-Macon Woman's College, 1961), 35.

49. Frances Mayes, "10,000 Rules to Live By," *The Virginia Quarterly Review* (Fall 1989): 718.

50. Ibid, 719.

51. Summary of Judiciary Committee Statement, Randolph-Macon Woman's College, Lynchburg, Va., 3 January 1961.

52. William F. Quillian Jr., statement to assembled student body, Randolph-Macon Woman's College, Lynchburg, Va., 3 January 1961, 1.

53 Ibid.

54. Mary Edith Bentley Abu-Saba, interview by Theresa J. Carroll, transcript, 15 November 1993.

55. Rebecca Owen, interview by Carolyn Bell, transcript, New York City, 29 May 1994.

56. Ibid.

57. William F. Quillian Jr., "1958 Annual Report of the President to the Board of Trustees," presented to Board of Trustees, Randolph-Macon Woman's College, Lynchburg, Va.

58. William Quillian, letter to Randolph-Macon alumnae in Lynchburg, Virginia, 1961, 3.

59. Rebecca Owen, interview by Carolyn Bell, transcript, New York City, 29 May 1994.

60. "Students Status Not Affected by Sentences," *Lynchburg News,* 7 February 1961, 8.

61. Mitchell Fordyce, letter to William F. Quillian Jr., 7 February 1961, Lynchburg, Va.

62. Rebecca Owen, interview by Carolyn Bell, transcript, New York City, 29 May 1994.

63. "Students Jailed for Sit-in Demonstration," *Concern* (Washington, D.C.: General Board of Church and Social Concerns of the Methodist Church, 1961), 4.

64. Clayborne Carson, *In Struggle: SNCC and the Black Awakening of the 1960s* (Cambridge, Mass.: Harvard University Press, 1995), 32.

65. Elsie Carper, "Six Students Drop Trespass Appeal, Plead Guilty and Then Are Jailed," *Washington Post,* 7 February 1961, 1(A).

66. Duncan Howlett, "Thirty Days in Jail," sermon, All Souls Church, Unitarian, Washington, D.C., 1961. It would later be determined by the Randolph-Macon administration that any form of celebration at the time of the release of Owen and Bentley should be discouraged. As Quillian confirmed in his written response to alumnae questions, "this release was accomplished very quietly" (Quillian letter to Randolph-Macon alumnae).

67. Mary Edith Bentley and Rebecca Owen, "Students Involved in Sit-in Explain Reasons for Action," *Randolph-Macon Woman's College Sun Dial,* 2 March 1961.

68. Mary Edith Bentley Abu-Saba, interview by author, tape recording, Greensboro, N.C., 22 January 1996.

69. Ibid.

70. Ibid.

71. Ibid.

72. Niebuhr, *The Children of Light, the Children of Darkness,* 84–85.

73. "College Seniors Overfed, Complacent to Educator, Seeking Future Teachers," *Washington Post,* 7 February 1960, 12 (C). Rosenhaupt is reported as stating, "Today's young people don't ride hobby horses of controversy as young people should. . . . We'd prefer a man with an ill-founded bias to the man who stands for nothing at all."

74. Dietrich Bonhoeffer, *Letters & Papers from Prison* (New York: Macmillan, 1971), 5.

75. Ibid., 279.

76. Rebecca Owen, "What Is Christ for Us Today? A Study of the Life and Thought of Dietrich Bonhoeffer," senior honors paper, Randolph-Macon Woman's College, Lynchburg, Va., 1961.

77. Yvonne Jeffries Johnson, interview by author, tape recording, Greensboro, N.C., 20 January 1996.

78. Lillian Smith, *Now Is the Time* (New York: Viking, 1955), 48.

79. Charles Cole, et al., "Divinity Students Support Sit-ins," *Lynchburg News,* 15 January 1961. Quillian received both his B.D. and his Ph.D. degrees from Yale University.

Part Two

□□□

Contemporary Social Contexts
for Struggle

5.

Trying to Be God in the World
The Story of the
Evangelical Women's Caucus and the
Crisis over Homosexuality

S. SUE HORNER

◻◻◻

In their introduction to *Recovering Biblical Manhood and Womanhood,*
John Piper and Wayne Grudem write:

> A controversy of major proportions has spread through the
> church. . . . [There is] great uncertainty among evangelicals. Men
> and women simply are not sure what their roles should be. Tradi-
> tional positions have not been totally satisfactory, because they
> have not fully answered the recent evangelical feminist argu-
> ments. Moreover, most Christians will admit that selfishness,
> irresponsibility, passivity, and abuse have often contaminated
> "traditional" patterns of how men and women relate to each
> other.
>
> But the vast majority of evangelicals have not endorsed the
> evangelical feminist position, sensing that it does not really reflect
> the pattern of Biblical truth. Within our churches, we have had
> long discussions and debates, and still the controversy shows
> signs of intensifying, not subsiding. Before the struggle ends,
> probably no Christian family and no evangelical church will
> remain untouched.[1]

Since the early 1970s there has been a growing feminist movement
within evangelicalism.[2] Two organizations, the Evangelical Women's
Caucus (EWC)[3] and the Christian feminist magazine *Daughters of
Sarah*, grew out of neoevangelicalism—which sought, beginning in the
1950s, to counter separatist fundamentalism—and out of "second-
wave" feminism, one of the liberation movements that emerged in
the 1960s in American society. EWC was organized in 1974 after the

inaugural meeting of Evangelicals for Social Action, and developed
into a national organization that still sponsors biennial conferences
and publishes a newsletter, *Update*. *Daughters of Sarah*, a Christian
feminist magazine committed to an ecumenical, dialogical perspective, was published from 1975 to 1996. The magazine, which grew out
of a consciousness-raising collective, was based in Chicago and in its
final three years of publication relocated to Garrett-Evangelical Theological Seminary in Evanston. The original vision of co-founders
Nancy Hardesty and Lucille Sider Dayton was that *Daughters of Sarah*
would serve as the publication for the activist EWC organization. But
despite significant overlap in message and audience, this partnership
did not occur, due primarily to perceptions of philosophical differences and financial instability in both organizations.[4]

Evangelical, or "biblical," feminism brings several challenges to
evangelicalism. First, an evangelical biblical feminist hermeneutic is
often understood as destabilizing the evangelical notion of biblical
authority, and second, feminist activism for social change, or what is
understood as "cultural engagement," is problematic for many evangelicals. These two concerns gave rise in the mid-1980s to two additional organizations addressing gender roles. One was a EWC splinter
group, Christians for Biblical Equality (initially affiliated with Men,
Women and God, a British organization within the London Institute
for Contemporary Christianity) formed in 1987 in reaction to perceived theological changes in EWC, as well as to differences over how
to address social issues like homosexuality and abortion. Christians
for Biblical Equality sees its calling as preserving the early mission of
EWC; namely, to bring to women and men in evangelical and conservative churches the good news of "the biblical basis for freedom in
Christ."[5] At the same time an anti-feminist group, the Council on Biblical Manhood and Womanhood, organized with the purpose of promoting a traditional understanding of gender roles. Their view
suggests that even though women and men are equally created in
God's image, they also are created for distinct roles. They see an evangelical feminist position as distorting God's plan for humankind as set
out in the Bible.

In 1977, shortly after the formal beginning of an evangelical feminist movement, Ina J. Kau wrote a master's thesis on "Feminism in
the American Evangelical Movement." Kau suggested that these religious feminists had found values in feminism that transcended evangelical values. She claimed that these emerging evangelical feminists
had a unified vision of feminism. She defined this vision in a manner

similar to Betty Friedan's in *The Feminine Mystique*, arguing that traditional roles and societal structures and expectations for women were preventing them from developing into mature, responsible adults who functioned both in careers and the family. Kau suggested that these feminists recognized that orthodox evangelical teaching on women's roles stunted women's development as much as societal expectations did.

Evangelical feminists also wanted to preserve family values and many values of evangelicalism in their desire to become "all they were meant to be." This tension, Kau predicted, would effect changes in both evangelicalism and feminism. One challenge she forecast was disagreement and potential cleavage over evangelical hermeneutics. To support this contention, Kau referred to a "letters-to-the-editor" debate on biblical interpretation and authority that appeared in the March and May-June 1976 issues of *Sojourners*, an evangelical social issues magazine. The participants were the movement's leaders, Sharon Gallagher, Virginia Ramey Mollenkott, and Nancy Hardesty. Kau also wondered if some of the "radical" agenda issues of secular feminism, like homosexuality, or some of its methods, like feminist activism, might cause middle-class, biblical- and spirituality-oriented evangelical feminists to step away from, or significantly recast, their "feminist" values and behaviors.[6]

My study of evangelical feminism, in particular the history of the Evangelical and Ecumenical Women's Caucus (EEWC), reveals that the tensions and potential revisions of evangelicalism and feminism that Kau foresaw in the mid-1970s were prescient. Evangelical feminists did find feminism a helpful resource for challenging the dehumanizing or at least limiting experiences of women within an evangelical ethos. They also found that the list of values they embraced from both evangelicalism and feminism could be seen as fluid in terms of priority. This chapter examines a stage in the life of EEWC: the period from 1984 to 1986, when a schism in the organization led to a broadening of its identity and the emergence of a second evangelical feminist organization. First, a brief outline of EEWC's history reveals that its ambivalence over social engagement, particularly the issue of homosexuality, had been present since its earliest days.

Evangelical Feminist Beginnings

We acknowledge that we have encouraged men to prideful domination and women to irresponsible passivity. So we call both men

and women to mutual submission and active discipleship.[7]
—Nancy Hardesty, *The Chicago Declaration*, 1973

I see five distinct periods in the nearly thirty-year history of the Evangelical and Ecumenical Women's Caucus. Its first two years saw the birth of EWC from the 1973 organizing meeting of Evangelicals for Social Action, and its growth to the point of its 1975 inaugural national conference in Washington, D.C. With that conference EWC began a process of institutionalization from 1975 to 1984. During this time it co-sponsored, with Fuller Theological Seminar, its largest national conference, in Pasadena, California, in 1978; worked on the Equal Rights Amendment campaign; and began to show signs of ideological fissures. In its "adolescent" years between 1984 to 1988, EWC split over the role of its resolutions, particularly a resolution on the civil rights of homosexual persons. One effect of the split was the formation of Christians for Biblical Equality in 1987. The years from 1988 to 1994 represent a reorganization period within EWC, symbolized by a name change to Evangelical and Ecumenical Women's Caucus (EEWC), as well as changes in the by-laws and statement of faith in 1990. Finally, after the global, religious feminist Re-Imagining Conference of 1993, EEWC, despite financial and membership challenges, repeatedly re-imagined itself and continued to hold national conferences (Chicago in 1994, Norfolk, Virginia, in 1996, Grand Rapids, Michigan, in 1998, Chicago in 2000, Indianapolis in 2002).

Within the evangelical world of the 1960s some of the wider discussion on feminism was known, but many acknowledged women simply with an intuitive sense of fairness or an experiential awareness of gifted women who preached and taught without recognition as "preachers or teachers of the Word." In 1966 Letha Scanzoni, then author of books on youth and sexuality, wrote a piece for the evangelical magazine *Eternity* on women's roles in church, family, and society. In the article, "Woman's Place: Silence or Service," she challenged the inconsistencies and even absurdities of a tradition that taught women's submission yet lived with numerous examples of women teaching, leading, writing, and increasingly present in professional and business life. However, she was also careful to make the disclaimer, "this article is not intended as an impassioned clamor for women's rights or female pastors!"[8]

In 1968 Scanzoni wrote a second article for *Eternity* on understanding marriage as partnership, rather than a dictatorship, benevolent or not. Again, her analysis introduced the evangelical audience of *Eternity* to sociological insights on marriage as "equalitarianism" and the culturally shaped ("socially-constructed") nature of "masculine" and "feminine" characteristics, such as intuition, reason, and sensitivity. Her analysis retained the Pauline concept of "headship" but recast it as "loving direction by a husband."[9]

Indeed, these early evangelical challenges to women's secondary role often equivocated between women's right to be "all they were meant to be" and the familial roles dictated by the Pauline concept of headship. One year later, in 1969, Scanzoni approached *Eternity* editor Nancy Hardesty about researching a book on "Christian Woman's Liberation," which five years later was published as the co-authored *All We're Meant to Be: A Biblical Approach to Women's Liberation.*[10]

The discussion of changing women's roles did not go unnoticed by the leaders of evangelicalism. In December 1970 *Ladies' Home Journal* printed renowned evangelist Billy Graham's "Jesus and the Liberated Woman," which Nancy Hardesty described in 1974 as the "classic statement of Christian male chauvinism."[11] Dismissing women's liberation arguments, Graham pronounced that "The Problem That Has No Name" (a reference to Betty Friedan's language in *The Feminine Mystique*) was boredom; namely, a spiritual problem of failing to accept one's God-given duty. God's plan for men is to be husbands, fathers, and protectors; and for women to be wives, mothers, and homemakers—what he called "queens" in the home. He understood gender roles as "appointed destiny"—equal but with respective stations and roles in all social institutions. He acknowledged that Christ brought women new prestige, but Christ did not free women from the home.[12]

Three years later Scanzoni's writing took on a stronger, less tentative voice as evidenced in her 1973 article in *Christianity Today* on "The Feminist and the Bible." Here she definitively declares the compatibility of feminism and Christianity, focusing on the historical legacy of the nineteenth-century women's rights movement, a "fervently religious" enterprise. Her opening paragraph sets the tone: "Many Christians dismiss the women's liberation movement as a kooky modern fad. . . . This image of women's lib is unfortunate; it misses the whole point of the movement and encourages the widespread suspicion that Christianity and feminism are incompatible."[13]

During this same period, educators Roberta Hestenes and David Scholer, in Washington and Massachusetts respectively, offered courses (one at a church and the other at a seminary) on women and the Bible, oblivious of each other's existence. And in 1974 Fuller Seminary theologian Paul Jewett published *Man as Male and Female*, a study of men and women's relationships.[14] Asserting that both men and women are created in the image of God, Jewett made a case for the equality of the sexes. Some within the evangelical community questioned his hermeneutic as challenging the authority of the Bible. In fact, his work was extensively debated at Fuller Seminary and nearly cost him his job. Nevertheless, evangelical voices were challenging gender stereotypes. But it was not until Evangelicals for Social Action was founded in 1973 that enough networks overlapped to give rise to a collective feminist consciousness sufficient to shape a movement.

Evangelicals for Social Action

On Thanksgiving weekend in 1973 some fifty evangelical leaders gathered at a YMCA hotel on South Wabash Street in Chicago's Loop. Six women, four white and two black, including Nancy Hardesty, Sharon Gallagher, and Dr. Ruth L. Bentley, attended the workshop on evangelicals and social concerns convened by a planning committee of eleven, chaired by Ron Sider, then dean of the Philadelphia campus of Messiah College. The committee consisted of editors, academics, and directors of prominent evangelical ministries: John Alexander, editor of *The Other Side;* Myron Augsburger, president of Eastern Mennonite College; Frank Gaebelein, headmaster emeritus of the Stony Brook School and former co-editor of *Christianity Today;* Paul Henry of Calvin College; Rufus Jones, general director of Conservative Baptist Home Mission Society; David O. Moberg, chair of Marquette University's department of sociology and anthropology; William Pannell, the only African American on the planning committee, vice president of Tom Skinner Associates (a New York City ministry to gangs); Richard Pierard, professor at Indiana State University; Lewis Smedes, professor at Fuller Theological Seminary, and Jim Wallis, editor of the *Post American* (renamed *Sojourners* in 1974).[15] Each of them had a vision of Christian faith that included social justice. They did not accept the received wisdom of the broader evangelical world that "politics is too dirty for devout believers,"[16] and they sincerely concluded that now was the time to "transcend the unholy dichotomy of evangelicalism and social concern."[17]

Each participant had been asked to come with "concrete proposals for evangelical social concern." Nancy Hardesty, former editor at *Eternity*, now assistant professor at Trinity College and doctoral student at the University of Chicago Divinity School, wrote a direct and clear letter to Ron Sider at the end of August. In it she outlined statements on women's rights, abortion, and pornography. She also asserted that "Christian organizations are going to have to clean up their own houses before they can speak to the world." She itemized some of those issues: equal access for women to the ministry, seminaries, and denominational administration; revision of hiring, pay, and benefit practices; and the development of day-care centers, vocational counseling and training, and family counseling.[18]

Before addressing such specific initiatives, however, the primary goal of the workshop was to draft a declaration on social justice. The planners saw this as a "historic moment." Evangelicalism was growing; liberal, mainstream Protestantism was in decline. Here was an opening for a reformed evangelicalism. Evangelicals needed to repent of the sin of indifference, its mindless support of the status quo, and move into a "balanced biblical concern for both social restructuring and individual conversion."[19]

Ultimately, after lively debate, the participants drafted the so-called Chicago Declaration. In its ten paragraphs, gender issues were covered in two sentences near the end of the document. Hardesty's contribution read: "We acknowledge that we have encouraged men to prideful domination and women to irresponsible passivity. So we call both men and women to mutual submission and active discipleship."[20] Hardesty remembers hearing about Billy Graham's response to the Declaration. The only phrase he found objectionable was "irresponsible passivity."[21] Apparently Graham hesitated to deem the notion of passive women irresponsible.

This was a historic meeting on many accounts, and the national press so noted. A fairly long article, "Social and Political Activism Is Aim of Evangelical Group," by Marjorie Hyer, appeared in the *Washington Post* the next Friday. She began: "A disparate band of men and women spent Thanksgiving weekend in a dingy hotel room trying to launch a religious movement that could shake both political and religious life in America."[22] Hyer also quoted William Bentley, who said, "This was the first time since 1920 that we've [black and white evangelicals] gotten together." Religion editor Roy Larson of the *Chicago Sun-Times* said that "some day American church historians may write that the most significant church-related event of 1973" occurred with the appearance of the "Declaration of Evangelical Social Concern."[23]

The group decided to meet again, and on Thanksgiving weekend in 1974, over one hundred invited participants met and debated strategy and the theological soundness of the action proposals presented by each task force. The women's caucus initiated a "torrent" of proposals. They were no doubt empowered by Hardesty's recent contributions to the cause of evangelical women. Her book (co-authored with sociologist Letha Scanzoni), *All We're Meant to Be: A Biblical Approach to Women's Liberation*,[24] had just been released. She was also meeting with a group of women from Chicago's North Park Theological Seminary who had decided to publish a newsletter, *Daughters of Sarah*. Its purpose was to establish a network of women and men who wanted to explore Christian feminist issues. The just-completed inaugural issue included an article by Hardesty, a biblical exegesis of Genesis 1 and 2, "Woman: Helper or Companion?"[25]

The women's caucus presented twelve proposals and all were approved. This meant that the participants recognized each action as a "valid means" for implementing the Declaration of 1973. The proposals included developing regional conferences to build a grassroots movement; using *Daughters of Sarah* as a national clearinghouse for dissemination of Christian feminist materials; evaluating Sunday school curricula for sexist bias and publishing the results; promoting equal opportunity for women's education in evangelical colleges and seminaries; examining Christian bookstores for sexist materials; educating Evangelicals for Social Action on the use of non-sexist language; compiling a directory of evangelical feminists; and endorsing the Equal Rights Amendment.[26]

In order to coordinate the varied projects, the task force agreed to form the Evangelical Women's Caucus, sharing the *Daughters of Sarah* mailing address. The women who developed the evangelical feminist agenda represented the nation geographically and imagined themselves on the cusp of a major transformation of gender roles, behaviors, and attitudes in the evangelical world.

The *Chicago Sun-Times* religion editor, Roy Larson, once again covered the workshop. He reported that the most intense debate arose from the proposals presented by the women's caucus. Statements calling for support of the Equal Rights Amendment and the use of non-sexist language and content in church publications were readily accepted. The issue that divided the group was the ordination of women. After long and "anguished" debate, the resolution was reworded and pledged members to "work towards giving women all the rights, privileges and responsibilities of membership in the Church of Jesus Christ." Still, the actions of Evangelicals for Social Action represented a new era in evangelicalism. The number of sign-ers of the Declaration had grown from fifty-three in 1973 to over one thousand, including some of the most prominent evangelicals in the country.[27]

Of course, others within the evangelical/fundamentalist community decried the "liberal" slippery slope of this gathering. Noted fundamentalist preacher Bob Jones branded Evangelicals for Social Action members as socialists-communists.

> There is something pathetic about these "New Evangelicals," who are preachers of a watered-down gospel. . . . Under the pretext of "the social emphasis of the Gospel," [they] align themselves with the enemies of the Gospel and of the Word of God. Pretending to look forward to the coming of Christ, they hurry to help build the government of the Antichrist.[28]

Despite the mixed reception by the broader evangelical/fundamentalist world, the group's third workshop met on Labor Day weekend 1975 at North Park College in Chicago (now North Park University). This time the event did not flourish. Not only was attendance lower; there were confrontations and charges of racism and sexism, resulting in the meeting being adjourned one day early.[29]

EWC Emerges

Unaffected by the discord within Evangelicals for Social Action, EWC held its first national conference in Washington, D.C., later in the fall of 1975. It was a huge success. The planning committee consisted of Judy Brown Hull of Broadway Presbyterian Church in New York, Cheryl Forbes of *Christianity Today*, Karin Granberg Michaelson of Wesley Theological Seminary, and Heidi Frost of Faith at Work. Nearly four hundred women and a dozen men attended, representing a wide spectrum of the Christian churches in thirty-six states and Canada. The planners had kept the registration fee modest at twenty-five dollars and built in extra monies to create a three thousand–dollar common transportation pool. Still, they were surprised at the overwhelming response; some sixty local people were turned away.[30]

The theme was "Women in Transition: A Biblical Approach to Feminism." Major papers on biblical interpretation and women's history were presented, as well as forty workshops covering biblical interpretation, politics, economics, marriage, singleness, self-esteem issues, and psychology.[31]

Virginia Ramey Mollenkott opened the conference asserting that "the Bible supports the central tenets of feminism." Lucille Sider Dayton and Don Dayton spoke on the nineteenth-century roots of evangelical feminism. Nancy Hardesty offered this definition of biblical feminism as conceptualized by EWC: "the commitment of those Christians who believe it is essential to have a personal relationship to God through Jesus Christ, who accept the Bible as God's inspired word, who have a deep concern for love and justice between the sexes, and who desire to find the whole counsel of God on this issue." Letha Scanzoni gave the final address, emphasizing that for "women, a whole new world is opening up."[32]

In the summary of the conference, Wes Michaelson noted that there was very little political emphasis. In fact, only two resolutions were passed: one an affirmation of the Equal Rights Amendment, which eighteen participants voted against; and one supporting the efforts of Roman Catholic sisters meeting that same weekend in Detroit to discuss ordination and the leadership issues in the Catholic church. Only eight participants opposed this. It was also duly noted that Elizabeth Elliot Leitch, probably the best-known "traditionalist" evangelical woman, was also in attendance and quite vocal regarding her disagreements with the feminist vision presented as "biblical." (By 1987 she would be affiliated with the traditionalist Council on Biblical Manhood and Womanhood.)

Clearly, EWC represented a "small minority protest against the prevailing culture of evangelicalism." For example, by the mid-1970s evangelical "traditionalism" was represented by books like Helen Andelin's *Fascinating Womanhood*,[33] which sold 400,000 copies, and Marabel Morgan's *The Total Woman*,[34] at one point the nation's top-selling nonfiction book. Equally popular were Larry Christenson's *The Christian Family*[35] and the seminars on the family sponsored by Bill Gothard, founder of the Institute in Basic Youth Conflicts.[36] Nevertheless, this gathering of emerging evangelical feminists was energized to challenge the traditionalists and indeed change the church. Remarkably, nearly five thousand dollars was donated in the closing service to further the work of EWC.[37]

In 1978 the largest conference EWC ever organized was held in Pasadena, California, co-sponsored with Fuller Seminary. Its planning committee was composed of Phyllis Hart, Roberta Hestenes, Liz Nordquist, Libbie Patterson, and Al Jepson.[38] Some eight hundred to a thousand women (sources vary on the number) and about fifty men from thirty-five states and a number of other nations filled the

Pasadena Holiday Inn Convention Center. Compared to the younger, counter-cultural tone of the 1975 Washington, D.C., conference, the 1978 conference drew more churchwomen in their mid-thirties.[39]

The theme, "Women and the Ministries of Christ," was addressed in eleven plenary sessions. Participants could choose from ninety-five workshops, all focused around three themes: women and the gospel of Christ, women and a needy world, and women and Christian discipleship. Workshop topics included biblical authority and biblical feminism; language, liturgy, and liberation; the Holy Spirit as female; battered women; the Equal Rights Amendment; sex roles; the single woman as pastor; "discovering our foremothers"; urban ministries; and assertiveness.

The tone of the conference was positive, both affirming and challenging. Planner Roberta Hestenes, then chair of Fuller's Ministry Division, asserted, "This conference indicates that biblical feminism has come of age." The questions were not about whether women can be ministers, but how women can develop their gifts in service to the church and society. Conference planner Liz Nordquist admitted that some attendees who supported "traditional" roles for women were disappointed at the lack of debate on the topic, but those voices represented a tiny minority. Further, Nordquist opined that the conference was not about drafting resolutions, but about actions. Women (and men), she said, needed to examine and change their attitudes on so-called "natural, God-given" gender roles and embrace the God-given talents of all persons. That unifying vision could be embodied in a network of evangelical women representing multiple denominational and theological emphases, "to unify on the essentials, and to agree to disagree."[40]

Controversial topics such as homosexuality and inclusive God language were not avoided, though discussions of homosexuality remained especially marginal. The issue of ordination and homosexuality had a few weeks prior been addressed at the General Assembly of the Presbyterian Church in San Diego. Consequently EWC conference planners made a concerted effort not to reduce the topic of biblical feminism to a debate over homosexuality. There were two workshops on the topic representing divergent views, and a debate was scheduled between Don Williams, author of *The Bond that Breaks: Will Homosexuality Split the Church?*,[41] and Letha Scanzoni and Virginia Ramey Mollenkott, who co-authored *Is the Homosexual my Neighbor?*[42] The debate was canceled, however, for fear of detracting from a "spirit of unity." In Claire Wolterstorff's write-up of the conference for the

Reformed Journal, she identified this "spirit of unity" as the apparent calm surface of a current-laden river. For example, on the topic of women's ordination, she noted that while there indeed was a refreshing, "quiet" affirmation of women's personhood, little attention was paid to "the unresolved tensions between emerging lay women, who wish for larger and more flexible roles in the churches, and ordained women, who are 'in but still out.'"[43]

On Saturday, EWC Organization Day, its institutionalization became official. The day began with a stirring speech, "Marching On!" by Letha Scanzoni. She characterized evangelical feminists as prophets, directed by God, and not a passing fad, as critic Richard Quebedeaux had charged in his recent book *The Worldly Evangelicals*. She stated, "The EWC is much more than a warmed-over, imitative, Christianized version of secular feminism. We did not become feminists and then try to fit our Christianity into feminist ideology. We became feminists because we were Christians."[44] Scanzoni suggested that evangelical feminists could act as a bridge "between the secular feminist movement and those Christians who are fearful, misinformed, and afraid to take a new look at woman's role because they believe to do so is to go against Scripture." In a blessing for the new organization, Scanzoni ended the address by quoting Luke: "While they were talking and discussing together, Jesus himself drew near and went with them" (Luke 24:15).[45]

For five years, between 1979 and 1984, EWC/EWCI did in fact function as a bridge organization. It was building bridges ecumenically, across denominational divides. It was building bridges between "secular" and religious feminism, primarily through its involvement with the National Organization for Women and its support of the Equal Rights Amendment campaign in 1981 and 1982. It was building bridges of knowledge, learning and uncovering the histories of women in evangelical history and in denominational histories. It was reconceptualizing, or at least re-examining, the dualisms of personal salvation and societal salvation.

Founding coordinator Joyce Erickson spoke clearly on this topic in her December 1980 editorial, "Social Issues: How EWC Grapples." She acknowledged the current debates in the broader evangelical world and discerned some "confusion" about EWC as an "evangelical" institution, particularly its support of the Equal Rights Amendment. Erickson admitted that EWC members' opinions varied on the social issues of the day (such as abortion, nuclear power, and homosexuality), but its primary purpose was the promotion of a feminist interpretation of the Bible to the church and to society.

With regard to the myriad social issues, from ordination to equal pay, EWC provided a forum for discussion of any and all of them in relation to biblical and faith commitments. As a consequence of this dialogue, women and men could act responsibly out of an informed ethical reflection. EWC, then, was a biblical-centered, feminist, prophetic organization working to eliminate sexism in the church, building bridges between feminists and Christians, and enabling the development of full personhood expressed in actions by Christian women and men.[46]

Several years later, in 1983, Britt Vanden Eykel was hired as part-time field director of EWCI. Her role was to work with chapters and affiliates to expand membership nationally and internationally, and to represent the organization broadly in the feminist and Christian communities. Her academic background in political science (she was at the dissertation stage of a doctoral program at George Washington University) and her government work experience with the Commerce and State departments and as New England regional manager for the U.S. Department of Energy qualified her well for this task.[47]

Vanden Eykel viewed EWCI as an organization composed of committed and active individuals or small groups. Institutionally she saw EWCI engaged in coalition-building, particularly through its membership in the Religious Network for the Equality of Women and its informal relationship with Church Women United. But she did not think it should limit its sphere to women in the church only, and suggested that EWCI was perhaps as effective "within the pluralistic women's movement as . . . in reaching members of many evangelical denominations." She supported EWCI's "no official position on any social/political issue" policy (apart from the Equal Rights Amendment) and felt that to emphasize resolutions was to divert energy from action. She said, "As biblical feminists, we know that commitment is at least as important as correctness, that carefully chosen words can never become a substitute for action."[48]

Early on, EWC struggled with identity issues. For some from confessional Christian backgrounds, a statement of faith was an important symbol, while for others it was less so; they also had fewer concerns about changing offensive language. Nevertheless, in the September–November 1981 *Update*, the statement of faith was printed for the first time. Then, at the 1982 business meeting during the Seattle conference, members discussed language changes in the statement of faith, particularly words like "fellowship," "Lord," and "kingdom," but agreed to table the discussion. There was also tension over what actions EWC should take. The unease was apparent in discussions on two resolutions. The first affirmed continued support of the Equal Rights Amendment. The second called for a committee, chaired by Hardesty, to draft an open letter to opponents of the Equal Rights Amendment explaining a biblical feminist rationale for supporting it and emphasizing EWC's "support for the family of God in all of its configurations."[49] Forging an identity with compatible actions would become the central issue in the years after 1984.

The Schism

The EWC's sixth plenary conference, in 1984, "Free Indeed, the Fulfillment of Our Faith," was its longest, lasting five days. It attracted over 450 participants from thirty-three states, six Canadian provinces, and five foreign countries. In conference organizer Dorothy V. Meyer's account in the September 1984–February 1985 *Update*, she recalls members from Hawaii and New Jersey as the first to check in at the Wellesley College site. Her memories and review of this gathering focused on the great diversity of traditions and experiences and at the same time enjoined readers to focus on the center of evangelical feminism; namely, "God's teaching on female-male equality to the whole body of Christ's church." Workshop choices were numerous, some sixty-five sessions, covering ground as diverse as urban ministry, feminine imagery of God, the personal story of a Puerto Rican biblical feminist, biblical exegesis of 1 Corinthians 11:2–16, women and work, biblical understandings of power, and analyses of female submission.[50]

Plenaries were equally challenging and diverse. Union activist and minister Addie Wyatt reflected on meanings of freedom, incorporating her own story along with the words of Sojourner Truth and Martin Luther King Jr. Actress Roberta Nobleman took the role of Julian of Norwich in a dramatic presentation, and Ruth Schmidt, president of Agnes Scott College and a founding member of EWC, reminded all that servanthood is chosen behavior, not assumed. Women's gifts were center stage in worship and eucharist, by now an expected tradition at EWC conferences.

At the annual business meeting, several resolutions in new arenas were advanced. The executive council offered two: one on the "elimination of military armaments and nuclear weaponry" and one encouraging members to participate in the political process. The next three were offered by the membership on the subjects of homosexuality, racism, and pornography. Of these, the text of the first included taking "a firm stand to support with love homosexual persons in an attitude of justice which is against the oppression involved in sexism, racism, classism, heterosexism, or homophobia."

Divided theological positions on homosexuality resulted in an emotional discussion of the appropriateness of EWC taking a stand on any controversial political issue. Some objections rose from employment concerns. EWC members who taught or worked at conservative institutions feared that any statements on homosexuality could be cause for dismissal. After a lengthy discussion, the vote was tabled. The membership seemed willing to resolve the issue by appointing five five-member task forces composed of people with varying viewpoints to discuss each issue. Each task force would poll the membership and try to arrive at some consensus, which would be reported at the 1986 conference.[51]

The summer 1985 issue of *Update* reported the results of the membership poll taken shortly after the Wellesley conference. Forty-six percent voted for the resolution supporting the Equal Rights Amendment but felt no other resolutions should be passed. Forty-eight percent wanted EWC to be politically active, both passing resolutions and working on a range of issues that affect women. The article quoted extensively from the poll questionnaires, revealing the diversity of the membership. Some felt "taking stands . . . was part of a Biblical imperative" and limiting broader concerns was a sign of self-centeredness. Others felt any foray into divisive issues had the effect of diluting "the unique thrust of EWC." For many the mission of EWC was to support women in conservative churches by educating them in biblical feminism, and controversial issues detracted from "original objectives."

It was also noted that members could join other organizations to work on specific justice issues. One respondent noted that the National Organization for Women had increasingly been distracted by internal divisions and was losing its effectiveness; she would hate to see EWC so immobilized. The two issues cited as most divisive were abortion and homosexuality. Members expressed concern over the endorsement of homosexual "lifestyle" and the injustice of gay members' invisibility in EWC. *Update* co-editor Sharon Gallagher summarized the findings by noting that there were strong arguments on both sides. She also affirmed the view that Christianity calls one to more than personal salvation or empowerment; however, in the wide range of justice issues that Christians could be active in, some could be argued for biblically, others clearly not, and some were unclear. She ended the article by asking, "Is it better to struggle for an organization that exactly expresses the commitment I hold, or to belong to one that is broad enough to accommodate other sisters and brothers whose equally strong convictions may center on different or opposing issues?"[52]

At the seventh EWC conference in Fresno on July 6–10, 1986 the issue came to a head. Resolutions were the touchstone issue, but the broader concerns were the mission of EWC, the recognition of homosexual members (estimated at twenty to thirty persons, or some five percent of the membership), how to handle diversity and consensus, and even the viability of the organization. EWC was now twelve years old, and some described the struggles and passions of this conference as an "adolescent" moment in its growth.[53]

Titled "Free Indeed: Empowered for Action" and chaired by Kathryn Klassen Neufeld, the conference was designed to address, with depth and breadth, EWC's central goal as stated in the by-laws: to "present God's teaching on female-male equality to the whole body of Christ's church; and to call women and men to mutual submission and active discipleship." Anticipating a large response from the nearly twenty thousand people on the mailing list, planners had booked the Fresno convention center.[54] Eighty-one workshops were scheduled, as well as women-centered worship and communion, and an opening celebration replete with a hundred-voice choir, a sculptress, a poet, instrumental groups, and dancers.

The plenary sessions were equally powerful and diverse. Addressing the theme of action and power, presenters included EWC members Virginia Ramey Mollenkott, Princeton New Testament doctoral candidate Linda Mercadante, New Testament professor Scott Bartchy of UCLA, and actress Roberta Nobleman. In her performance of "Solo Flight," Nobleman dramatically told the story of Rev. Jeannette Piccard, who in 1934 became the first woman balloon pilot and at the age of seventy-nine became one of the first women ordained in the Episcopal Church.

In another session, Betty Hanna-Witherspoon, executive director of the San Fernando Valley Fair Housing Council, discussed how twenty years of work in urban planning had contributed to her understandings of racism and sexism: it was her work with children and youth that made her an "existential feminist." She also underscored the role of the Bible in sustaining her work. In another plenary, New Testament scholar Elisabeth Schüssler Fiorenza challenged Bartchy's evangelical biblical hermeneutic by calling for a new model of biblical interpretation that distinguishes the liberating words from the androcentric, patriarchal aspects of the text. But, no matter how challenging her new hermeneutic was to an evangelical understanding of the biblical text, focus quickly shifted to the viability of EWC itself at the business meeting that followed the Schüssler Fiorenza plenary.

The meeting was chaired by co-coordinators Barbara Gifford and Britt Vanden Eykel and began with the usual business. The first disturbing news was financial. Not only was the organization $5000 short in income, but the conference was running a $10,000 deficit because of low attendance. (Fewer than half of EWC's nearly 650 members had registered.) As if that weren't troubling enough, the final item of "Old Business," a report by Nancy Hardesty on the resolutions tabled at the 1984 Wellesley conference, evolved into three resolutions being proposed from the floor and ultimately passed by eighty members with sixteen opposed and twenty-three abstentions. Resolutions one and two were on racism and violence against women. It was resolution three that provoked furor and lengthy discussion, causing "confusion, conflict and hurt for many." It stated: "Whereas homosexual people are children of God, and because of the biblical mandate of Jesus Christ that we are all created equal in God's sight, and in recognition of the presence of the lesbian minority in the Evangelical Women's Caucus International, EWCI takes a firm stand in favor of civil rights protection for homosexual persons."[55]

The focus of the Wednesday morning open-mike session shifted from sharing feminist journeys to airing members' divergent views on what had happened at the business meeting. Executive director of Faith at Work, potter, author, and EWC member, Marjory Zoet Bankson facilitated the discussion, but what became apparent was that the membership was "heart-breakingly polarized." The last person at the microphone was Los Angeles businessperson and philanthropist Margo Goldsmith, who announced that an anonymous donor had covered the $15,000 shortfall. The next day it became known that Goldsmith was responsible and had given the money to remove the "intolerable burden." Now solvent, EWC's biggest concern was finding consensus on its mission.[56]

Virginia Ramey Mollenkott, the last scheduled speaker, challenged members to expand EWC's agenda and to not be content to work only for personal empowerment. "Feminism," she said, "involves opposing the age-ist, racist, classist, heterosexist systems of patriarchy. We are feminist and therefore we are political; by definition political." Clearly, many in the organization concurred with this closing charge, but the question many left with was "What kind of action is right for us now?"[57] The Minnesota conference chairperson, Cathy Kroeger, had decided it was no longer possible to host the next biennial conference, titled "Women of Peace," although it was already slated for July 21–25, 1988, at conservative Baptist General Conference Bethel College and Seminary in St. Paul, and chapter members were already promoting it by selling packets of Minnesota wild rice. By the end of the Fresno conference, the future of EWC looked bleak, or at best changed. In the fall *Update* EWC national secretary Catherine Bailey aptly began her account of the business meeting with a quote attributed to foremother Rev. Jeannette Piccard, "Without turbulence, there is no movement."[58]

The executive council retired to Bass Lake, California, to sort out the "Fresno conference fiasco," already conscious of troubling publicity. The California news media was not subtle and took quite a run at the organization. *The Fresno Bee*'s coverage included an interview with Bartchy and Hanna-Witherspoon on biblical feminism and an article headlined "Women's Caucus Endorses Gay Rights" that focused on the controversies. The article began with reference to the resolution on the civil rights of homosexuals and, without mentioning Virginia Ramey Mollenkott's name, it quoted from the plenary in which she "declared that biblical passages about homosexuality have been misinterpreted and that scripture does not speak about homosexual orientation." Reacting to the quote, organizer Neufeld stated that Mollenkott was speaking for herself, not for the organization. The article also observed that the "Boston chapter was reported to be 'devastated' by the resolution" and that the Minnesota chapter had withdrawn as host of the 1988 conference. Further, it quoted a local evangelical leader, Pat Kissell, who had decided to resign from EWC: "I am not against civil rights, but I know exactly where it is leading. It's leading to the Evangelical Women's Caucus becoming a support group for lesbians."[59]

A week later, after the council meeting, *Los Angeles Times* religion writer John Dart wrote a similar article, headlined "Evangelical Women's Caucus Backs Gay Rights." Dart suggested that EWC had been "dogged for years by accusations from other evangelicals that it is a 'lesbian support group'" and quoted the resolution's author, Anne Eggebroten of Costa Mesa: "We have not said that theologically homosexual behavior is OK with God; we took a stand on civil rights." Additionally, coordinator Britt Vanden Eykel of Glendale was extensively quoted. She reaffirmed EWC's mission and acknowledged that the council had struggled with the cost of taking a stand on this issue; namely, the unity of the organization. She noted that council members had spent the weekend at Bass Lake studying scripture, trying to determine God's will. She also admitted: "We've been operating out of fear for a number of years and decided it's time to confront that fear."[60]

The weekend council meeting immediately following the Fresno conference was painful, but members decided to allow the resolutions to stand.

> EWCI was reaffirmed as a vital organization . . . yet our faith remains central. . . . EWCI remains committed to outreach to our sisters and brothers in conservative churches, yet we must also formally reach out to include our sisters of color, abused women and children, and Christians with a homosexual orientation. Such steps are frequently out of our "comfort zone" and may create much conflict within us. Yet we recognize that without change, or "turbulence," there is no movement.[61]

By the end of July, Vanden Eykel had written two letters, one to the membership and one to Minnesota chapter member Susan McCoubrie, given that Cathy Kroeger and Alvera Mickelsen were unavailable. She urged the Minnesota chapter to reconsider hosting the 1988 conference.[62] In her general letter to the membership (which she also attached to the appeal to Minnesota). Vanden Eykel outlined the events of the business meeting and offered recent background on resolution procedures, a summary of the council's discussions at Bass Lake, and hope for reconciliation and consensus on future actions. She quoted EWC's purpose as stated in the by-laws and warned against loss of focus as "EWC is the only organization with the specific purpose of calling the evangelical church to accountability on the women's issue." Further, she suggested members with broader social justice concerns hold dual memberships with organizations like Sojourners, Evangelicals for Social Action, and Evangelicals Concerned, a gay and lesbian evangelical group founded by Dr. Ralph Blair in 1976. Vanden Eykel rebuked Mollenkott for confusing the issue.

> One of the speakers at the Fresno conference demanded that, if we are to continue calling ourselves Biblical feminists, we must also take a stand endorsing abortion, affirming the homosexual lifestyle, and condemning heterosexism. Some feminists have apparently diverged from the path that EWC is on, and perhaps

must go on to work for their agenda through some other vehicle. EWC cannot take theological positions such as these without consensus and the guidance of the Holy Spirit and the Word of God. In addition, our membership is committed to reconciliation between the sexes, not separatism.

The letter ended commending the organization for taking a stand on the *civil rights* of homosexual persons and urged members to dialogue, recover trust, and recommit themselves to EWC.[63]

In the fall of 1986, *Christianity Today* carried a news article by Beth Spring, "Gay Rights Resolution Divided Membership of Evangelical Women's Caucus," which reported on the Fresno conference. She also reported on Cathy Kroeger's plans for a new organization focusing solely on "biblical" feminism; Kroeger feared that EWC was becoming too extreme for women in conservative churches and in other countries. Kroeger had a mailing list of thirty-seven women, a meeting place at the North Central Center for Christian Studies in St. Paul, Minnesota, and connections with a two-year-old British evangelical group called Men, Women and God, affiliated with theologian John Stott's London Institute for Contemporary Christianity.

The *Christianity Today* article also noted that Kroeger had two strong supporters in retired Bethel College journalism professor (and former EWC Minnesota chapter head) Alvera Mickelsen and author and educator Gretchen Gaebelein Hull. Mickelsen did not think the focus on civil rights was the issue. Quoting from the resolution, she said, "The crucial phrase was not 'civil rights' but rather, 'in recognition of the presence of the lesbian minority in EWCI.' That's what the battle was about—official recognition of lesbianism as being congruent with EWCI." Hull, who had not attended the Fresno conference, resigned from EWC because of its shift from a single focus to a "multiple agenda that changes the character of the organization."[64]

Both Mollenkott and Hardesty were identified in the article as "advocates of homosexual rights and recognition" and as exercising "strong influence in EWCI." Vanden Eykel defended the resolution, emphasizing that it was not an endorsement or theological statement of homosexual practice. Further, she noted that biblical feminism is not generally well received by evangelicals. She said, "We have not been palatable to the conservative church with any part of our message....There is a limit to how much we can sacrifice our principles." Hardesty added that EWC had been political since its inception at the 1973 meeting that also spawned Evangelicals for Social Action. She viewed this bold step as a sign of maturity. The article concluded with a statement by Evangelicals for Social Action chair Ron Sider, who definitively expressed opposition to "practicing homosexuality," as he called it, while at the same time allowing for civil rights for all people. He said, "We want to do everything we can to promote a biblical feminism that does not condone practicing homosexuality. At the same time, we have no interest in mounting negative campaigns against anyone."[65]

The Aftermath of the Fresno Conference

The spring 1987 issue of *Update* did not focus on the aftermath of Fresno; rather, it depicted a strong organization. It focused on women and psychology, a "herstory," book reviews, and Fresno workshop reports. It was in the letters section—albeit barely three pages long—that reactions to the fallout from the homosexuality resolution were aired. Some members expressed support for the risk the organization had taken, while others spoke of outrage and pain at the perceived manipulation of the business meeting by a minority of members. Mollenkott felt ill-treated by accounts in *Update* and wanted members to know that "nobody is a villain." Eggebroten pointed to "manipulative politics" on both sides and said, "The power expended in trying to avoid a vote on this resolution was certainly as great as the power expended in trying to bring it to a vote."[66]

There were only two other references to the Fresno event in the issue. Out of nine chapter reports, the only negative one was from the Minnesota chapter, expressing regret over their withdrawal from EWC, but also acknowledging that they found themselves "severely hampered in our work as biblical feminists." The other reference was the "birth announcement" of an organization called Christians for Biblical Equality, headquartered in Minneapolis. Along with subscription information for its newsletter, *Priscilla Papers,* the article noted that concern was expressed in its inaugural issue "that others in the evangelical movement for equality 'have lost their Biblical moorings.'"

Since 1986 EEWC has struggled financially but survived. It has also revisited the "identity" topic many times. Prior to the 1990 conference, when its name was changed to the Evangelical and Ecumenical Women's Caucus, an "identity" article appeared in *Update*. Foremother Anne Eggebroten recounted the history of the group's struggles over its name, its statement of faith, and its purpose. She reminded members of the group's impact, especially in light of the formation of an anti-feminist group in 1987, the Council on Biblical Manhood and Womanhood.[67] She also characterized the post-Fresno "split" as characteristic of evangelicalism; when evangelicals cannot agree, they separate and start something new. In fact, using what some might call a "traditional" evangelical tactic of drawing boundaries, Christians for Biblical Equality was having some success by identifying themselves as "*not* EWC, *not* dangerous."

After commenting on the wide range of denominational Christian feminist groups, Eggebroten suggested that perhaps the enigmatic EWC's major role was as a stubborn witness to an inclusive form of evangelicalism. In response to queries about EWC's reason to exist, its unique mission, and even its now-tiny constituency, she offered that perhaps "we are called to be, more than to do." She also suggested that EWC had often been a place for "short-term therapy," an affirmation of the "empowerment" quality of the organization. Eggebroten pointed out that more than 2,400 people had been EWC members, despite a relatively small continuous core. The article was a reminder that the progressive, dialogical qualities of the organization, replete with all manner of attachments to evangelicalism, both "advances the gospel and overthrows the patriarchy."[68]

The story of EEWC continues. The members are ecumenically evangelical—though some prefer to drop the "evangelical" nomenclature. The members are feminist, with all the diversity that feminisms encompass in the new millennium. Despite all this difference, these women (and some men) are fully committed to women's full equality in the church and the "kindom" of God. Their vision is one of "being God in the world"; [69] God in all her expansive fullness.

Notes

1. John Piper and Wayne Grudem, eds., *Recovering Biblical Manhood & Womanhood: A Response to Evangelical Feminism* (Wheaton, Ill.: Crossway, 1991), xiii.

2. Evangelicalism includes the belief in the authority of the Bible, the need for personal faith in Jesus Christ alone, and the responsibility to evangelize others. In short, evangelicalism includes those who embrace the message of evangelist Billy Graham. Christian fundamentalism, a subset within evangelicalism, has been characterized as consisting of angry, militant, separatist evangelicals who oppose modernity. Historically, fundamentalism emerged at the turn of the nineteenth century in reaction to evolutionary theories and historical biblical criticism. It called for a return to the five "fundamentals" of

Christianity; namely, verbal inerrancy of Scripture, the divinity of Jesus Christ, the virgin birth, a substitutionary theory of the atonement, and the physical resurrection and bodily return of Christ.

3. The Evangelical Women's Caucus (EWC) has had three name changes. It was known as EWC from 1974 to 1980; the Evangelical Women's Caucus International (EWCI) from 1980 to 1990; and the Evangelical and Ecumenical Women's Caucus (EEWC) from 1990 to the present. Here I use EWC when referring to the organization prior to 1990, and EEWC thereafter.

4. Nancy A. Hardesty, *Nancy A. Hardesty and the Evangelical Women's Caucus: An Oral History,* interview by Karen Kidd; Claremont, Calif.: Oral History Program, Claremont Graduate School, 12 June 1992, 24, EEWC Papers, Union Theological Seminary, Sue Horner, EEWC archivist.

5. *Priscilla Papers* 1:2 (Fall 1987), EEWC Papers.

6. Ina J. Kau, "Feminism in the American Evangelical Movement," (master's thesis, Pacific School of Religion, Berkeley, Calif., 1977), 97–99, EEWC Papers.

7. Ronald J. Sider, *The Chicago Declaration* (Carol Stream, Ill.: Creation House, 1974), 2, EEWC Papers.

8. Letha Scanzoni, "Woman's Place: Silence or Service," *Eternity*, February 1966, 15, EEWC Papers.

9. Letha Scanzoni, "Elevate Marriage to Partnership," *Eternity*, July 1968, 12–14, EEWC Papers.

10. Scanzoni and Hardesty, *All We're Meant to Be: A Biblical Approach to Women's Liberation* (Waco, Tex.: Word, 1974).

11. Nancy A. Hardesty, "Women's Liberation: An Annotated Bibliography," *Post American*, August–September 1974, 29, EEWC Papers.

12. Ibid., 42–44.

13. Letha Scanzoni, "The Feminist and the Bible," *Christianity Today*, 2 Feb. 1973, 10, EEWC Papers.

14. Paul Jewett, *Man as Male and Female: A Study in Sexual Relationships from a Theological Point of View* (Grand Rapids: Eerdmans, 1975).

15. Sider, *Chicago Declaration*, 9–10, 22.

16. Ibid., 18.

17. Ibid., 13.

18. Hardesty to Sider, 29 August 1973, Evangelicals for Social Action Papers, box 1, folder 11, Billy Graham Center Archives, Wheaton, Ill.

19. Sider, *Chicago Declaration*, 17.

20. Ibid., 2.

21. Hardesty, *Oral History*, 16.

22. Marjorie Hyer, "Social and Political Activism Is Aim of Evangelical Group," *Washington Post*, 30 November 1973, Evangelicals for Social Action Papers, box 3, folder 10.

23. Martin E. Marty quotes Larson in *Context: A Commentary on the Interaction of Religion and Culture*, 15 March 1974, Evangelicals for Social Action Papers, box 3, folder 10.

24. Scanzoni and Hardesty, *All We're Meant to Be*.

25. *Daughters of Sarah* (newsletter), 1974, Evangelicals for Social Action Papers, box 3, folder 8.

26. News release, 1974, Evangelicals for Social Action Papers, box 3, folder 8.

27. Roy Larsen, "Evangelism God's "Truth in Action,'" *Chicago Sun-Times*, 7 Dec. 1974, Evangelicals for Social Action Papers, box 2, folder 18.

28. Bob Jones, Editorial, *Faith for the Family*, September/October 1974, Evangelicals for Social Action Papers, box 3, folder 10.

29. Judy Brown Hull, Evangelicals for Social Action, An Open Letter, Thanksgiving Week 1975, Evangelicals for Social Action Papers, box 4, folder 7.

30. Wes Michaelson, "Neither Male Nor Female: The Thanksgiving Conference on Biblical Feminism," *Sojourners* (January 1976): 10–12.

31. EWC Conference brochure, 28–30 November 1975, Evangelicals for Social Action Papers, box 4, folder 14.

32. Michaelson, "Neither Male," 10–11.

33. Helen Andelin, *Fascinating Womanhood* (Santa Barbara, Calif.: Pacific, 1965).

34. Marabel Morgan, *The Total Woman* (New York: Pocket Books, 1975).

35. Larry Christenson, *The Christian Family* (Minneapolis: Bethany Fellowship, 1970).

36. Kathleen Storrie, "The Modern Movement for the Submission of Women," *Canadian Woman Studies* 5 (Winter 1983): 9, EEWC Papers.

37. Michaelson, "Neither Male," 12.

38. Roberta Hestenes and Lois Curley, eds., *Women and the Ministries of Christ* (Pasadena, Calif.: Fuller Theological Seminary, 1979), xi, EEWC Papers.

39. Phyllis E. Alsdurf, "Evangelical Feminists: Ministry Is the Issue," July 1978, *Women and the Ministries of Christ*, 359.

40. Ibid.

41. Don Williams, *The Bond That Breaks: Will Homosexuality Split the Church?* (Los Angeles: BIM, 1978).

42. Letha Scanzoni and Virginia Ramey Mollenkott, *Is the Homosexual My Neighbor? Another Christian View* (San Francisco: Harper, 1978).

43. Claire K. Wolterstorff, "Encouragement and Unanswered Questions: Evangelicals Discuss Women's Issues," *Reformed Journal*, August 1978, in *Women and the Ministries of Christ*, 363–64, EEWC Papers.

44. Letha Scanzoni, "Marching On!" in *Women and the Ministries of Christ*, ed. Roberta Hestenes and Lois Curley (Pasadena, Calif.: Fuller Theological Seminary, 1979), 126–34, EEWC Papers.

45. Ibid.

46. Joyce Erickson, "Social Issues: How EWC Grapples," *Update* 4 (December 1980): 2, EEWC Papers.

47. "Britt Vanden Eykel Named to New Field Director's Post," *Update* 6 (December 1982–February 1983): 3, EEWC Papers.

48. Andy Moor, "Politics: A Biblical Feminist View of the 1980s," *Update* 6 (December 1982–February 1983): 6, EEWC Papers.

49. "Membership Approves Resolutions," *Update* 6 (September–November 1982): 8, EEWC Papers, Sue Horner, EEWC archivist.

50. Dorothy V. Meyer, "At Wellesley, We Were 'Free Indeed': Reliving Our Sixth Plenary Conference," *Update* 8 (September 1984–February 1985): 1–10, EEWC Papers.

51. Kathryn Neufeld, "To Resolve—or Not to Resolve?" *Update* 8 (September 1984–February 1985): 1314, EEWC Papers.

52. Sharon Gallagher, "What Does Our Diversity Mean?" *Update* 9 (Summer 1985): 1–4, EEWC Papers.

53. Joanne Ross Feldmeth, "Surviving Our Adolescence," *Update* 10 (Fall 1986): 1–15, EEWC Papers.

54. National Conference Update, 24 Jan. [1986], EEWC Papers.

55. Catherine Bailey, "Not 'Business As Usual,'" *Update* 10 (Fall 1986): 5–6, EEWC Papers.

56. Feldmeth, "Surviving," 4.

57. Ibid., 15.

58. Bailey, "Not 'Business,'" 5.

59. "Women's Caucus Endorses Gay Rights," *Fresno Bee*, 12 July 1986, A10, EEWC Papers.

60. John Dart, "Evangelical Women's Caucus Backs Gay Rights," *Los Angeles Times*, 19 July 1986, part 2, p. 19, EEWC Papers.

61. Catherine Bailey, "Summer Council Meeting," *Update* 10 (Fall 1986): 7, EEWC Papers.

62. Britt Vanden Eykel to Susan McCoubrie, Rosemont, Minnesota, 23 July 1986, EEWC Papers.

63. EWCI coordinator Britt Vanden Eykel to EWC Sisters, 23 July 1986, EEWC Papers.

64. Beth Spring, "Gay Rights Resolution Divided Membership of Evangelical Women's Caucus," *Christianity Today*, 3 October 1986, 40–43, EEWC Papers.

65. Ibid.

66. Your Turn, *Update* 11 (Spring 1987): 10–12, EEWC Papers.

67. In 1987 the Council on Biblical Manhood and Womanhood (CBMW) formed and drafted the "Danvers Statement," which asserted the rationale, purposes, and affirmations of the new organization. In August 1995 a newsletter, *CBMW News,* began publication "to set forth the teachings of the Bible about the complementary differences between men and women, created equal in the image of God, because these teachings are essential for obedience to Scripture and for the health of the family and the Church." In the inaugural issue of *CBMW News* (August 1995) one article announced the intention to report on churches and organizations that affirmed either egalitarian or complementarian positions. To qualify as complementarian it was necessary to agree that "some governing and teaching roles within the church are restricted to men" and that "wives should forsake resistance to their husbands' authority and grow in willing, joyful submission to their husbands' leadership." Four organizations were named as egalitarian—Presbyterian Church,

U.S.A., United Methodist Church, Fuller Theological Seminary, and InterVarsity Christian Fellowship.

68. Anne Eggebroten, "EWC: Called To Be," *Update* 13 (Fall 1989): 1–3, EEWC Papers.

69. This phrase was expressed by Anne Eggebroten, interview with author, tape recording, Santa Monica, Calif., 7 January 1997.

Bibliography

Archival Documents

Evangelical and Ecumenical Women's Caucus Papers. Sue Horner, Evangelical and Ecumenical Women's Caucus archivist. The Archives of Women in Theological Scholarship, Union Theological Seminary, New York, New York.

Evangelicals for Social Action Papers. Billy Graham Center Archives, Wheaton, Illinois.

Publications of Evangelical Feminism

Daughters of Sarah, Nov. 1974–Winter 1996.
Priscilla Papers, 1987–.
Update, summer 1977– .

Books

Andelin, Helen. *Fascinating Womanhood*. Santa Barbara, Calif.: Pacific, 1965.

Christenson, Larry. *The Christian Family*. Minneapolis: Bethany Fellowship, 1970.

Jewett, Paul K. *Man as Male and Female: A Study in Sexual Relationships from a Theological Point of View*. Grand Rapids: Eerdmans, 1975.

Morgan, Marabel. *The Total Woman*. New York: Pocket, 1975.

Piper, John, and Wayne Grudem, eds. *Recovering Biblical Manhood and Womanhood: A Response to Evangelical Feminism*. Wheaton, Ill.: Crossway, 1991.

Scanzoni, Letha, and Nancy Hardesty. *All We're Meant to Be: A Biblical Approach to Women's Liberation*. Waco, Tex.: Word, 1974.

Scanzoni, Letha, and Virginia Ramey Mollenkott. *Is the Homosexual My Neighbor? Another Christian View*. San Francisco: Harper & Row, 1978.

Williams, Don. *The Bond that Breaks: Will Homosexuality Split the Church?* Los Angeles: BIM, 1978.

6.

Diaspora Economics
Filipino American Families and Globalization

JOCELYN ECLARIN AZADA

🔲🔲🔲

> You have to realize that the Filipino people are in diaspora. We are
> in our wilderness journey, our exile, looking for the promised land
> that is livelihood.
>   —Reynaldo Lopez
>   Philippine Seafarers Organizing Ministry

> It is the current moment of capitalism as a global mode of pro-
> duction that has necessitated the maintenance of family ties and
> political allegiances among persons spread across the globe.
>   —*Nations Unbound*

Mobility—of culture and people, information and markets, capital
and labor—is a hallmark of globalization. In the scheme of an export-
oriented national economy without enough jobs for its people, workers are the Philippines' greatest export. As millions of Filipinos find
their livelihoods outside their homeland, scholars have rightly identified a Filipino diaspora. The destination for thousands of Filipino
immigrants every year is the United States. Focusing on conditions
from 1965 to the present, this chapter examines some of the effects of
this migration on the Filipino family in the context of the macroeco-
nomic conditions determining this flow of migration. Some patterns
can be seen in contemporary Filipino American families' creative
adaptations—despite some harmful consequences—to a complex historical context: globalization and the Filipino diaspora.

Filipino Culture and Family Values

For Filipinos, one's family is the "primary source of individual and
social identity and material and emotional support and security."[1]

The Filipino family is defined more broadly than the nuclear family of father, mother, and children. The Filipino family branches bilaterally, including extended relatives, from first cousins to third cousins and their families.[2] Further, the kinship bonds are broadened through the Catholic sacraments of baptism, confirmation, and marriage. Participating in these sacraments are godparents, who covenant to provide social, spiritual, emotional, moral, and material support to their godchildren whenever possible.[3]

Filipino culture defines family roles, expectations, and norms in detail. The father is the head of the household, the primary income earner. He takes charge of disciplining children and undertakes major household chores. The mother governs the family; she manages the household budget, oversees the family's health, and manages its social, relational, and educational activities. Borrowing from the language of corporate organization, the father is the chief executive officer, holding the ultimate decision-making and financial power. The mother is the chief operating officer, running the family's day-to-day operations, including managing the family budget. She bears most of the responsibility for child-rearing but receives help from grandparents and other kin who play major roles in children's lives. Siblings are expected to contribute to the chores of the household, and older siblings even participate in the disciplining of younger ones. In adulthood, siblings act cooperatively to provide assistance in various forms to their parents, elder relatives, and other relatives who may need help.[4]

Gender roles in the household are "less rigidly demarcated" in Philippine society compared to other Asian countries.[5] Men may assist with cooking, cleaning, or looking after children, and Filipina women are typically not confined solely to the domestic sphere, but participate in the labor force at a rate of 39.2 percent.[6] Sexist disparities still persist, however. Although domestic responsibilities are shared, women still shoulder at least two-thirds of the household duties. The added power that comes from managing household finances becomes a stressor when money is short. Finally, men can operate by a double standard that justifies domestic violence, extramarital affairs, and male dominance.[7]

Filipinos cherish certain family and kinship values. These include respect for older relatives, maintenance of close family ties with extended family kin, and love and concern for children.[8] These values are demonstrated through such practices as care and support for parents in old age, monetary assistance provided to relatives (whether nearby or overseas), and providing educational funds and assistance to children. Thus, traditional Filipino families emphasize intergenerational relationships and often act as economic cooperatives for the betterment of the entire family. Financial assistance can be requested and given for a whole spectrum of needs—from basic subsistence to medical emergencies, business investments, and immigration expenses.

Individual needs are subordinated to the family's common good, and helping the family collectively is viewed as one's primary responsibility. Major decisions—such as those involving employment, education, or health—are often made in consultation with the nuclear family or even some members of extended family.[9] For example, the oldest adult daughter in a family may be advised to pursue nursing as a profession because it pays well and allows for easy entry into the United States. With a salary as a registered nurse in a U.S. hospital, she would then be able to send money back to the Philippines and financially assist her younger siblings in their schooling. Under U.S. immigration laws, she could also serve as the primary sponsor for the family to immigrate to the United States, thus improving the whole family's condition.[10] In the same way, a consideration of the family's well-being is a significant dimension of the decision to immigrate.

Philippine Immigration to the United States

Immigration History
In the 2000 census, Filipinos were the second most numerous Asian subgroup, with a population of 1.8 million.[11] Filipinos also claim the longest history of Asian immigrants in this country. In 1763 a small number of Filipino sailors jumped ship off the *San Pablo*, a Spanish galleon sailing as a trade vessel between the Philippines and Mexico, then two Spanish colonies. Known as the "Manilamen," they began the first Filipino settlement in North America, just outside New Orleans.

Philippine immigration to the United States has been summarized generally in three waves, with the first wave occurring between 1910 and 1945, the second between 1945 and 1965, and the final wave after 1965. Each of these waves has been characterized by distinct demographics determined by immigration policy. As with immigrant communities in general, the demographic makeup of the Filipino immigrant community—its gender ratios, its family constitution, its economic, geographic, and occupational distribution—has depended on fluctuating and conflicting economic and racial concerns.[12]

Throughout this century, United States immigration policy has been contested with each recalculation of the tradeoff between economic need and racial climate. In expanding economies requiring unskilled—and today, skilled—labor, the doors to the fabled land of opportunity have opened and welcomed immigrants. In recessionary economies, when immigrants are perceived as a threat—to the economic security and/or political identity—of the majority population, that flow is restricted, and immigrants are scapegoated. The tensions fostered by this intersection of racial and economic exploitation have at various times culminated in extreme xenophobia, fueling, for example, the internment of over one hundred thousand Japanese Americans in World War II and the cruelty of border patrol officials along the Mexico–U.S. border.

The first wave of Filipino manual workers came in 1910, laborers for Hawaii's sugar plantations, California's agricultural fields, and Alaska's canneries. Enduring harsh and lonely working conditions at subsistence level wages, they also experienced systematic mistreatment and ill will in a harsh society. They faced segregation and physical abuse and were denied citizenship, the right to own property, and the right to intermarry. Furthermore, labor recruitment practices and exclusionary legislation limited the migration of Filipina women. Numbering one hundred thousand at its height, 90 percent of this first wave was comprised of men.[13]

Yen Le Espiritu notes the impact of gender imbalances on Asian immigrant men, women, and families generally during this period of American history.[14] These implications certainly apply to Filipinos in this period, with their ten-to-one ratio of males to females. First, unattached men were a much more mobile and exploitable labor force. Second, the gender ratio discouraged the formation of nuclear families with children who would then be American citizens. Third, the responsibilities and costs of child-rearing remained with the kinship group—headed by women—in the Philippines.

Faced with an environment hostile to the Filipino family, Filipino male laborers were forced to redefine family in other terms. They did this in two ways: through bachelor societies and also through transnational families. Filipino bachelors rearranged the way they met their various needs: boarding houses provided lodging and food, social needs were met at gambling and social halls, and bachelors fulfilled their sexual needs with prostitutes. They also stretched and redefined family to include non-kin. They formed kin-like organizations with the few Filipino nuclear families in proximity for mutual aid, companionship, and security—what they missed from their extended families back home. Predominantly Catholics, they adopted families and families adopted them through sacraments like baptism, confirmation, and marriage. In Hawaii, the routine participation of as many as two hundred godfathers in a single ceremony attests to the inclusion of bachelors in the family structure.[15]

For men with families in the Philippines, separation from wives gave rise to a "transnational family," or split household.[16] According to Espiritu, such families survived because they coordinated their economic activities: Wives, along with other kin in the Philippines, were responsible for raising the family, while the husband supported them with his earnings. This division of labor had both positive and negative effects. Wives enjoyed a greater degree of control over the household and independence from their husbands; however, a woman also had to manage a family without the assistance and companionship of a partner. Meanwhile, husbands still controlled the income flow. They also missed the companionship, but were less accountable sexually than their wives, who were expected to remain faithful to their distant husbands.[17]

After World War II, conditions for Filipinos in the United States improved. During the war, Filipino nationals who fought alongside U.S. soldiers in the Philippines were hailed for their bravery and loyalty. Similarly, Filipino Americans recruited for the U.S. Navy were naturalized in mass inductions. With the civil rights movement and other foreign policy concerns (discussed below), the United States relaxed its legal restrictions based on race. The major demographic impact of the 1945-to-1965 wave was the admittance of the wives and family of military personnel through the War Brides Act of 1945, balancing the gender ratios somewhat. A small number of elite foreign exchange students, called *pensionados,* were also admitted. Under the terms of these educational exchanges, the *pensionados* would later return to their home countries to take leadership positions. By the end of the second wave, there were almost 200,000 Filipinos in the United States, many of them reunited families, and the gender ratio decreased to two males for every female.[18]

The demographic profile of the community changed dramatically and its numbers swelled with the Immigration Act of 1965. This legislation would permit two main streams of immigration from the Philippines and other Asian countries: families and highly educated, highly skilled workers. From 1965 to 1970, most Filipino immigrants were admitted as professionals with occupational visas. From the late 1970s to the present, family reunification visas have predominated, as family members follow their relatives in a migration chain to

America. In the last thirty-five years, the Filipino American population has multiplied almost tenfold, from 176,310 in 1960 to 1.4 million in 1990 and 1.8 million in 2000.[19] Between 1990 and 2000, the Philippines ranked third behind Mexico and China in annual numbers of immigrants to the United States.[20]

Census information from the last three decades provides a sketch of the demographic changes prompted by the 1965 legislation. By the 1980s, women comprised half of the Filipino American population.[21] In 1990 its rates of family constitution paralleled the larger United States society; 78.3 percent of Filipino families were headed by a married couple, compared to 78.6 percent for the general U.S. population. Similarly, 16.4 percent of Filipino families were headed by a single female, compared to 16.5 percent for the general U.S. population.[22] Labor force participation is higher for females than for males. In 1990 75.4 percent of Filipina females worked outside the home, compared with 65.3 percent of their male counterparts.[23] In terms of occupational distribution, 63.3 percent of adult Filipinos in the United States were employed in professional managerial occupations; 18.3 percent as service or farm workers, 9.5 percent as sales/clerical workers and 8.9 percent as craftsmen or semiskilled manufacturing operators.[24]

Immigration and Global Economic Restructuring

In *Global Economic Restructuring and the New Asian Immigration* (1994), Paul Ong and other Asian American scholars analyze post-1965 Asian immigration in the context of globalization, particularly in the Pacific Rim. Their examination considers the changes in global economic capitalism since the end of World War II as pertinent to understanding post-1965 Filipino immigration to the United States. Since World War II, trade policies aimed at deregulating and liberalizing markets have allowed for fewer trade barriers and greater access to markets.[25] As a result of these policies, the authors argue, worsening economic conditions in the Philippines have provided the push toward immigration. At the same time, greater economic opportunity in the United States, a historic relationship between the two countries, and the acceptance of Western culture and capitalist ideology on the part of Filipinos has provided the pull to America.[26]

The Push toward Immigration: The Philippines' Brain Drain

With the end of World War II and the beginning of the Cold War, the United States pursued foreign policies of containment in the Asia Pacific region. Its intensive military interventions, monetary aid, and development assistance were proactive efforts to contain communism and, ostensibly, lay the foundations for "democracy" throughout the region. Critics of these policies note that such initiatives were designed to reinforce U.S. political economic hegemony, disseminate Western capitalist ideology, and secure Asian markets for globalization.[27]

Within a newly independent Philippines, the United States, its former colonizer, established an educational system as part of its post–World War II reconstruction package. The curricula and organization of Philippine public elementary and secondary schools were patterned after the American system, right down to the use of English as the language of instruction. In this way, a Western-oriented education was made accessible to most Filipino children. With greater numbers of educated children came a greater demand for colleges and universities. Such institutions of higher learning further articulated a decidedly Euro-American culture and imparted the ideology of modern development and capitalism through native-born professors trained in Western schools.[28] The prevalence of higher education produced a sizable managerial-professional class—white-collar workers in the medical, legal, financial, and business sectors.

Ong and his colleagues noted a convergence of factors predisposing these Filipino professionals to immigrate to the United States.[29] First, as prescribed by Western development theory, the Philippine government had committed to an export-oriented strategy of entering the world economy. Such a strategy is predicated on a supply of cheap labor to attract foreign capital, with little opportunity for well-educated labor; in effect, *the Philippines was educating workers its domestic economy could not absorb*. Second, the training of professionals and managers—which emphasized English fluency along with Western attitudes and values—was more suited to the needs of advanced capitalism rather than the needs of the Philippines, a developing Asian country. Lastly, countries such as the United States could offer higher wages, professional opportunities, and possibilities for a brighter economic future not available in the Philippines. With the Immigration Act of 1965, thousands of Philippine professionals left their homeland, culture, and families in search of this future.

The Pull toward the United States: Global Restructuring

Global economic integration in the late twentieth century is characterized by the disappearance of commercial borders, an expanding service and information sector, and the internationalization of the production of goods and services.[30] In the United States, corporations "downsize," retaining professional personnel for primary capitalizing activities, such as finance, marketing, management, and research and development. These highly valued workers perform specialized service or information functions in the centers of global commerce, so-called global cities such as New York or Los Angeles. Traditional manufacturing activity is either shifted to developing countries or remains in the United States by utilizing cheap immigrant labor. Since the 1960s, the United States has deindustrialized. In its labor market the number of highly paying jobs in the manufacturing sector have decreased, and the number of poorly paid *and* highly paid jobs in the service sector have increased.[31] The "duality" of post-1965 Asian immigration in general and Filipino immigration in particular reflects this division of labor.[32] Filipino immigrants today are employed in both the highly paid, highly educated sector and in the lower- and lowest-paying service and manufacturing jobs.

Changes: Gender, Work, and Families in the Filipino Diaspora

Immigrant Gender Relations and Work

For immigrants, gender relations are construed by the changes in women's and men's relative positions of power in the country of settlement. Yen Espiritu, in a study of Asian American gender relations, suggests a general pattern that is relevant to Filipino American gender relations as well.[33] Upon immigration to the United States, Asian men confront institutionalized racism and a subsequent loss in social and earning power. Asian women then must enter the work force to compensate for losses in male income. As a woman's contribution to the household income increases, so too does her power to challenge sexism in the home. Espiritu further comments on possible differential effects by class.

Gender Relations in the Professional Managerial Class

Two studies of gender dynamics in professional minority couples support Espiritu's thesis.[34] In a study of Taiwanese couples in New York in 1992, researchers found that professional men married to professional women do a greater share of housework than Taiwanese men in other classes. With similar results, Beatriz Pesquera studied Latino couples and found that professional men married to professional women also perform a greater share of the household chores than Latino men in other classes.[35]

Pesquera attributes this finding to three factors: (1) the diminishing earning gap between the men and the women, (2) the time demands of the women's careers, and (3) the women's ability to pressure husbands into doing their share of the household chores. She cautions us with two caveats to these findings. First, the women in these couples still performed a greater share of the household duties than the men did. Second, the women had to negotiate for the responsibilities the men shared, suggesting an a priori male assumption that women should do the greater share of the housework.[36]

Espiritu applies these findings to the lives of Filipina women in the medical field, particularly nurses, and suggests that for them, numerous conditions may increase the parity of gender relations in the home. First, these women may enter the United States as the principal immigrants under the professional preference; their husbands would then enter as dependents. Second, these nurses tend to work shifts that increase their income—double shifts and graveyard shifts—thereby increasing both the value of their work hours and decreasing their hours available for housework. Finally, most Filipina nurses work with co-ethnics; strong female support groups may help them challenge the household division of labor.[37]

Gender Relations in the Working Class

For poor Asian women in general, Espiritu posits the following dynamic, which may be applied to poor Filipino families.[38] A study by an organizing and advocacy group based in California, the Asian Immigrant Women Association (AIWA), found that most women workers in the low-wage microelectronics and apparel industries were married to men who were also employed in the low-wage sector as cooks, janitors, and the like. Job opportunities differ for low-wage Asian workers depending on their gender. Working-class Asian women may find work in both the service and manufacturing sectors and in small-scale ethnic enterprises. Working-class Asian men, however, are more limited in their work options and mostly placed in the ethnic enterprise sector. Women are the preferred workers for microelectronics manufacturers, for example, for their dexterity (due to their smaller hands) and lower wage requirements. Despite exploitation, more job opportunities for women may give them an advantage in their gender relations at home.

Following Espiritu's general pattern, as lower-income women's earnings become more important to the family, the women's value in the home increases, and so does her ability to contest sexist gender relations in the home. However, these women, who are more vulnerable than professional women due to *both* gender and economic oppression, may be more constrained in asserting gender equality than their professional-class counterparts. Additionally, in the face of both gender and economic exploitation, the family is a source of security and moral support. Women may accept certain patriarchal expectations in order to maintain family harmony. Thus, poorly paid women workers may leverage their wage-earning clout to redefine gender roles more equitably but not to the same degree as professional women.[39]

The New Transnational Families in the Filipino Diaspora

Approximately seven million people, or 10 percent of the country's total population, work outside the Philippines, with an estimated two million residing in the United States.[40] These workers are mandated by law to return 50 percent of their earnings to the Philippine government as remittances.[41] In 1999 overseas remittances totaled almost seven billion dollars, and in 2000 the total was six billion dollars[42]— the economy's greatest share of foreign exchange for the Philippines. Through its Philippine Overseas Employment Administration, the Philippine government vigorously promotes and encourages migratory labor. Filipinos supply temporary and permanent, skilled and unskilled labor in more than one hundred countries throughout Southeast Asia, the Middle East, and Europe, and including Australia, Canada, and the United States.

Transnational Families
Jonathan Okamura's recent book, *Imagining the Filipino Diaspora: Transnational Identities, Relations and Communities* (1998), explores the nature of the Filipino diaspora. The transnational character and social construction of diaspora communities are the most significant dimensions of his analytical framework. He writes:

> By this proposition, I mean that diasporas should be understood as consisting of transnational linkages between an ethnic minority and its homeland (or cultural center) and its counterpart communities in other host societies. As for being socially constructed, diasporas should be viewed as resulting from the development and maintenance of those transnational relations that link them culturally, economically and politically with their homeland.[43]

Thus he distinguishes a diaspora from an "expatriate, exile, ethnic, minority, refugee, migrant, sojourner and overseas community."[44] For Okamura, the Filipino diaspora is constituted by the collective consciousness and the cultural, economic, and social practices connecting Filipinos to their homeland as well as to other Filipino communities throughout the world.

The Filipino value of family figures prominently in transnational linkages. Separated by economic necessity, Filipino Americans have adapted by using travel, information, and communications technologies to preserve their families. In true globalized fashion, Filipino families maintain their relatedness by exchanging flows of money, goods, information and communication across national borders and time zones. Three of these practices—the sending of remittances, *balikbayan* pilgrimages and long-distance communications—are discussed below.

A primary practice linking overseas Filipinos with their families is the sending of remittances and cash contributions to relatives back home. A survey of 17,000 families conducted in 1986 by the Philippine Census Office found that over five percent of these households consider "cash receipts, gifts and other forms of assistance from abroad . . . a primary source of income."[45] Approximately 568,000 families (3.2 million individuals) a year report being supported by family members overseas.[46] The Filipino value of helping siblings and relatives with educational expenses is observed in many families across national borders, and cash contributions for education are like "family grants" that will eventually benefit the entire family. Other material gifts sent to relatives back home include expensive consumer goods, like designer clothing and shoes, linens, watches, and electronics, and even canned foods or staples.

Filipinos in the United States plan for and save money for vacations home. These journeys home—halfway around the world—are pilgrimages loaded with great cultural and social significance. The traveler is called a *balikbayan,* which means "one who returns home." *Balikbayan* visits often coincide with special times, like Christmas, the annual town fiesta, or family events.[47] Filipinos who return home to their town fiesta are treated as honored and special guests at parties where the whole town is present. These fiestas are elaborate rituals in which the transnational family and kinship relationships are cemented and nurtured.

According to airline regulations, passengers to the Philippines can carry two boxes weighing a total of seventy pounds for no extra charge. In Philippine culture, these are called *balikbayan* boxes, and are filled with gifts, called *pasalubong,* for all family members, from immediate family to extended relatives. Most traveling Filipinos save diligently for these gifts and carry the maximum two boxes, jampacked with gifts that signify success and the American lifestyle. For many poor Filipinos, these gifts are tangible symbols of the new "Filipino Dream": making it in America.[48]

Telecommunications facilitate regular information flow to and from the homeland. Ethnically targeted advertising directed at Filipinos in all Filipino publications indicate the monetary and emotional value of long-distance phone calls placed to the Philippines.[49] These ads generally appeal to the heartstrings, written in the Filipino language and picturing Filipino family members sharing a special moment on the telephone. Given a community that makes up less than 1 percent of the United States population and generates scarce attention from the media in general or business in particular, Okamura notes the significance of this campaign:

> I do not doubt that similar advertising campaigns are directed at other immigrant populations, but I also assume that there are several larger and more prosperous racial/ethnic groups that have not been so targeted because they are conceived as not being concerned to affirm transnational relations. . . . Telecommunications companies consider Filipino Americans to be a lucrative and expanding market in the highly competitive telecommunications field.[50]

Other telecommunications innovations, such as cell phones and the Internet, are also used to maintain regular contact if families have access to these forms of communication. Cell phone text messages, in particular, have become the medium of choice for many Filipinos:

> Each 160-character message costs 1 peso (U.S. 2 cents) within the Philippines and 10 pesos internationally, making this possibly the cheapest place on earth to get hooked on texting. . . . A typical cell phone costs the equivalent of $50; most people buy prepaid cards that, for $6, cover the cost of 300 domestic messages. I MISS YOU; SEND MONEY; DO YOUR HOMEWORK—it's how OFWs [overseas Filipino workers] and their families remain families. Rosaria Reyes, the Filipina domestic helper killed by a suicide bombing in Israel last year, transmitted a message to her son the night before her death: MATULOG KA NA. Go to sleep already.[51]

Children of Filipino Immigrants: Second-Generation Filipino Americans

In the United States, Filipinos have created the least institutionally complete ethnic community of the four largest Asian subgroups.[52] A low rate of entrepreneurship and Filipino-owned businesses accounts for the virtual absence of Filipino ethnic enclaves in large cities. A weak business sector, in turn, translates into weak political leverage. Socially, group cohesiveness has not been reinforced by traditional stabilizing agents such as churches or community organizations. The disunity observed in the United States, sadly, has generally been attributed to experiences Filipinos bring with them from back home. A colonial history along with regionalistic and linguistic diversity in a country of over a thousand islands and two hundred dialects has historically made unity difficult to achieve for the Filipino people.

Studies are just beginning to document the effects of a weak cultural and group identity on second-generation Filipino Americans—the American-born children and grandchildren of Filipino immigrants. Few cultural or language schools have been established to promote Filipino culture or pride in Philippine heritage.[53] The immigrant linguistic paradigm of losing native-language fluency by the third generation is dramatically altered for the Filipino community: Most *second-generation* Filipino Americans are not able to communicate in the first language of their parents.[54] Finally, a worrisome statistic emerged from a study conducted in San Diego by the Centers for Disease Control and Prevention in 1996. In a study of adolescent mental health, 46 percent of Filipino high school students surveyed indicated that they had seriously considered attempting suicide in the previous year. Of that group, half—23 percent—actually did attempt to commit suicide in the previous twelve months.[55]

Although much more research needs to be done in order to draw definitive conclusions, some have already been suggested. For Filipino American children and young people, a lack of connection with their Philippine background and culture contributes to a weak sense of identity and lack of self-esteem. Intergenerational conflict may ensue, as Filipino immigrant parents struggle to pass on their own cultural values while their children try to succeed in the dominant culture, with a very different value system. Children and adolescents thus must negotiate the challenges of understanding and integrating two cultures—Filipino and mainstream American. When the internal conflict between the cultures becomes too great, with few supports to reconcile it, American-born Filipino youth lose their Filipino identities and the self-pride and knowledge that come from a healthy integration.

On the other hand, where programs and organizations support "Fil-Ams" in their search for identity and cultural heritage, the response is tremendous. Studies of ethnic identity among Filipino American college students in California document a desire to reclaim their roots. These students engage in a process of "decolonization" and consciously select, reject, and redefine notions of what it means for them to be Filipino. "Born-again" Filipinos, they draw from Philippine—rather than American or even Filipino American—culture and traditions to help them adequately realize their sense of self.[56] That cultural traditions from the Philippines resonate so deeply with Filipino Americans—some of whom may have never even set foot in the Philippines—is striking. Indeed, the next generation of Filipino Americans may find themselves only by reaching back to where they came from. The Filipino community in the United States would do well to support such opportunities for its children and youth.

A Special Case: Overseas Contract Workers

The costs of *balikbayan* visits, expensive gifts, and long-distance communication are manageable for overseas Filipino Americans who are stable economically, have settled as permanent residents or even United States citizens, and can afford such practices. The implications of family separation are much different, however, for overseas contract workers, the approximately 800,000 Filipinos occupying the lowest paying sectors of the global economy. These workers are highly susceptible to economic exploitation and unsafe working conditions.[57] According to the 2001 Survey on Overseas Filipinos, about a third are employed as physical laborers in manufacturing, transport, mining and construction, and over half of the female workers work as domestic helpers or cleaners.[58] Low pay and separations are detrimental not only to the worker, but to the worker's family.

Numerous organizations throughout the world now provide assistance to these workers and advocate for their rights. One such Philippines-based organization, Kakaampi, is dedicated to helping families address the impact of immigration. Kakaampi's research documents the social problems affecting families of migrant workers who are left behind in the Philippines. Foremost among these problems is marital breakdown as a result of prolonged separation. Incidents of drug abuse, juvenile delinquency, and early pregnancy have also been observed in families of migrant workers adversely affected by the stress of overseas labor.[59]

In a conference sponsored by Kakaampi, migrant workers and their families engaged in painful discussion regarding the strain of overseas employment. Wives and husbands remaining in the Philippines complained about delayed or dwindling remittances, neglect of family responsibilities, and extramarital affairs. Migrant workers complained about family members overspending, not disciplining children, and making constant financial requests.[60]

The challenges facing migrant worker families are enormous. In addition to the hardships faced by the workers themselves—cruel and alienating conditions, discrimination, extreme economic exploitation—the families also suffer. With migrant workers and their families, Kakaampi has identified the issues of livelihood, education, child health care, nutrition, and youth development as primary concerns. With these families, Kakaampi has instituted a savings and loan cooperative, a food cooperative, a child care center, health education programs, and a youth development program. By Kakaampi's accounts, the Youth Sector program is its most active program. Here youth learn to appreciate issues related to overseas migration and become conscious of their role in helping to strengthen the family. They are then encouraged to participate and take leadership in the positive initiatives listed above.

Conclusion

Since 1965, Filipino families have changed and adapted to the global economy. As people of the global South, they have been especially vulnerable to the repercussions of globalization on work and livelihood chances in their home country. For Filipino families, the choice to immigrate must be viewed in this context: The workings of the global economy at the "macro" level determine the economies of Filipino households, while the construction of traditional extended Filipino families has its effects on the "micro" level.

Notes

1. Jonathan Y. Okamura, *Imagining the Filipino Diaspora: Transnational Relations, Identities and Communities* (New York: Garland, 1998), 33.

2. Aurora Tiu and Juliana Sustento, *Depression and Other Mental Health Issues: The Filipino American Experience* (San Francisco: Josscy-Bass, 1995), 110.

3. Ibid., 111.

4. Ibid.

5. Sylvia Chant and Cathy McIlwane, *Women of a Lesser Cost: Female Labour, Foreign Exchange and Philippine Development* (London: Pluto, 1995), 6.

6. National Commission on the Role of Filipino Women, *Women, Employment and Economic Activities,* website: http://www.ncrfw.gov.ph/info_resource/employment.htm. December 2001.

7. Chant and McIlwane, *Women of a Lesser Cost,* 11.

8. Okamura, *Imagining the Filipino Diaspora,* 33.

9. Ibid., 35.

10. Tiu and Sustento, *Depression and Other Mental Health Issues,* 111. See also Okamura, *Imagining the Filipino Diaspora,* 35, and Paul Ong, Edna Bonacich, and Lucie Cheng, eds., *The New Asian Immigration in Los Angeles and Global Restructuring* (Philadelphia: Temple University Press, 1994), 83.

11. U.S. Department of Commerce, U.S. Census Bureau, DP-1, *Profiles of General Demographic Characteristics,* website: http://www.census.gov/Press-Release/www/2001/demoprofile.html.

12. Ong et al., *The New Asian Immigration,* 45.

13. Maria P. Root, ed., *Filipino Americans: Transformation and Identity* (Thousand Oaks, Calif.: Sage, 1997), 12.

14. Yen Le Espiritu, *Asian American Women and Men: Labor, Laws and Love* (London: Sage, 1997), 17–18.

15. Ibid., 23–24.

16. E. N. Glenn, "Split Household, Small Producer, and Dual Wage Earner: An Analysis of Chinese-American Family Strategies," *Journal of Marriage and the Family 45* (1983): 35–46; quoted in Espiritu, *Asian American Women and Men,* 24.

17. P. Hondagneu-Sotelo, *Gendered Transition: Mexican Experiences in Immigration* (Berkeley: University of California Press, 1994); as quoted in Espiritu, *Asian American Women and Men,* 26.

18. Root, *Filipino Americans,* 13.

19. Ibid., and U.S. Department of Commerce, U.S. Census Bureau.

20. U.S. Department of Commerce, U.S. Census Bureau, *Profile of the Foreign-Born Population in the United States: 2000, Current Population Reports, Special Studies,* website: http://www.census.gov/prod/www/abs/for-born.html.

21. Root, *Filipino Americans,* 14.

22. Ibid., 16.

23. Ibid., 18.

24. Ibid.

25. Ong et al., *The New Asian Immigration,* 16.

26. Ibid.

27. Walden Bello, *Dark Victory: The United States, Structural Adjustment and Global Poverty* (London: Pluto, 1994).

28. John M. Liu and Lucie Cheng, "Pacific Rim Development and the Duality of Post-1965 Asian Immigration to the United States," in Ong et al., *The New Asian Immigration,* 82.

29. Paul Ong and John M. Liu, "U.S. Immigration Policies and Asian Migration," in Ong et al., *The New Asian Immigration,* 57, and Paul Ong, Edna Bonacich, and Lucie Cheng, "The Political Economy of Capitalist Restructuring and the New Asian Immigration," in Ong et al., *The New Asian Immigration,* 26.

30. Ong et al., *The New Asian Immigration,* 17.

31. Espiritu, *Asian American Women and Men*, 61.

32. Liu and Cheng, "Pacific Rim Development," in Ong et al., *The New Asian Immigration*, 94.

33. Espiritu, *Asian American Women and Men*, 63.

34. Hsiang-Sui Chen, *Chinatown No More: Taiwan Immigrants in Contemporary New York* (Ithaca, N.Y.: Cornell University Press, 1992), cited in Espiritu, *Asian American Women and Men*, 69.

35. Beatriz Pesquera, "'In the Beginning He Wouldn't Even Lift a Spoon': The Division of Household Labor," in A. de la Torre and B. M. Pesquera, eds., *Building with Our Hands: New Directions in Chicana Studies* (Berkeley: University of California Press, 1993), 181–95, cited in Espiritu, *Asian American Women and Men*, 69.

36. Espiritu, *Asian American Women and Men*, 69.

37. Ibid., 70.

38. Ibid., 71–73.

39. Ibid., 77.

40. Philippine Overseas Employment Administration, *Stock Estimates on Overseas Filipinos 2000*, [website] http://www.poea.gov.ph/Stats/st_stock2000.html.

41. Okamura, *Imagining the Filipino Diaspora*, 126.

42. Philippine Overseas Employment Administration, *Remittances of Overseas Filipinos 2000*, website: http://www.poea.gov.ph/Stats/st_remit84-2000.html.

43. Ibid., 14.

44. Ibid., 16.

45. Ibid., 135.

46. Ibid.

47. Ibid., 123.

48. Ibid., 125.

49. Ibid., 129.

50. Ibid.

51. David Diamond, "One Nation, Overseas," *Wired* (June 2002), website: http://www.wired.com/wired/archive/10.06/philippines_pr.html.

52. Leny Mendoza Strobel, "Coming Full Circle: Narratives of Decolonization Among Post-1965 Filipino Americans," in *Filipino Americans*, 67.

53. Strobel, "Coming Full Circle," in Root, *Filipino Americans*, 62–79.

54. Ong et al., *The New Asian Immigration*, 43.

55. http://www.med.upenn.edu/cmhpsr/PDF/AsianAmericanReport.PDF.

56. Strobel, "Coming Full Circle," in Root, *Filipino Americans*, 62–79.

57. Philippine Census Bureau, *2001 Survey on Overseas Filipinos*, website: http://www.census.gov.ph/data/pressrelease/2002/of01tx.html.

58. Ibid.

59. M. Fe Nicodemus, "Separated by Opportunity: The Impact of Overseas Migration on the Family," *Communities: The Newsletter of Shared Communities* 3, no. 2 (1998): 5–6.

60. Ibid., 5.

Bibliography

Basch, Linda G., Nina Glick Schiller, and Cristina Szanton Blanc. *Nations Unbound: Transnational Projects, Postcolonial Predicaments, and Deterritorialized Nation States*. London: Gordon and Breach, 1994.

Bello, Walden. *Dark Victory: The United States, Structural Adjustment and Global Poverty*. London: Pluto, 1994.

Chan, Hsiang-Sui. *Chinatown No More: Taiwan Immigrants in Contemporary New York*. Ithaca, N.Y.: Cornell University Press, 1992.

Chant, Sylvia, and Cathy McIlwane. *Women of a Lesser Cost: Female Labour, Foreign Exchange and Philippine Development*. London: Pluto, 1995.

Diamond, David. "One Nation, Overseas." *Wired* (June 2002), website: www.wired.com/wired/archive/10.06/philippines_pr.html.

Donato, K. M. "Understanding U.S. Immigration: Why Some Countries Send Women and Others Send Men." In *Seeking Common Ground: Multidisciplinary Studies of Immigrant Women in the United States*, ed. D. Gabaccia, 159–84. Westport, Conn.: Greenwood, 1992.

Espiritu, Yen Le. *Asian American Women and Men: Labor, Laws and Love*. London: Sage, 1997.

Glenn, E. N. "Split Household, Small Producer and Dual Wage Earner: An Analysis of Chinese-American Family Strategies." *Journal of Marriage and the Family* 45 (1983): 35–46.

Hondagneu-Sotelo, P. *Gendered Transition: Mexican Experiences in Immigration*. Berkeley: University of California Press, 1994.

Lai, T. "Asian Immigrant Women: Not for Sale." In *Race, Class and Gender: An Anthology*, ed. M. L. Anderson and P. H. Collins, 163–90. Belmont, Calif.: Wordsworth, 1992.

National Commission on the Role of Filipino Women. *Women, Employment and Economic Activities,* website (December 2001): http:www.ncrfw.gov.ph/info_resource/employment.htm.

Nicodemus, M. Fe. "Separated by Opportunity: The Impact of Overseas Migration on the Family." *Communities: The Newsletter of Shared Communities* 3, no. 2 (1998): 5–6.

Okamura, Jonathan Y. *Imagining the Filipino Diaspora: Transnational Relations, Identities and Communities*. New York: Garland, 1998.

Ong, Paul, Edna Bonacich, and Lucie Cheng, eds. *The New Asian Immigration in Los Angeles and Global Restructuring*. Philadelphia: Temple University Press, 1994.

Pesquera, Beatriz. "'In the Beginning He Wouldn't Even Lift a Spoon': The Division of Household Labor," in A. de la Torre and B. M. Pesquera, eds., *Building with Our Hands: New Directions in Chicana Studies* (Berkeley: University of California Press, 1993), 181–95.

Philippine Census Bureau, *2001 Survey on Overseas Filipinos,* website: http://www.census.gov.ph/data/pressrelease/2002/of01tx.html.

Philippine Overseas Employment Administration, *Remittances of Overseas Filipinos 2000,* website: http://www.poea.gov.ph/Stats/st_remit84-2000.html.

Philippine Overseas Employment Administration, *Stock Estimates on Overseas Filipinos 2000,* website: http://www.poea.gov.ph/Stats/st_stock2000.html.

Root, Maria P., ed. *Filipino Americans: Transformation and Identity.* Thousand Oaks, Calif.: Sage, 1997.

Tiu, Aurora and Juliana Sustento. *Depression and Other Mental Health Issues: The Filipino American Experience.* San Francisco: Jossey-Bass, 1995.

U.S. Department of Commerce, U.S. Census Bureau, *Profile of the Foreign-Born Population in the United States: 2000, Current Population Reports, Special Studies,* website: http://www.census.gov/prod/www/abs/for-born.html.

U.S. Department of Commerce, U.S. Census Bureau, DP-1, *Profiles of General Demographic Characteristics,* website: http://www.census.gov/Press-Release/www/2001/demoprofile.html.

7.
The Garifuna *Dugu* Ritual in Belize
A Celebration of Relationships

BARBARA FLORES

□□□

This chapter examines the spiritual worldview of the Garinagu people of Belize through the lens of the *dugu* ritual system. The distinct aspects of the ritual embody the traditional Garifuna worldview and religious practices. After a brief look at the roots of Garifuna philosophy, located in West African and Amerindian worldviews, this chapter provides a comprehensive, descriptive overview of the *dugu* and analyzes how its enduring practice sustains a strong sense of ethnic identity among the Garinagu.

The Garinagu People of Belize

The contemporary Garinagu, who live in the Central American nation of Belize, trace their roots to the coming together of Carib Indians (known as Kallinagos) of the Lesser Antilles with West Africans brought on slave ships to the Caribbean by European colonial masters. Their encounter and intermarriage resulted in a new ethnic group, the Garinagu, with its origins on the Caribbean island of St. Vincent. This emerging group, referred to by the British as "Black Caribs," later reclaimed their ancestral name, Garinagu. (The term *Garinagu* is the plural form and refers collectively to the whole people. The singular form *Garifuna* is also the name of the language and is used as an adjective.)

Garifuna spirituality is thus rooted in both West African and Amerindian traditional religions, integrating their core elements. The Garinagu people have reconfigured the basic orientations of both West African and Carib Indian worldviews into a new pattern of meaning, symbols, and expression. Therefore, any discussion of Garifuna spirituality warrants a look at these two worldviews.

The African Philosophical Worldview

According to Peter Paris,

> African slaves brought their worldviews with them into the dias-
> pora. Though different in many respects, they all shared one pri-
> mary feature, namely their belief in a sacred cosmos created and
> preserved by a Supreme Deity. In fact, everything they thought and
> did reflected the sacred nature of the cosmos. . . . Their cultural cre-
> ations—their songs, music, dances, stories, art—transcended any
> secular-sacred dichotomy.[1]

Patrick Kalilombe puts this succinctly: "For Africans, life is a totality;
culture is holistic."[2] He goes on to say:

> The universe is seen as a common heritage, its diverse compo-
> nents as potential partners in the shared project of existence.
> There is, therefore, a feeling of mutual dependence among the dif-
> ferent parts: human beings, the animal world, vegetation, the ele-
> ments, the heavenly bodies, the departed as well as the diffuse
> forces, visible and invisible, that circulate all around. . . . Success
> in living depends very much on how well these different parts
> interact, negotiating carefully and "respectfully" the common
> resources available to all.[3]

Included in that partnership is one's relationship to the ancestors.
Referring to the tradition of ancestral rites, E. Bolaji Idowu explains
that

> the proper meaning of ancestral cults derives from the belief of
> Africans that death does not write 'finish' to life, that the family
> or community life of this earth has only become extended into
> the life beyond in consequence of the 'death' of the ancestors.
> Thus the cults are a means of communion and communication
> between those who are living on earth and those who have gone
> to live in the spirit world of the ancestors.[4]

John S. Mbiti also affirms the significance of this connectedness, this
relationship of reciprocity with the ancestors. Referring to the manifes-
tation of ancestral presence in "spirit possession," he points out that

> spirit possession seems to occur in all African societies, though in
> different forms. . . . The possession is sometimes harmful, but at

times it is useful and may even be induced through dance and drumming. The departed appear generally to the older members of their surviving human families, for a friendly visit, to inquire about family affairs, to warn of impending danger, or to demand a sacrifice or offering or the observation of a particular request or command.[5]

According to Mbiti, any severance in the relationship of reciprocity calls for ritual offerings and sacrifice to restore "the ontological balance between God and man, the spirits and man and the departed and the living."[6]

The Amerindian Philosophical Worldview

The central features of the Amerindian worldview bear striking similarities to the African. For the Amerindian, the spirit world is in all of life, including the forests, the seas, the rivers, and all of creation.

Fr. Raymond Breton, one of the first European missionaries to visit and work among the Carib Indians of St. Vincent, in 1647 wrote early accounts of his perceptions of their understanding of God:

> They have a natural sentiment of some Divinity or some superior obliging power which has its residence in the Heavens. . . . They also invoke their false gods when they desire their presence but that is to be done by the *boyez*, that is to say their priests or to say better their Magicians. . . . Every *boyez* has his particular God or rather his familiar Devil which he invocates by the singing of certain words, accompanied with the smoke of tobacco—this is always done at night time.[7]

Breton explains that the invocation is done "to be healed of some disease with which they are troubled. And when they are recovered they make wine and assemble in rejoicing."[8]

Breton's reference to the role of the *boyez*[9] essentially describes a shaman. Significant research has been conducted by anthropologists on the role and function of shamans among Carib Indians. Ellen Basso in her study speaks of "the importance of shamanism as a means for expressing local group solidarity in the face of potential hostility from both human and non-human outsiders. The individual shaman is seen as a person with unusual abilities who must act as a mediator between the world of human needs and that of dangerous ever-threatening non-human forces."[10]

The same tone is maintained by Nancie Gonzalez in describing her research on the Island Caribs' notion of the spirit-world. Gonzalez says: "The Island Caribs were said to believe that after death the spirits might become mischievous, annoying and even bringing harm to the living. To avoid this, the Caribs made spirit offerings of food and drink."[11] On the particular function of shamans, she writes that the "shamans *(buwiyes)* consulted the spirits on behalf of afflicted people, and were also helpful to the society at large in predicting the outcome of battles, counteracting sorcery, and exacting revenge on enemies."[12]

Byron Foster illustrates the points of similarity between the rituals as historically practiced by the Island Caribs and as currently practiced among the Garinagu. The features of a séance demonstrate this link.[13]

Island Carib Séance	Garifuna Séance
Performed by shaman *(boye)*	Performed by spirit medium *(buyai)*
Performed at night	Performed at night
Audience aligned along sides of hut	Audience seated in main hall of cult house
Offerings of cassava and cassava beer	Offerings of raw rum and cash
Shaman lit cigar and summoned spirit helper	Medium blows cigar smoke through doorways and ascends to the roof
Spirit helper *(ioulouca)* descended and responded to questions concerning the afflicted and warfare	Spirit helper *(hiuruha)* descends and responds to questions concerning affliction
Spirit helper stamped his foot on the ground prior to departure	Spirit helper referred to as stamping his foot on the ground prior to departure in leading spirit medium's account of her initiation-affliction

Thus, in spite of major historical shifts, development, and social change within the Garifuna diaspora, including assimilation into other cultures and adaptation to new homelands, there is a clear traceable continuity from both the African and Amerindian worldviews to the contemporary Garifuna worldview and its concomitant ritual system.

Douglas Taylor, in his extensive research on the Garinagu, further concluded that in "the cultural syncretism which resulted from the merging of Negro, Carib and Arawak strains in St. Vincent, the Ignerian [Arawak] elements came to predominate in the realm of religion, no less than in that of language; and that these greatly resembled in general pattern, what has been reported for corresponding parts of the related Tainan [Arawak] culture of the Greater Antilles."[14]

The Garifuna Worldview: The Concept of God

For the Garinagu, all of life begins with God. The name given to God is *Bungui*. God is perceived as the creator and the preserver of life. Ultimate authority resides in God. The home of God is located in *seiri,* which metaphorically is in the original Garinagu homeland, St. Vincent. According to Jerris Valentine, *seiri* "is the place where God sits and to this place, the spirit of every Garifuna goes after he or she dies."[15]

Valentine claims that the Western concept of "images of God" is nonexistent within Garifuna understanding of God. The Garinagu have a name for God and have attributes for God but do not have images of God. Furthermore, if they did have images, he claims, these images would be primarily feminine. Valentine's claim is based on the attributes given to God in the Garifuna language. For example, if one refers to the greatness and power of God, the feminine word is used in that description. The word used is "Tuguchu," which is translated as "the mother of"; taken to the superlative degree the word becomes "Tagutu," for example, Tagutu Idibu, "the grandmother of trees."[16] "The Garifuna sees majesty, greatness, power, wisdom and knowledge as some attributes of God."[17]

The notion of God as creator and preserver appeared often in ethnographic interviews for this study; traditional healers repeatedly used the expression *"Bungui waba, ahari larigi, wagia harigi."* In its literal translation, these connotes a hierarchy of relationships—"God as Creator guides and leads, our ancestors walk in God's footsteps, we walk in theirs." In this formula God is creator of the universe, a steadfast God who can never be contained, a God who cannot be fathomed, but a God who is reliable and relational. The ancestors provide the pattern of life. The living are reliant on God's guidance and on that of the ancestors. The hierarchical order is one of connection, immanence, and a relationship of reciprocity.

Garifuna Spirituality: Ancestors, Community, and Healing

For the Garinagu the notion of ancestry is of great import. Individuals are expected to live their lives in a harmonious relationship with their kin, with their ancestors, and with their environment. There is a deep sense of respect for elders within a community. For this reason the title used to greet an elder is of importance. For example, a female adult who approximates the age of one's mother would be referred to as *oufuri,* translated as "aunt." Any woman older than one's mother would be *agutu* or "grandmother." The elders are perceived as wisdom figures who have gained greater understanding and experience about life.

The deep reverence for an elder and the relationship of reciprocity is sustained and intensifies after a person dies. It is the basis of the notion of "I am because we are." This notion is also grounded in the Garinagu's perception of time as cyclical. According to Marilyn Wells, "Positive acts such as high fertility, bravery, honor, veneration of ancestors increase the amount of power available to the group, living and non-living. The generation of power through actions of the living provides the non-living with greater resources by which they may in turn help the living."[18] This reciprocal relationship results in health, well-being, and equilibrium for the extended family. In an ethnographic interview, Roy Cayetano affirms and elaborates on this aspect of Garifuna philosophy:

> The basic idea is that there should be harmony, a balance in the relationship between the individual and everything around him including the social, spiritual and the environment in which he is an integral part. We see our oneness with the world around us. Our existence and our future are inextricably linked with the world and the environment. When I speak of the environment, I mean the social, spiritual, physical. By social we speak of people and their relationships. By spiritual there is also our relationship with our ancestors and those who are yet to come. The past, present and future life are all one. I think if an individual sees himself as one, social, physical, spiritual, he thereby has obligations as to how to relate with others. If he deals with them right, everything will be real. When he begins to fail in his obligations, bad things begin to happen, like disease, illnesses and misfortune. One has to step in since things are thrown out of balance and in order for this balance to be re-established it is necessary for certain rituals to happen.[19]

Here Cayetano refers to ritual offerings to redress wrongs or disharmony within a family. The Garinagu have five primary rituals that that serve as times and moments for healing and for re-establishing relationships and unity among family members. These practices are briefly outlined here.

1. *Beluria:* The nine days of prayer following the death of a family member. The ninth day is a day of celebration and feasting.

2. *Chugu:* The offering of food to the ancestors.

3. *Lemeci:* The commemorative ritual occurring one year after a person has died. The family members who have observed this mourning period by wearing black clothing mark the anniversary as the end of

that period. The ritual generally includes prayers at the home and a Catholic mass followed by the sharing of food and dancing.

4. *Amuyedahani:* The bathing of the dead to assist the person on the way to *seiri.*

5. *Dugu:* The major ritual of healing and thanksgiving, done at the request of the ancestors.

During my visit to Dangriga, Belize, in the summer of 1999, I participated in an *amuyedahani,* the ritual of bathing the dead. It was held on the feast day of St. Bernard, the Catholic patron saint, which was also the birthday and wedding anniversary of the deceased. At his baptism as an infant, he had been given the name Bernard because he was born on that date, August 20. Bernard had been a vibrant and well-liked individual who had died rather suddenly the year before, leaving behind his wife and three children.

Preparations for the ritual began at about 4 A.M. at Bernard's home; participants arrived at about 4:45. The first part of the ritual was conducted in the yard, where a tarpaulin had been set up adjacent to the house to create a makeshift room. Inside that space a hole had been dug earlier in the morning. Around the hole were three buckets, the first holding water from cassava *(gainji),* the second water from the Caribbean Sea, and the third rainwater. Next to the buckets stood a lit candle and a pint of strong rum. Each participant individually went in, dipped a gourd (calabash) into each bucked, and poured the liquid into the hole. As each person poured the water, we spoke to Bernard and told him that we were bathing him. Different messages were given to him by family members. After this part of the ritual, all of the participants walked over to Sacred Heart Church, where a mass was offered for Bernard on this, his patron saint's feast day. As we prayed and sang traditional Marian hymns that morning, I once again marveled at how the Garinagu have blended their spirituality with Roman Catholicism. After the Catholic mass, the family and friends returned to the home of the deceased, where Garifuna dancing took place and food was shared.

Garifuna Spirituality: Community and Nature in Relationship

Traditionally the Garinagu have perceived the land, the earth, and the environment as sacred. There is a deep connection to the earth and an obligation to respect and care for it. Earth is seen as symbolic of life. This notion is evident in the process of making cassava bread. The daily bread of the Garinagu, *ereba* is made from the cassava root known as manioc or tapioca. In the process of making cassava bread, nothing is wasted. The Garinagu believe that the cassava root and the bread made from it are gifts from God, so the cassava peelings are buried and returned to Mother Earth. The continued cycle of life and regeneration is of great significance.[20] Jerris Valentine elaborates: "Our [Garifuna] people believed that God in Her goodness will provide and make the earth yield plenty. Therefore there is respect for the land. We leave the tender parts of the cassava in the ground for its nourishment so that we can come back—and if not us—others after us can return to the harvest and be fed."[21]

This notion of respect and reverence for the earth was affirmed in an ethnographic interview with traditional healer Ebu Tola from Honduras. She spoke of the care with which traditional healers gather herbal medicines:

> You don't just go the forests and gather bushes like that—you have to throw away some pennies. You bless the area with holy water and then ask permission. You ask permission of the plant that you are going to gather. You are asking for some bushes to prepare medicine for such and such people so that you can lift those persons up with the power of this plant. You have to ask permission. And when it is afternoon you don't go and bother the plant. It is forbidden for the *buyei* [traditional healer] to go get plants in the afternoon for medicine. You go during the day when the plants are awake because at that time in the afternoon they will be sleeping. If the bushes are sleeping, they will be no good. There will be no energy but during the day the bushes are awake so they have the energy that you need.[22]

A further example of the Garinagu working in collaboration with nature was described by a *buyei* in what she referred to as a tribute to the sun. These are songs sung at sunrise and sunset during the *dugu* ritual. She explains: "We have a tribute to the sun because the sun is an element essential for life. So we sing this song to the sun. When the sun goes down at five P.M. or six P.M. there is another song for the setting of the sun. It's like giving thanks for the day but also a sense of sadness that the day has ended."[23]

Roy Cayetano concurs with this description: "There are songs that are sung before sunrise to bring out the sun, so to speak, and there are songs to push the sun in at sunset. These are beautiful songs which have a tone that signifies how special each rising is and how the setting of the sun parallels death or a loss."[24] In the *dabuyaba*, the

Garifuna temple or "ancestral house," many individuals spoke of these tributes as beautiful moments of deep communion.

Garifuna Ritual: The Role of the *Buyei*

Within the Garifuna tradition the *buyei* is the shaman or traditional healer. Foster describes the buyei as "a specialist in the use of bush medicine and amulets, but it is her possession by spirit helpers *(hiuruha)* which makes her a buyai. . . . The buyai, then, is one possessed by hiruruha, the spirits of the mediums of the past. Generally, the living medium claims descent from the medium whose spirit possesses her."[25] In my own interview with *buyei* Baba Mariano, he spoke of his great-grandfather as the one who offered him guidance in his calling. Foster notes that "mediumship need not, however, be hereditary."[26]

The stories of the callings of the *buyeis* I interviewed corroborate this statement. All three spoke of becoming physically ill for extended periods of time, with no conventional medical explanation for their illness. They also perceived their resistance to assuming the call as worsening their physical condition. They spoke of being drawn into isolated areas in the forests and of insights for healing revealed to them in dreams.

Ebu Manu spoke of her own call at the young age of nineteen and her repeated refusal and resistance. She became ill for a period of four years. It was through her willingness to surrender to the call that she began to comprehend the meaning of her role. In her words, "You cannot refuse because you are born with this call. Male or female, a person is born with this call." On their role and function, the *buyeis* I interviewed spoke confidently of the specific guidance they receive from their spirit helper. Each spoke of being counseled in dreams and in consultation sessions with the spirits.

My involvement is rooted in my commitment to the cultural integrity and resistance to colonialism of my people, the Garinagu. In my own experience of Ebu Manu at the *dugu* in Barranco, I saw a deep peacefulness and confidence as she coordinated and moved through the performance of the ritual. I was struck by her attentiveness to the many details and her quiet but pastoral presence in her interaction with the participants.

Garifuna Ritual: Spirit Possession

Garifuna tradition includes this phenomenon, defined as "the belief that 'spirits' take possession of humans on certain occasions and/or in certain ritual settings."[27] Spirit possession during a *dugu* ritual generally occurs after its high point, the *mali* ceremony of appeasement or placation. Sebastian Cayetano comments that females are possessed far more often than males, because the females tend to be "more tuned into the spirits and have a more intimate connection with them."[28] According to Ebu Manu, spirit possession in the *dugu* ritual ordinarily occurs after the *mali* ceremony because the gestures within the *mali* summon the spirits and draw them into the *dabuyaba* and into the body of a living relative.

Jan Platvoet identifies four features of spirit possession:

> First, the person who has entered into it [a trance] is "dissociated" to a greater or smaller degree; i.e. he or she is to a certain degree out of [normal] touch with his or her social environment. Second, that person often exhibits a certain loss of muscle and motor control. . . . He or she may be in a state of considerable bodily agitation. This state is termed hyperkenesis. Third, in that state, he or she is acting out a character and role that are markedly different from his or her normal self. Finally, the person often does not remember what he or she has said or done during the period of ritual dissociation.[29]

Among the Garinagu, Douglas Taylor describes three stages of spirit possession using three Garinagu verbs. *Adereha,* "to stiffen," indicates a slight jerkiness of movement and fixity of gaze; *agoburiha,* "to 'be-anciented,'" indicates a state of full possession; and *aueha,* "to pass out,"[30] indicates a temporary period of unconsciousness. Ebu Manu commented in an interview that if a person's body is overcome by the spirit, the individual does not have the strength and motor control to stand upright. The body becomes limp. Her remedy, to enable the individual to dance, is to massage the joints with raw rum.

In my own observation of a spirit possession at the *dugu* in Barranco, I wrote the following description.

> Today I observed what seemed like a beautiful family reunion. A woman danced around the *dabuyaba* and as she danced around the room she became possessed by her ancestral grandmother and began to speak in the grandmother's voice. The comments in the *dabuyaba* were that this was the voice of the woman's grandmother. With her eyes closed, she began to call on her grandchildren and each was brought to her. She hugged each person and inquired about their lives.

This powerful moment was indeed a meeting of the living and the dead. The living person literally and physically assumes the persona of the ancestor and a communion takes place. In the process of spirit possession, Garinagu lay claim to their identity as they become one with the ancestors in the context of family gathering.

The *Dugu* Ritual: Garifuna Performance of Healing

The *dugu* ritual of healing and thanksgiving is a convergence of the elements of the Garifuna worldview. Its continued survival and practice, in spite of ongoing attempts at erasure, speak of its embeddedness in the Garifuna psyche. Essential to their identity, its bodily practice has indelibly inscribed itself in the Garifuna psyche, thus evolving into a form of historical documentation.

The depth of significance of the *dugu* ritual is aptly expressed in these words of one Garifuna tradition bearer: "The whole *dugu* embodies the totality of the Garifuna tradition. If the *dugu* disappears, then you can say the Garifuna are finished. The *dugu* holds everything Garifuna together. Their food, their dances, their music."[31]

The *dugu* ceremony is complex in its structure. It is multi-vocal and encompasses themes of thanksgiving, healing, and social kinship. Derived from the verb *adugura,* which literally translates as "to kick" or "to step on,"[32] the word *dugu* denotes "treading on."[33] This term suggests a connection to an earlier Island Carib practice: "After a burial, when they thought the body had disintegrated, the Island Carib family gathered at the tomb, wept and *trod down the grave with their feet. . . .*"[34]

The *dugu* ritual is generally held during the months of July and August, primarily for pragmatic reasons: travel is easiest during the summer. The participants at a *dugu* are extended-family members; some may be from neighboring Garifuna communities, but some may come from farther away.

For the Garinagu, one of the primary functions of the ancestors is the maintenance of harmonious relationships and reciprocity among family members and across generations. If reciprocity is broken and relationships are not intact, the ancestors intervene. This intervention occurs in a variety of ways, for example, in the form of dreams and illnesses.

Generally, in the case of illness, conventional medicine would be the first recourse. The lack of positive results would normally lead a family to consult with a *buyei*. Several of the interviews I conducted referred to the *dugu* as alternative medicine for the Garinagu. Roy Cayetano compares a *buyei* consultation with a visit to a psychiatrist.

> If something is wrong, instead of going to the psychiatrist one would consult the *buyei*. There are certain things a

psychiatrist cannot handle. There can be illness within the family. It may not be the sick person that goes to the consultation but someone on his or her behalf. The *buyei* sings and the spirit comes down into the *buyei*. There is a bridge of the gap between the spirit and the *buyei* so the revelation of information is possible. The spirit is asked and it then states the nature of the problem. It is very personal. If it reveals that there is a need for a *dugu*, it gives the details.[35]

If it is the ancestors' request that the family gather for this ritual, every aspect of the manner in which it is to be performed is revealed to the family. Even though the details of every *dugu* vary according to the requests of the ancestors and the preferences of the officiating *buyei*, the main elements are standard.

One woman poignantly described her experience of a revelation:

I was in attendance at the healing ceremony of a relative. It was during this ceremony that I was summoned by a woman. She held me by the hand and drew me into the circle of dancers. The woman was speaking but the voice coming from her was a male voice. It was the voice of my great-grandfather. He told me that my own daughter's illness was due to disharmony in the family and that the ancestors were requesting a family reunion in the form of a *dugu*.[36]

And so it was from that point onward that these particular family members began to collaborate and negotiate, preparing for the subsequent performance of this elaborate ritual of *dugu*.

Because of the extensive scope of the *dugu* ritual celebration, preliminary preparation requires that family members share responsibilities and spend extensive amounts of time in planning. This preparation includes the ancestors, who communicate multiple messages to relatives through dreams: messages about their expectations for the celebrations, but also messages about the quality of the patterns of their relationships during the time of planning and preparation.

The planning stages of a *dugu* ritual bring families together in a spirit of cooperation and reconciliation that is actually the initiation of the healing process. One *dugu* participant passionately described the challenge: "It is a gathering of families and the re-establishing of relationships. The entire thing about reconciliation, it's there, it's deep, it's challenging and sometimes it's raw and because it's so raw you don't want to get into it. Because it's so raw you want to run away from it but it's there."[37]

The therapeutic effect of these gatherings for one individual was described in this manner: "The *dugu* heals at a psychological level and a physical level. It heals relationships that have gone sour. It helps us to look at each other and recollect where we are as a family. It gives one a sense of belonging, of validation, of affirmation, and that brings a level of psychological healing."[38]

Indeed, as I have listened, the conversations referring to the healing power of the *dugu* rite echo and reiterate its transformative effect through the qualitative change experienced in one's way of life and family relationship. Some of the values expressed reflect solidarity, connection to history and the cosmos, healing of broken spirits, and renewal of body and spirit.

The planning period for a *dugu* requires a minimum of a year, particularly for the notification of relatives, raising money, and procuring food. Huge expenses are involved in the total project. The food acquisition includes the planting and harvesting of the cassava root and the rearing of the sacrificial pigs.

The *dugu* ritual is approximately a week-long event. It is celebrated in a *dabuyaba*, or ancestral house, under the guidance of the *buyei*, or traditional healer. It includes elements of drumming, chanting, dancing, and feasting. The *dugu* in which I participated in Barranco included the following sequence of events:

Thursday evening	A formal and symbolic ceremony handing over the *dabuyaba* to the sponsoring family of the *dugu*
Friday morning	Trip of selected members to the cays (islands) to fetch seafood
Saturday	Preliminary preparations for *dugu* continue
Sunday	Church service in the *dabuyaba*
Monday	Official beginning of *dugu*
	Return of fishing boats from the cays
	Ceremonial entrance of the foods and implements for the *dugu*
Tuesday	Offering of ritual foods to the ancestors
Wednesday	Primary day for offering of *mali*
Thursday	Official closing of ritual and bidding of farewell

Construction of a *Dabuyaba*

The *dabuyaba* (ancestral house) for the *dugu* is generally constructed near the beach, facing east toward the Caribbean Sea. A new *dabuyaba* is built if it is requested by the ancestors. If so, the process begins with the gathering of palm leaves. *Buyei* Tola commented that "the palm tree for the Garifuna is important and it is reliable. The whole plant is used. The inside of the fruit is used for food. The leaves are used as shelter and the root is used for medicine."[39] The *buyei* refers here to the cohune palm tree. Among the Garinagu in Belize, the cohune palm is generally used, but the particular type of leaf used for the thatching of the *dabuyaba* varies according to availability.

The gathering of leaves and materials for the new temple constitutes a ritual of purification. While participants methodically chop and gather the leaves, the drums are played. The land where the *dabuyaba* is to be constructed is incensed, blessed with holy water, and sprinkled with rum.

Sebastian Cayetano offers an account of the building of his family *dabuyaba* in Barranco.

> When the *dabuyaba* was built, the ground had to be blessed. It was an international meeting at the groundbreaking ceremony. The *gayusa* [musicians for the *dugu*] from Livingston [Guatemala] came over, the *gayusa* from Punta Gorda and the buyei also came over and it was a great meeting to bless the grounds. After the grounds were blessed, there was drumming and singing. As the traditional ritual says there were three pints of raw rum that had to be placed in each hole that holds the posts, the supporting frame of the building. These [pints of rum] are sealed and placed into the hole in order to ensure that the ancestors are brought in from the very beginning. So the rum was in the hole before the posts were placed in the hole and before the holes were covered up.[40]

Each particular section of the *dabuyaba* has its specific use. Of primary significance is the center, referred to as *tanigi dabuyaba*, the "heart of the ancestral house." Anthropologist Byron Foster refers to this central place as "the heart-centre, the source of vitality."[41]

According to Sebastian Cayetano, "the center is the heart of the *dabuyaba*. During the *mali* ceremony, that center becomes the central focal meeting point to which everything is drawn."[42] In stressing its importance, Cayetano pointed out that during the construction of their family *dabuyaba*, a hole about four feet deep was dug in the center and five pints of raw rum were placed in it.[43]

In the event that a new *dabuyaba* is not requested by the ancestors, the one to be used must be incensed, blessed with holy water, and sprinkled with rum. In an official ceremony, the *dabuyaba* is passed from the original owners to the family currently sponsoring the *dugu*.

The size of the *dabuyaba* varies according to the number of participants. The one in Barranco is approximately sixty feet long. The building has several sections, each with a particular purpose. The first section, by the entry, is the *dubase,* an open-sided area attached to the main temple. Hammocks are strung in every direction here; one person called it "a corridor where one goes for relaxation and fresh air after the dancing."[44] From the *dubase*, one enters into the main section of the temple, the *gauinare*, where the dancing occurs. This main section leads into a partitioned room, one side of which is designated as the *guli*, the inner sanctum of the *buyei*. Adjacent to the *guli* is the place where the table is set with food and offerings for the ancestors. Every *dabuyaba* I visited stands close to the beach and faces east.

During my first visit to the *dabuyaba* in Barranco, I was honored to be invited into Ebu Manu's *guli*. Her altar was adorned with several small statues of Roman Catholic saints, a picture of the Sacred Heart, and a painting of Nuestro Señor de Esquipulas (an image of a Black Christ common in Central America). There were also lit candles, a notepad, and a pen. Lying on the altar were a slender stick about twelve inches long and several pairs of gourd rattles. In explanation Ebu Manu lifted the stick and compared it to the Bishop's staff. This stick, referred to as *mureo,* and the *sisira* (gourd rattles) form her symbols of power. Her spirit helper is present in the presence of these two symbols.

I was intrigued by this explanation, which was confirmed with a varied but similar explanation by another *buyei*. Ebu Tola also spoke of the significance of the *sisira* but used the term *"mureba"* for the stick, comparing it to Moses' staff. *"Mureba* is the stick used for medicine. When preparing medicine the stick is placed in it. When a *buyei* goes to see a person who is ill she rubs it on the person's body. The stick is a plant used for purification. With regard to the *sisira,* they are used for the ancestors to rest in. When someone is sick, they are rubbed on the person's body to lift the illness."[45]

Aduguhatiun

A major aspect of the *dugu* ritual is the *aduguhatiun*, the trip to the cays by a predetermined group of males and females to gather seafood for the celebration. In a three-day journey, they are to fetch the favorite seafoods of the ancestors. Generally the group leaves early

Friday morning and returns at sunrise on Monday. Prior to the group's departure, the *buyei* prepares each person with herbal baths. The departure and arrival of the *aduguhatiun* is done in a grand ceremonial style. For their departure, all the *dugu* participants walk in procession to the beach to bid them farewell, led by the *buyei* playing her *sisira* and by the drummers.

The return of the *aduguhatiun* from the cays also is conducted in ceremonial style. My notes describe this solemn aspect of the *dugu* in which I participated in Barranco.

> Monday, August 9, 1999
> At sunrise, the boats are spotted approaching the beach. Their approach from the south is slow, deliberate, solemn and ceremonial. The Caribbean Sea, as if understanding the significance of the event, is smooth and shimmering like a sheet of glass with the sun's reflection. As the silhouetted boats become more visible, Garifuna flags can be seen flying in a light southerly wind. Even sea crabs from the catch dangle from the masts. The occupants of the boat are adorned with palm-frond hats. The crowd on the beach, led by the *buyei,* stand under a slight drizzle in anticipation, awaiting with songs and drums. As the boats arrive on the shore, the *buyei* is the first to welcome, bless, and greet them. They are welcomed with warmth and deep gratitude as the "catch" is proudly displayed. Many helpers assist in unloading the boats and the group, with equal ceremonial style, returns in procession to the *dabuyaba,* led by the *buyei* with the drums and the *sisira*. There is excitement in the air and great anticipation as the celebration is truly about to begin. The catch is brought into the center of the temple to be purified with incense and rum. There is singing and dancing. Indeed, they came laden with crabs, fish of different varieties, including red snappers and barracudas, and a turtle. There was much rejoicing with song and dance. I was deeply moved when in the height of excitement, Ebu Manu made her way to me through the crowd and offered me two of the crabs that had been caught. For me, to be offered part of the catch given by the ancestors was a gesture of acceptance.

Symbolically, this journey from the cays also marks the arrival of the ancestors to the ceremony from the historical ancestral home of St. Vincent. Dr. Joseph Palacio offers the following explanation: "The sea is a kind of floating universe and in this floating universe, the *ahari*, the spirits, are finding their way. So you bring them along with you into the temple so that they too will be a part of the *dugu*."[46]

The Preparation of Food

According to Sidney Mintz,

> for us humans . . . eating is never a purely biological activity. . . .
> The foods eaten have histories associated with the past of those
> who eat them; the techniques employed to find, process, prepare,
> serve, and consume foods are all culturally variable, with histories
> of their own. Nor is the food ever simply eaten; its consumption
> is always conditioned by meaning. These meanings are symbolic,
> and communicated symbolically, they also have histories.[47]

These words certainly apply to the food offerings at a *dugu* ritual. The
foods that are offered are the favorite foods of the ancestors. These are
foods connected to the homeland of St. Vincent and to the daily life
of the Garinagu; the foods from the Caribbean Sea and bread made
from the cassava root grown specifically for this ritual. The additional
nontraditional meats of chicken and pork signal the specialness of the
celebration.

The preparation of each food is ritualized, and a sacrificial pig is
offered at the request of the ancestors. The pig is brought to the
dabuyaba complex, purified, slaughtered, and dressed. It is cut in half,
and the halves are hung overnight at the north and south doors of the
dabuyaba. One explanation offered for this action is that the ancestors
may clearly see that what they have requested is being done. The
meat is prepared the following day and is included in the main offering of food.

The cassava root that has been specifically grown and harvested for
this event is ritually baked into fresh cassava bread in the *dubase* of
the *dabuyaba*. The root is first purified by the buyei with a sprinkling
of rum. The women then peel and grate it, standing in a circle and
expressing themselves in song and body movement with great ani-
mation. A sense of togetherness and connection to the ancestors is
expressed through inclusion in the circle.

The Setting and Offering of Food: *Adagaruduguni*

For all Garinagu, the setting and offering of food to the ancestors during the *dugu* ritual is an extremely elaborate, systematic, and meticu-
lous process. (In Sidney Mintz's words, "Consumption is, at the same
time, a form of identification and of communication."[48]) Long tables
are set in one section of the *guli*. The *buyei* and her assistants then pre-

pare the tables, covering them first with a layer of banana leaves, followed by cassava bread. The bread serves as a placemat for other
foods.

The procession with the food offerings begins with the immediate
family sponsoring the *dugu*. All participants stand in double file at the
entrance of the *guli* and process inside with their foods. Each recites a
silent prayer of offering and hands the plate over to the *buyei*, who
sets it on the table. The table is beautifully laid with every kind of Garifuna dish and drink.

After every family has offered food to the ancestors, communal
prayers are offered. At the *dugu* in Barranco these included Catholic
devotional prayers. The prayers began with the Apostles' Creed, the
Lord's Prayer, and two Hail Marys. This was followed by an abbreviated version of a litany to the Holy Rosary and two songs, a favorite
Garifuna hymn, "*Ida Liansan,*" and the traditional "Grace before
Meals." After all these prayers, the *buyei* commended the table of offerings to the ancestors. She told them that this food was theirs and to
partake of it. The moment carried a deep sense of reverence and
solemnity as relatives and participants sat in the *dabuyaba* talking in
hushed voices, waiting for the ancestors to symbolically have their fill.

The food offered to the ancestors remains on the table for about
four hours before it is disposed of. The disposition is conducted in various ways. There is agreement that some food is buried in the earth
and some is thrown into the sea. According to Ebu Tola, "the food
offered to the ancestors is placed into barrels thrown into the sea and
buried. It depends on the request of the ancestors. Burying the food
nourishes the earth. And if we throw it in the sea, the goddess of the
sea will provide us with more abundance of fish."[49]

Food is also distributed to those in the community who are needy.
In Roy Cayetano's words, "The *dugu* recognizes the needy. There is a
certain amount of food that is buried and returned to the earth, but in
Dangriga, food is given to the shut-ins."[50]

The ceremony of offering food is usually followed by dancing and
spirit possession.

Dances in the *Dugu*

Within the *dugu*, there are generally four types of dance. These
include "*abaimahani*—a semi-sacred song and dance of the women;
the *amalihani*—a song and dance of supplication; the *awangulahani*—
a dance of rejoicing; and the *hugulendii. . . .*"[51]

Accompanying the dances are the *garawoun* (drums). Three large drums are used for the *dugu*. The central drum is referred to as *lanigi garawoun,* literally the "heart drum," the leading instrument that guides the other two. Byron Foster says that "drumming is explicitly associated with life, the clamour of the earth," and the drums are believed to attract the spirits. The drums are the antithesis of death, and the term for the central drum, 'heart drum,' suggests that the rhythms symbolize the heartbeat."[52]

Roy Cayetano elaborates on the significance of the drums: "I see the heart drum as representing life and the other two drums as representing past life and the life to come. Together they represent all of life, life in totality, life throughout the ages, life that beats."[53] Indeed, within the *dugu,* dynamism and vitality prevail as the drums reverberate in unison.

Accompanying the drumming are the gourd rattles. The rattles symbolize the authority of the *buyei* who acts as the mediator between earth and the spirit. Later, the upward gestures the *buyei* makes with the *sisira* during the *mali* will summon the ancestral spirits.

The Symbolism of Color in the *Dugu*

A symbolic aspect of the *dugu* ritual is the specially dyed clothing worn by a select group of females directly related to the ancestors being honored. The group is referred to as *afounahountina;* its number varies at the *buyei's* discretion. Throughout the proceedings the *afounahountina* maintains an active leadership role and a close connection to the central activities of the *dugu*. The dyed clothing is regarded as sacred and is of major ritual significance. The fabric chosen is unbleached cotton, which is hand-dyed in arnotto or *gusewe,* resulting in an orange-reddish color.

Anthropologist Marilyn Wells describes *gusewe* as "a deep red powder gathered from the Bixa Orellana . . . also known as arnotto, achiote, roucou, and urucu. The powder may serve as a paint, a dye for cloth and a seasoning for foods."[54] The tradition of using *gusewe* can be traced back to the Island Caribs in St. Vincent, who used it as body paint for occasions of primary significance. Later its use among the Garinagu in Central America became connected to "occasions of a religious nature."[55]

One can speculate that this color may offer another link to the African roots of the Garinagu. According to Victor Turner, among the Ndembu people of Africa, the symbolism and use of color for ritual decoration was of primary importance. To the Ndembu, in Turner's observations, red had a dual interpretation: it signified both goodness and danger, and was always associated with activity and power.[56]

According to Marilyn Wells, within contemporary Garifuna practice, the use of *gusewe* signifies "the prevention or treatment of spirit-caused illness"[57] and "communication between the *buiai [buyei]* and nonmalevolent spirits."[58]

The *Gayusas*

Another special role among *dugu* participants is that of the musicians, or *gayusas*. This group is ordinarily comprised only of women, who acquire the songs to be used at the *dugu* through dreams. Cayetano says that "some of the most experienced *gayusas* are those who are more in tune with the spirits. They would be inspired with a melody in a dream and they would teach these songs to the other members of their group."[59] The songs of the *dugu* "are accompanied by three drums playing a simple triple meter to which participants dance the hugulendii, a shuffle step of great antiquity . . . [from] as long ago as about 1640."[60]

The following is the text of a song that is commonly used in the *dabuyaba*. It refers to the theme of reciprocity.

> *Katoun Funa sa Tinaru boun Katoun*
> *Alugudaheina nubara*
> *Katoun funa sa tinaru boun katoun*
> *Ounaba bana ibiri wau*
> *Aganba namuga bumagien*
> *Ounaba bana mawau*
> *Ounaba bana ibiri wau*
> *Aganba namuga bumagien*
> *Tibe sa gien bichugu*
> *Tibe biaratu mawau*
> *Tibe bisubudi ibiri wau*
> *Subudi tibu gien anichugu*
> *Tibe biaratu mawau*
> *Tibe bisubudi ibiri wau*
> *Subudi tibu gien anichigu*

> What is the truth? Answer me—Let me hear from you.
> You know a lot. You can do a lot.
> You are intelligent. You are wise.
> You have wisdom . . .

Cayetano explains this song as a dialogue between a grandson and an ancestor. The grandson is on a quest for truth. He appeals to the wisdom of his grandfather.

Movement in the *Amalihani (Mali)*

As we move into the main *dugu* dance—the *mali*—the focus remains at the heart-center of the ancestral house. The dance's name is derived from *amalihani,* the placating dance. "The *mali* is the part of the *dugu* that heals. It heals divisions among relatives and friends across generations."[61]

Prior to beginning the *mali*, "the medium bathes her *sisira* [gourd rattles] with raw rum and, entering the main hall from her sanctuary, announces the name of the ancestor to receive the *mali*. The heart drummer takes the dance's pulsating rhythm, and, as the dancers chant in accompaniment, the medium moves to face the three drummers in the center of the cult house."[62] In the rhythm of this movement the *buyei* begins in the west, moving counterclockwise. With great solemnity she goes to the center of the *dabuyaba*. With this gesture, "all the singing ceases and the medium bends forward and down to shake her gourd rattles close to the heart drum, which has also been lowered to the floor, just above the ground at the center of the house. The medium then gestures upwards with her rattles momentarily, before lowering them again to the center point. This sequence is repeated as the dance rotates through the cardinal points."[63]

It is the actions of the *buyei* and the drummers at the center of the hall that transfer the ancestors from below ground to above ground. It is the moment of transition. It is the moment in which the ancestral spirits rise and make their way into the *dabuyaba*, the ancestral house, and into the bodies of the dancers.[64]

Roy Cayetano provides a compelling description and analysis of the *mali*.

> The action of the *mali* typically starts in the west and then to the center, and here we say the earth and the drums whisper. If the drum is seen as representing life, past, present and future then you see the earth as an entity that ties all life together because it is the same earth that our ancestors fought, died, walked on. They drew sustenance in friendship and support. It is the same earth that we have an obligation to look after and pass on. The earth is important. The land is important. Life and this unifying principle ties us all together.

As the *mali* proceeds the dancing occurs. From the center we move to the south and then back to the center where the drums and the earth whisper. Then we move from the east to the center again, then to the north and then the center again and end up at the starting point. If you look at the shape described by these movements, you get a cross within a circle. The cross is a universal symbol and not a Christian cross. It is a universal cross because the sun rises in the east and sets in the west. This is a universal principle and everybody understands that. You also know that people orient themselves in space according to where the sun rises and where it sets. The *dabuyaba* is oriented east-west. Churches are usually oriented east-west, and when we are buried we are oriented east-west. If you have this east-west orientation, it also helps to organize space. As you look at all the space around you, you get a cross within a circle, exactly the same as we described in the *mali* which is really the part of the *dugu* that heals. The reason it heals is because it enacts and reinforces oneness and if you're talking oneness, you are talking wholeness. You are at one with everything around you, you are at one with space and time, with the universe. You're at one with the Great Spirit. At one also means atonement. That is the cure of the *dugu* because it emphasizes oneness, wholeness, all that you are.[65]

Cayetano continues with a summary of the depth of meaning attributed to the *mali:*

In the *mali* we pull space into the center, into the here, and we pull time into the now so that all things are pulled together into the here and now. It symbolizes the oneness of the Garifuna people. It symbolizes the oneness of all the children of the Great Spirit, and if we remember that we are one, then we will be truly holy and healed.[66]

Aguduhani and the *Dugu's* Healing Powers

The ritual's final official feature is the *aguduhani,* which signifies whether the *dugu* has gained the approval of the ancestors and whether they are pleased with the sponsoring families' conduct in planning and executing it. My notes describe the atmosphere of the *dugu* in Barranco as it drew to a close:

Thursday, August 12, 1999
    It is the final morning of the *dugu* celebration. The participants are weary after several nights of dancing. However, there is a

strong feeling of connection amongst the participants. The experience of spirit possession had a joyful tone. The ancestors convened and gathered families together and spoke to them of the ills in the family. They appealed to them to heal the divisions or whatever might be the source of conflict and tension among themselves. They also offered counsel and advice to the young.

All were now anticipating the *aguduhani*. For this rite, a table is set in the center of the *dabuyaba* and the *buyei* pours rum on the table in the sign of a cross, then burns it with a match. A live blue flame is an indication that the spirits were happy and pleased with the proceedings of this event. At this moment in Barranco, there was spontaneous applause and tremendous relief.

In further analysis, the complex *dugu* ritual is replete with symbolism that serves various functions. The *dugu* is concerned with the unity and social well-being of a people, but also with the individual human person in his or her own existential being. The primary concern is the human being in relationship to all of life.

In the therapeutic healing process that is *dugu*, the Garinagu people move toward creating a sense of harmony among and within themselves. The incisive words of a woman from another indigenous culture capture the essence of its practice: "This search for equilibrium that forms a part of our indigenous identity comes from the teaching of our ancestors, and is an integral part of our spirituality. So we say that spirituality isn't finished, but rather is constantly being renewed for full humanity."[67]

As I have listened during the process of conducting fieldwork, I have gained deeper insights into Garifuna spirituality as a way of being, a way of embodying life-in-relationship. The challenge of the Garifuna perspective is to live life with an awareness of one's historical time frame, a sense of indebtedness and gratitude to the ancestors, and a sense of responsibility to present and future generations. The family and community's faithful response to the ancestors' call for harmony and equilibrium through this embodied experience of the *dugu* is a key communal locus for discovering the "divine." It is also catalyst that effects transformation. This transformation becomes manifest in the qualitative change experienced in the extended family's way of life.

As relatives becoming better acquainted during the pre-celebration gatherings, the network of solidarity in present social relations expands and solidifies, along with a deeper understanding of the implications of living faithfully in concert with the ancestors. When the extended family reunifies, the interconnectedness that occurs transcends the particularity of the moment, and connects deeply into history, not in a linear mode of being but in a convergence point for multiple layers of healing. In the words of Malidoma Some,

> Ritual is an art, an art that weaves and dances with symbols, and helping to create that art rejuvenates participants. Everyone comes away from a ritual feeling deeply transformed. This restoration is the healing ritual is meant to provide. Ritual is central to village life, for it provides the focus and energy that holds the community together, and it provides the kind of healing that the community most needs to survive.[68]

As the *dugu* ritual undergoes a resurgence among the Garinagu, new hermeneutical lenses are being employed. These new interpretations place less emphasis on ancestor placation and more on social harmony, linkage with ancestors, and the promotion of unity and community. In the village of Barranco, for example, a *dugu* celebration recently inspired a new initiative with important political and economic implications.

Sebastian Cayetano describes the significance of this development:

> Before our *dugu* in Barranco in 1998, people in the village were pulling apart. There was seemingly no hope. But during the *dugu* and after the *dugu* the concerned people came together to discuss the issues that were affecting our village and this has continued. It was after the *dugu* that we had the first home-coming to Barranco. In that home-coming we organized. We were concerned about the school building, about the completion of the bridge, about the road to the village and about the water-system. Today Barranco has an all-weather road and the bridge is complete. It has a concrete school building with four classrooms and the water system is being worked on. Also coming out of the *dugu* were our efforts to build a new concrete Church. Four walls are already up. Last year for the second homecoming there a thousand people gathered in Barranco. And the people generated income by making food and drinks for sale. The bridge has made the village accessible. It is the giving of self without counting the cost.[69]

Critical Perspectives and Conclusion

To sum up the discussion in this chapter, the complex *dugu* ritual serves various functions. In its more contemporary interpretation, it is concerned with individual and social well-being in relationship to all of life. It is about the maintenance of a sense of balance of all beings within the community. It fosters a vision for individuals to develop virtues such as harmony, respect, and concern for all.

The *dugu* ritual is a critical place and a critical "space" where the Garinagu can unapologetically claim their identity and continually recreate themselves, always remaining connected to the homeland and to the ancestors. In this regard it has been and continues to be a space for the maintenance of Garifuna autonomy. This space promotes a consciousness that sustains and empowers, giving life a view different from the reality imposed by the colonizer. It is a time and space transformed into a moment of pedagogy, a teaching moment in which the younger generations can witness and grow in the Garifuna way of life.

The *dugu* ritual links and connects both families and communities. Within the ritual there is an element of indulgence. Food and drink abound, as do dancing and music; loving attention is given to a sick relative or to an individual possessed by the spirits. It is a time for "letting go." This indulgent attitude generates energy. There is a nurturing spirit that affirms, nourishes, and heals the soul. One feels deeply that this is the spirit that has contributed to individual and corporate Garifuna survival.

An essential element of the Garinagu's historical resistance to colonization, from the original homeland of St. Vincent to the present day, has been the safeguarding of the *dugu* as a space of Garifuna freedom, subverting their oppressors. This sacred space of *dugu*, which the Garinagu believe has been uniquely given to them by God and the ancestors for healing, has indeed become the catalyst for transformation as the Garinagu ward off the evils of oppression and potential erasure. In spite of assault from various historical colonial forces, the *dugu* ritual, in its ongoing physical enactment and its current resurgence, has remained a means and a witness to the survival, resistance, and empowerment of the Garinagu.

Notes

1. Peter J. Paris, *The Spirituality of African Peoples: The Search for a Common Moral Discourse* (Minneapolis: Fortress Press, 1995), 34.

2. Patrick A. Kalilombe, "Spirituality in the African Perspective," in *Paths of African Theology,* ed. Rosini Gibellini (Maryknoll, N.Y.: Orbis, 1994), 119.

3. Ibid., 123.

4. E. Bolaji Idowu, *African Traditional Religion: A Definition* (London: SCM, 1973), 186.

5. John S. Mbiti, *Concepts of God in Africa* (New York: Praeger, 1970), 266.

6. Ibid., 179.

7. Père Raymond Breton, "Observations of the Island Carib: A Compilation of Ethnographic notes from Breton's *Carib-French Dictionary (1665)* Trans. Marshall McKusick and Pierre Verin. Human Relations Area Files, New Haven, Conn., 278. Translated from Old English by the author.

8. Ibid., 279.

9. Spellings of the word *boyez* vary, but the term refers to the Garifuna traditional healer.

10. Ellen Basso, "Introduction: The Status of Carib Ethnology" in *Carib-Speaking Indians: Culture, Society and Language,* ed. Ellen Basso (Tucson, Ariz.: Arizona University Press, 1977), 16.

11. Nancie Gonzalez, *Sojourners of the Caribbean: Ethnogenesis and Ethnohistory of the Garifuna* (Chicago: University of Illinois Press, 1988), 83.

12. Ibid.

13. Byron Foster, "Celebrating Autonomy: The Development of Garifuna Ritual on St. Vincent," *Caribbean Quarterly* 33 (1987), 78–79. Foster states that the data on Island Carib séance was drawn from R. Breton and A. de la Paix, *Relation de L'Ile de Guadeloupe,* trans. T. Turner, Human Relations Area Files, 1958; and Jean Baptiste du Tertre, *Histoire Génerale des Antilles Habitées par les Français* (orig. 1667) (Paris: Édition et diffusion de la culture antillaise, 1978), 396.

14. Douglas Taylor, "The Black Carib of British Honduras" in *Viking Fund: Publications in Anthropology,* ed. A. Irving Hallowell (New York: Wenner-Gren Foundation for Anthropological Research, 1951), 140.

15. Excerpt from a public lecture, "Garifuna Spirituality," presented by Rev. Jerris Valentine in New York City, 3 July 1993.

16. Ibid., 3.

17. Ibid.

18. Marilyn Wells, "Circling with the Ancestors: Hugulendii Symbolism in Ethnic Group Maintenance," *Belizean Studies* 8:6 (November 1980), 3.

19. Phyllis and Eldred Roy Cayetano of Dangriga, interview by author, tape recording, 15 August 1999, Dangriga, Belize.

20. Rev. Jerris Valentine, interview by author, tape recording, 16 August 1999, Dangriga, Belize.

21. Rev. Jerris Valentine, "Traditional Social Life, Garifuna Perspective and the Contribution of the Garifuna Woman" (unpublished paper, January 1996), 4.

22. Ebu Tola and Felix Miranda, interview by author, tape recording, 20 January 2001, Bronx, New York.

23. Ibid.

24. Roy Cayetano, interview.

25. Foster, "Celebrating Autonomy," 19.

26. Ibid.

27. Jan G. Platvoet, "Rattray's Request: Spirit Possession among the Bono of West Africa" in *Indigenous Religions: A Companion,* ed. Graham Harvey (London: Cassell Wellington House, 2000), 80–81.

28. Sebastian and Fabian Cayetano, interview by author, tape recording, August 1999, Barranco, Belize.

29. Platvoet, "Rattray's Request," 82.

30. Taylor, "The Black Caribs of British Honduras," 123.

31. Excerpt from interview with Sebastian Cayetano, Garifuna tradition bearer, taken from Garifuna Journey Exhibition text, Museum of Anthropology, Chicago, Illinois.

32. Eldred Roy Cayetano, ed., *The People's Garifuna Dictionary: Dimureiagei Garifuna* (Belize City: Government Printery, 1993), 9.

33. Foster, "Celebrating Autonomy," 79.

34. Taylor, "The Black Caribs of British Honduras," 141.

35. Roy Cayetano, interview.

36. Mrs. Nunu Enriques, interview by author, tape recording, November 1998, Chicago, Illinois.

37. Ibid.

38. Ibid.

39. Ebu Tola, interview. She was the only source to speak of the significance of the palm tree.

40. Sebastian Cayetano, interview by author, tape recording, 25 February 2001, Belize City.

41. Byron Foster, *Heart Drum: Spirit Possession in the Garifuna Communities of Belize* (Belize City: Cubola Productions, 1986), 42.

42. Sebastian Cayetano, interview.

43. Ibid.

44. Ebu Tola, interview.

45. Ebu Tola and Felix Miranda, interview by author, tape recording, 20 January 2001, Bronx, New York.

46. Dr. Joseph Palacio, interview by author, tape recording, 20 August 1999, Belize City.

47. Sidney W. Mintz, *Tasting Food, Tasting Freedom* (Boston: Beacon, 1996), 6.

48. Ibid., 13.

49. Ebu Tola, interview.

50. Roy Cayetano, interview.

51. Wells, "Circling with the Ancestors," 4.

52. Foster, *Heart Drum*, 45.

53. Roy Cayetano, interview.

54. Marilyn Wells. "Spirits See Red: The Symbolic Use of Gusewe among the Garifuna (Black Caribs) of Central America," *Belizean Studies* 10 (1982), 10.

55. Ibid., 11.

56. Victor Turner, *The Forest of Symbols: Aspects of Ndembu Ritual* (Ithaca, N.Y.: Cornell University Press, 1967), 80.

57. Wells, "Spirits See Red," 12.

58. Ibid.

59. Sebastian Cayetano, interview.

60. Douglas Taylor as quoted in Carol and Travis Jenkins, "Garifuna Musical Style, Culture History" *Belizean Studies* 10 (1982), 19.

61. Roy Cayetano quoted from documentary, "Reconciliation and Mali Ceremony," filmed at St. John's Anglican Cathedral in Belize City. The taping was recorded by TV Station Channel 5.

62. Foster, *Heart Drum*, 43.

63. Ibid., 44.

64. Ibid., 43.

65. Roy Cayetano, interview.

66. Ibid.

67. Esther Camac, quoted by Janet May in *Women Healing Earth: Third World Women on Ecology, Feminism and Religion,* ed. Rosemary Radford Ruether (Maryknoll, N.Y.: Orbis, 1996), 46.

68. Malidome Patrice Some, *The Healing Wisdom of Africa: Finding Life Purpose through Nature, Ritual, and Community* (New York: Penguin Putnam, 1999), 24.

69. Sebastian Cayetano, interview.

Bibliography

Basso, Ellen, ed. *Carib-Speaking Indians: Culture, Society and Language.* Tucson, Ariz.: Arizona University Press, 1977.

Bolaji, Idowu E. *African Traditional Religion.* London: SCM, 1973.

Breton, Père Raymond. "Observations of the Island Carib: A Compilation of Ethnographic Notes from Breton's Carib–French Dictionary" (1665). Translated by Marshall McKusick and Pierre Verin. Human Relations Area Files, New Haven, Conn.

Cayetano, Eldred Roy, ed. *The People's Garifuna Dictionary: Dimureiagei Garifuna.* Belize City: Government Printery, 1993.

Foster, Byron. "Body, Soul and Social Structure at the Garifuna Dugu," *Belizean Studies* 9 (July 1981).

———. "Celebrating Autonomy: The Development of Garifuna Ritual on St. Vincent." *Caribbean Quarterly* 33 (1987).

———. *Heart Drum: Spirit Possession in the Garifuna Communities.* Belize City: Cubola Productions, 1994.

Gonzalez, Nancie. *Sojourners of the Caribbean: Ethnogenesis and Ethnohistory of the Garifuna.* Chicago: University of Illinois Press, 1989.

Jenkins, Carol, and Travis Jenkins. "Garifuna Musical Style Culture History," *Belizean Studies* 10 (1982), 10–16.

Kalilombe, Patrick A. "Spirituality in the African Context." In *Paths of African Theology,* ed. Rosino Gibelli. Maryknoll, N.Y.: Orbis, 1994.

May, Janet W. "Foreigners: A Multicultural Dialogue." In *Women Healing Earth: Third World Women on Ecology, Feminism and Religion,* ed. Rosemary Radford Ruether. Maryknoll, N.Y.: Orbis, 1996.

Mbiti, John S. *Concepts of God in Africa.* New York: Praeger, 1970.

Mintz, Sidney W. *Tasting Food, Tasting Freedom.* Boston: Beacon, 1996.

Paris, Peter. *The Spirituality of African Peoples: The Search for a Common Moral Discourse.* Minneapolis: Fortress Press, 1995.

Platvoet, Jan G. "Rattray's Request: Spirit Possession among the Bono of West Africa." In *Indigenous Religions: A Companion,* ed. Graham Harvey. London: Cassell Wellington House, 2000.

Some, Malidome Patrice. *The Healing Wisdom of Africa: Finding Life Purpose through Nature, Ritual and Community.* New York: Penguin Putnam, 1999.

Taylor, Douglas MacRae. "The Black Carib of British Honduras." In *Viking Fund Publications in Anthropology,* ed. A. Irving Hallowell. New York: Wenner-Gren Foundation for Anthropological Research, 1951.

Turner, Victor. *The Ritual Process: Structure and Anti-Structure.* Chicago: University of Chicago Press, 1969.

Valentine, Jerris. "Garifuna Spirituality," public lecture, July 1993 (photocopy).

————. "Traditional Social Life, Garifuna Perspective and the Contribution of the Garifuna Woman," unpublished paper, January 1996 (photocopy).

Wells, Marilyn. "Circling with the Ancestors: Hugulendii Symbolism in Ethnic Group Maintenance, " *Belizean Studies* 8 (November 1980), 1–9.

————. "Spirits See Red: The Symbolic Use of Gusewe among the Garif (Black Caribs) of Central America," *Belizean Studies* 10 (1982), 10–16.

8.

Across the Kitchen Table
Cuban Women Pastors and Theology

Margarita M. W. Suárez

🔲🔲🔲

It was Christmas Day 1999, and we'd been invited to Christmas dinner with Davila Caceres and her family at her father's house across the street from the church. I knew that her brother and his wife would be there, and Davila and her two sons and her father and stepmother. I knew that Cesar, her husband, wouldn't be there: he was conducting services at two churches in the interior of the province and wouldn't arrive home till late. I felt most privileged to have been invited. Davila and I hadn't known each other long, as I had arrived on the island a mere five weeks before.

What an incredible five weeks it had been! On November 15 we'd left our home in Oak Park, Illinois, at 4:30 in the morning. Rubén, my seven-year-old son, was still asleep when my husband carried him into the car, but he awoke right away, knowing that this day was the beginning of a six-month adventure. I had long dreamed of this adventure, fed by my earliest childhood memories—to live in the land of the palm trees, of Marti and Maceo and, of course, of Fidel. I wanted to continue the search for my roots and for my long-forgotten family. Rubén had been added to this hope and dream. For unlike me, with my lifelong struggle with the Spanish language, in this dream Rubén would be bilingual, able to speak the language of our heritage, *de la patria de su abuelo.*

All of this was made possible due to the fieldwork I needed to do for my doctoral dissertation. I'd chosen to investigate Protestant Cuban feminist theology, a topic many in the States found strange, asking, "You mean there is a Protestant church in Cuba?" or "Are there any women pastors in Cuba?" or remarking, "I didn't know that there was a viable church in Cuba." To each I would say, "Yes, there is a growing Protestant presence on the island with quite a few women pastors." On November 15 I didn't know where this trip would lead us, but I knew that we were in God's hands.

So here it was Christmas Day. (Elián Gonzalez had been rescued from the ocean five days after we'd arrived. The incredible political saga ensuing from his abduction by his U.S. family would continue until after our return.) Davila had a wedding to perform that morning. It was surprising that anyone would get married on Christmas Day, but as she explained it, the groom was the son of a good friend of the congregation and as the couple had no strong link to any faith tradition, the holiday didn't mean much to them. Davila believed that by marrying them in a Christian church, she might spark the possibility of a new faith within them. It would be God's work to see what would happen next.

While I took photographs and taped the ceremony, Rubén played with Cesar Marcos, Davila's son. After the wedding I joined them across the street to discover that the side patio of Davila's house was being set, with borrowed tables from the church, for over fifty people. I was just flabbergasted, overwhelmed at the generosity of the Caceres family. As this was the first time they'd invited me to their house, it was quite unexpected. As the weeks went by, I witnessed such generosity of spirit again and again—a Cuban quality my parents had told me about. *"Mi casa es su casa"* was one way they had described it. And so it was true. This was my house too.

This story is the first of several exemplifying how theological fieldwork, using ethnographic and auto-ethnographic research methodologies, can be a significant tool in learning about context theologies. The term *theological fieldwork* at first glance appears a bit strange. Theology is not known as an area of study requiring field investigation, as do the social and natural sciences. Since the advent of liberation theologies in the late 1960s, however, the concept of social analysis has gained great importance within some theological circles. Scholars have begun to critically analyze social location, economic and historical location, race, gender, and sexual orientation as components in the development of any theological statement. It has ventured into the realm of using social scientific methodologies in order to uncover, disentangle, and debunk "universal truths" that had silenced those considered marginal within Western society.

In the last thirty-odd years, theology has ceased to be a field whose practitioners are exclusively white, Western, and male. Latin Americans, African Americans, Native Americans, women, Latinas/os, Asians, Africans, and gay and lesbian peoples have all joined the ranks of theologians and have brought the concerns of social analysis to bear on theological reflection. It is no surprise, therefore, that the anthropological methodologies that help define the "cultures" within which societies are arranged are now part of the social analysis component of the liberation hermeneutic.

Anthropology, specifically cultural anthropology and ethnography, offers new sets of questions and direction to the theological enterprise. Some questions often considered anthropological in nature are already being asked by theologians, albeit without much awareness of their ties to cultural anthropology. These are questions about "the nature of Christian identity and communal traditions, the relations between social practice, on the one hand, and Christian beliefs and symbols on the other, and the character of apologetics and interreligious exchange."[1] I propose that the methods particular to ethnography can also be usefully employed to investigate a culture's adaptation of Christian belief.

Using reflexive ethnographic methodology, I lived among various women pastors, theologians, and Christian educators to learn the lived context of feminist theology in Cuba. (For most of the people I quote from here, I will use pseudonyms.) Reflexive ethnography, recently more prominent particularly among feminist ethnographers, requires the researcher to shift from the stance of "knowing professional" to that of humble participant. The researcher asks questions and is asked questions, but she does not assume she knows the answers because she has read many books. Instead, she tests her theories with her informants, recognizing their ability to name their own theological reflections, assumptions, history, and social location.[2] Reflexive ethnography challenges the investigator to acknowledge her own assumptions, history, and social location, owning and wrestling with her own biases through constant self-reflection. Reflexive ethnography presumes a passion for the people under investigation. There is no room for the detached observer in this schema. One needs to be vulnerable to the interventions of the moment, willing to share with one's informants the intimacies of one's own heart.

These concepts are rather new, as compelling to scholars of theology as they are to ethnographers. For many in theology, H. Richard Niebuhr's foundational work *Christ and Culture*[3] is the starting point for any cultural analysis within theology. Stated plainly, in Niebuhr's typology "culture" stands for "the world." In Kathryn Tanner's words, "What Christian theologians make of the world, of the practices and beliefs of the wider society, is viewed by Niebuhr as a judgment about culture."[4] He outlines a typology of five possible ways in which Christ (as embodied in the Christian community)[5] can interact with the

world: "Christ against Culture" (a separatist view), "The Christ of Culture" (an accommodationist view), "Christ above Culture" (a tri-
umphalist view), "Christ and Culture in Paradox" (a dualist view),
and finally "Christ the Transformer of Culture," Niebuhr's own stand.

Though this serves as a valuable starting place for discussing culture from a theological perspective, Niebuhr's definition of culture
places Christ and the world in competition with each other, for the
faithful. Culture, as the world, is understood as partially outside of
Christian community, something ultimately to be transformed by
Christ. Conversely, he places the Christian community outside of culture. It seems, however, that Niebuhr's definitions of both culture and
the Christian community are too narrow and have all the problems of
Western, specifically Christian, elitism. If one instead broadly defines
culture as "human activity," then the human practice of theology
arises out of culture and is therefore not, inevitably, in competition
with it.

Apart from Niebuhr's discussion, the study of culture has been
reserved for anthropologists. But the written ethnography, according
to Ruth Behar, can be a "strange cross between the realist novel, the
travel account, the memoir, and the scientific report . . . to be understood in terms of poetics and politics."[6] This suggests that although
ethnographic work falls within the field of anthropology, it is in itself
a multidisciplinary pursuit and its methodologies and definitions
could therefore be useful to many fields. Culture is recognized by
scholars in numerous fields as a concept essential to their own inves-
tigative work. Writing about culture or writing ethnographically does,
however, come with its own sets of ethical imperatives that have
changed over the life of anthropology as an academic discipline. The
"'new ethnography' [is] also expected to reflect a more profound self-
consciousness of the workings of power and the partialness of truth,
both in the text and in the world. The 'new ethnography' [will] not
resolve the profoundly troubling issues of inequality in a world fueled
by global capitalism, but at least it [will] seek to decolonize the power
relations inherent in the representation of the Other."[7]

For nearly a century, since anthropology has been recognized as a
scholarly field within the social sciences, anthropologists and ethnographers have investigated "primitive" cultures such as the Ilongot of
the Philippines,[8] the Neur in Africa,[9] or specific rites and rituals, such
as those for coming of age, death, and burial. These cultures have
often been considered part of Western Europe and America's cultural
past, a past that the West believes it has progressed beyond. These

peoples have been studied, in part, so that we cultural elites could know from whence we came even in the modern/postmodern age. Too, we are curious people and desire to know and understand other cultures. However, our desire to know "them" often does not come from a genuine interest in the people we are studying; rather, it is to show our superiority to or our difference from "them." When we see ourselves as the "professionals," with the "knowledge" to objectively analyze more "primitive" cultures, the result is often their exoticization for mass consumption. This, in turn, has created a few generations of scholars who have either romanticized "primitive" cultures or vilified them, but not known them.

When I first met Rosa, I was impressed by her clarity of vision, her administrative competence, and her intellectual innovation. From a distance she appeared self-assured, confident, and supremely able to handle any difficulty that came her way. Married to an Episcopal priest right after the triumph of the Revolution, she assumed the role of parish priest's wife; motherhood expanded that role. She also volunteered in her child's school and was a founding member of the local *Comité para la Defensa de la Revolución*. As a "militant Christian"[10] and revolutionary, Rosa was working, by the mid-sixties, as a teacher in the local elementary school. Subsequently she became a quasi-lay counselor there because she understood her work as ministry. When women were struggling with life problems, they came to Rosa: she was trustworthy, confidential, and always made the time for them. Highly respected in her work, she won awards for her participation in all aspects of revolutionary life.

Throughout these years she also upheld her congregation's expectations for the priest's wife. She administered and taught Sunday school and was involved as an adult facilitator in the Student Christian Movement. Eventually the bishop recognized her talent and encouraged her to continue the theological studies she had abandoned for marriage.[11] Had the church not been desperate for trained leaders, her talents might have gone unnoticed, but after the revolution, clergy and lay workers of every denomination departed the island in droves, leaving a dearth of trained professionals to serve the churches.

In 1986 Rosa was ordained an Episcopal deacon and four years later a priest. In 1993 she was named the first woman chaplain of the national women's organization of the Episcopal Church. In this role she worked to transform the gender-exclusive language in the liturgy, initiated "Bible studies from the woman's perspective, the study of gender theory, and many other things that were necessary for us to explore."[12] Yet for all that she had accomplished and overcome, for the great admiration of hundreds of people both inside and outside the church, Rosa felt small. Since her marriage, she had studied only irregularly, by correspondence or independently. Not only did she have no formal degree in theology, her preparatory schooling had ended with the ninth grade because her family couldn't afford private school, the only option in her small home town before the revolution. She snatched all of her further education whenever the opportunity presented itself. This lack of formal degrees made her feel both inadequate and insecure. It was apparent to me, however, that in her preaching and her teaching she was neither; rather, she was accomplished and authoritative.

This differentiation between her own opinion and mine speaks to the insight a researcher can gain by allowing informants to name their own life circumstances. Rosa came from very humble surroundings and pursued life to the fullest extent possible, given the limitations imposed upon her. She grasped every opportunity to learn and study, and she worked doggedly to achieve her dreams. Even so, she lives haunted by what she perceives she still lacks. She is all the more amazing to me as I reflect upon her inner struggle to feel self-assured.

In Kathryn Tanner's *Theories of Culture: A New Agenda for Theology*,[13] she outlines a series of critiques of classical anthropology, summarizing for the nonspecialist the field's current methodological approaches. She argues that modernist approaches should be discarded in favor of post-modernist approaches, which underscore the agency of the informants to name their cultures, and do not presume to divide the "professional" from the lay person. Modernist methodologies have many problems, she argues. First, "modern" anthropology sees culture as a given, unaffected by history; it dehistoricizes culture, ignoring the historical process that has influenced it, and indeed continues to do so.[14] Second, modernist methodologies tend to assume and seek an internal consistency within the cultural group, in order to appropriately interpret it. Wittingly or unwittingly the anthropologist, as the expert, controls the process of discovery by the very questions she asks and the persons she chooses as interlocutors. By discounting the differences within the culture, she avoids messy conflict or inconsistency.[15] Third, this assumed consistency leads to the appearance of consensus within the entire culture based on a small sampling of people with whom the anthropologist is acquainted.[16] The anthropologist can limit the number of her informants because all persons within the culture allegedly have similar social locations and similar understandings of the phenomena of the culture. Fourth, modernist anthropology has also insisted that culture holds the norms for social order, that "cultural forms themselves determine the manner in which those cultural forms direct action,"[17] privileging cultural forms over historical and economic factors. Tanner offers this example, in which what could be seen as reactionary in one setting could be subversive in another:

> . . . The idea that a woman's place is in the home might simply reinforce the status quo where increased economic opportunities for women are becoming a reality. One could also imagine, however, how the same ideal could be used to subvert the status quo where women have traditionally been forced into degrading lines of outside employment (for instance, prostitution). A domestic ideal for women might be used to keep women in the home; or, it might be used to argue for a general change in business ethics now that women have been integrated into the workforce.[18]

Fifth, when historical processes have been acknowledged within modernist anthropology, according to Tanner, a culture is seen as stable until "outside" forces generate change within it. The change is therefore not considered part of the fluidity of culture, nor is it intrinsic to the culture, but rather a force "externally generated,"[19] thus preserving culture as ahistorical. Last, she critiques modernist anthropology for creating "sharply bounded, self-contained units."[20] She argues that since "change, conflict, and contradiction are now admitted *within* culture, the anthropologist has no reason to insist [that] a culture's sharp boundaries [are] needed to protect a homogeneous, stable, and unified whole from outside dissension and disruption."[21]

Tanner's critique of modernist anthropological approaches as dependent on outside forces can be exemplified through the story of Magdalena, Rosa's daughter. While Rosa constantly struggled to receive a full and formal education, Magdalena has received numerous formal degrees, including a medical degree from a Cuban university, a *licenciatura* degree[22] from the Seminario Evangelico de Teología in Matanzas, and a master's degree specializing in pastoral care and counseling from a Brazilian seminary. Although Magdalena is not an ordained priest, her career often feels as though it is dependent on the discretion of the bishop, due to the policies and constitution of the seminary.

Magdalena is Rosa's second child. An excellent student, she eventually received a scholarship to study medicine. She met her husband while in medical school and they married. After receiving their degrees they wanted to work in a remote part of the island in a mountain village. As Christians they had to justify the assignment and allay official suspicions that they planned to evangelize while serving the village's medical needs. (It is important to remember that prior to 1991 believers were looked upon with extreme suspicion, due to some churches' early counterrevolutionary activity as well as the supernatural characteristics inherent in religious ritual.) Magdalena and her husband, however, convinced the authorities that they were not a threat to the revolutionary fervor of the village in which they wanted to serve. Rather, they explained, their faith taught them to use their gift to benefit humanity where the need was the greatest. They therefore understood their service to the revolution based upon their faith commitment. The authorities satisfied, they went to the mountains. Although the next two years were filled with hardships, they loved their work and they had each other and were happy.

One day all that changed when Magdalena's husband suffered a terrible accident. A sixteen-year-old boy throwing rocks at passing cars on the mountain road tossed one through his windshield and hit him in the head. He suffered a severe cranial injury and survived less than twenty-four hours.

Magdalena decided that she couldn't continue in medicine; the stress was too great. Whenever someone with a head injury came into the hospital, she froze and was incapable of working on the patient. At this same time, she received a vocation letter from the Episcopal bishop seeking candidates for the ordained ministry. As she prayed to know how she might continue through life, though in emotional torment, she heard a call to ministry. The bishop approved her call and sent her to study at the seminary. There, a professor of pastoral care and counseling saw in her the gift of counseling and suggested she continue her studies in this area.

In her final year at the seminary, while writing her thesis on issues of pastoral care, she applied for the opportunity to study in Brazil for a master's degree in practical theology with an emphasis on pastoral counseling. Still a candidate for ordained ministry, she discussed this possibility with the bishop. He did not deny her request but was less than enthusiastic, preferring her to consider, at a later time, to study in London, where he had friends. In the meantime Magdalena graduated and was assigned to work as an assistant to the priest in the province of Camagüey. Four months later the Brazil scholarship came through. "During this time, as a candidate for sacred orders, I had the right to be away from canonical residence for two years, and I could do what I wanted to with my life for those two years."[23] So she prepared both for her trip to Brazil and for her predeparture ordination to the diaconate, at the bishop's request.

Without explanation, the night before her ordination was to take place, she was advised to go to Brazil without ordination to the diaconate. A few months later, while in Brazil, she received notification from the bishop's office that she was being dropped from candidacy for sacred orders. Upon her return to Cuba with her master's degree in hand, the bishop asked if she would like to be ordained. In a recent interview, Magdalena recalled her response: "No, I would not like for you to ordain me, because I would like to work on my doctorate and I am thinking about other things. I have my own plans." In an aside to the interviewer, she added, "I would like to tell you this, because this is how I feel, that they wanted to ordain me but in order for me to move on to other possibilities, I had to work in Havana, and really I wanted to honor these other things."[24] Once she was ordained, the bishop could assign her anywhere in the country, and she didn't trust him to help her in accomplishing her goals.

Through this story Tanner's critiques of modernist approaches in anthropological research are validated, particularly in the areas of the assumptions of "internal consistency within the cultural group," "the appearance of consensus," and cultural stability only being affected by "outside forces." It is clear in Magdalena's story that there was no internal consistency within the cultural group known as the Episcopal church. Its authorities often advised one course of action, then precipitously changed their minds. Consensus was also absent; they acted upon her by erasing her candidacy without so much as a formal hearing or opportunity for her to make her case. Evidently the stability of the Episcopal church's culture did not depend on "outside forces." To Magdalena and Rosa, its authorities' actions often seemed incoherent, perhaps because of the church's internal struggle with sexism.

Magdalena, eminently qualified, is a strong woman, without benefit of a spouse to "contain" her. She poses a threat as an independent person who thinks for herself and challenges, by her very being, the authority of the male hierarchy. Rosa posed significantly less threat because of her own insecurities and the historical context in which she grew up, when women were taught to be subservient to their husbands and other male authority figures. Magdalena grew up during the women's revolution within the Cuban revolution, when women were learning to assert themselves within the family and in society. The church was not yet ready to allow feminists to enter the ranks of clergy, even though the society had been preparing these women to take their place at the tables of power for twenty years.

As I struggle to stay aware of these various methodological pitfalls in the field, it has been helpful to see the examples of anthropologists Renato Rosaldo and Ruth Behar. They, too, have struggled with positionality and reflexivity in their fieldwork, moving from a stance of ostensible objectivity to one of constant self-questioning and readjustment. Rosaldo was traditionally trained in anthropology, taking the approaches critiqued by both Tanner and di Leonardo until he underwent a life-changing experience. He and his wife, Michelle, also an anthropologist, had lived with the Ilongot people in the mountains of the Philippines for some thirty months in the late 1960s and again in 1974. One Ilongot practice defied Renato Rosaldo's understanding. The elder men of the Ilongot go on a headhunt to express their grief. For years Rosaldo tried to make sense of this tribal ritual but couldn't.

Rosaldo introduces his book *Culture and Truth: The Remaking of Social Analysis* with an essay titled "Grief and a Headhunter's Rage."[25] In it he recounts one Ilongot man's answer when asked why he went on headhunting raids to express his grief: "rage, born of grief, impels him to kill his fellow human beings. He claims that he needs a place 'to carry his anger.'"[26] This answer was, to Renato, too disingenuous to be plausible. He says,

> I brushed aside their one line accounts as too simple, thin, opaque, implausible, stereotypical, or otherwise unsatisfying. Probably I naively equated grief with sadness. Certainly no personal experience allowed me to imagine the powerful rage Ilongots claimed to find in bereavement. My own inability to conceive the force of anger in grief led me to another level of analysis that could provide a deeper explanation for older men's desire to headhunt.[27]

But when he confronted the Ilongot with his own rationale for their headhunting, they respectfully disagreed with his theory, reiterating once again their own connection of grief and rage.

The turning point came in 1981, when Renato and Michelle were doing different field research in the Philippines. Michelle met with an accident and fell to her death from a sixty-five-foot precipice. Renato was grief-stricken and enraged. And so he began to understand the

Ilongots in a way he had not before. He recognized that by using personal experience as tool for anthropological analysis, he ran the risk of being dismissed by his colleagues in anthropology. He argued, however, that his recognition of Ilongot rage within himself informed the "power of positionality" in his analysis. No longer did he see the ethnographer as the only "positioned subject, grasping human phenomena better than others." The peoples under study are also positioned subjects, able to critique and interrogate the ethnographer within their midst.[28]

Rosaldo's changed view of positionality also led him to re-evaluate his view of culture, no longer a static, self-contained whole, but a vibrant, changing array of crisscrossing intersections varying with the subjects' positionality. In other words, one's age, race, gender, class, sexual orientation, and other variables would, by necessity, affect one's interpretations of cultural phenomena. No longer should objectivity, neutrality, and impartiality be the fieldworker's desired norm. Rather, one must recognize that in analyzing any culture, social analysis must incorporate the positionality of the subjects under study, the positionality of the researcher, and the ability of the subjects to be fully engaged in the process of analyzing themselves along with the "professional" fieldworker.

My experience with Lea offers an example of the challenges a researcher can face in the field considering issues in positionality. I learned to respect my informant as a woman capable of critical analysis, even as I personally struggled with her theological position. Lea is a woman in her mid-thirties raising two children, ages seven and five, alone. She is the lay pastor of a growing Methodist congregation in Cuba's central Matanzas province. She is the only divorced pastor serving a congregation in the Cuban Methodist tradition. The Methodist Discipline in Cuba precludes anyone from serving a congregation if divorced. There is only one exception: if the divorce was due to the infidelity of the spouse.

Lea's church was the most difficult research site for me and the one where I had to confront my own assumptions and preconceptions most directly. The Cuban Methodist Church is growing in its charismatic zeal. It also tends to be the most theologically conservative of the "historic" churches—those established in Cuba by mainline United States Protestant congregations at the end of the Cuban War for Independence, also known as the Spanish-American War. (Other "historic" churches in Cuba include Presbyterian–Reformed, Episcopal, American Baptist, and Quaker.)

My difficulties were not only theological, they involved practical matters too. Lea's church had no printed program bulletins for its worship services (Davila's church, the first I had worked in, had bulletins, so I had assumed all Cuban churches had them). There was no overhead projector helping congregants with the words of the hymns, as some churches have. These lacks limited my participation in the worship services. Even though I am rather fluent in Spanish, learning the culture of a congregation and their worship style without those aids hampered my initial research there. Some proscriptions went against my grain too. While the sanctuary was rockin' and rollin' with guitars, drums, and other percussion instruments with a terrific sound system, I knew that secular dancing was not allowed by the Cuban Methodist Discipline. Both drinking and smoking were considered sinful, unacceptable to church membership.

While I could see in Lea a profound faith, my preconceptions about what this theology was instilling caused me to be circumspect. I wanted to remain more observer than participant. I didn't want to be swept into the waves of charismatic fervor that I witnessed around me. I didn't trust the faith of the membership, believing many to be using the church for their own benefit, during this *"periodo especial"* when economic times were strained to the breaking point and the church in Cuba had access to all kinds of aid from U.S. churches. This was not the kind of church I wanted to see growing so rapidly in Cuba. This was a church of traditionalist values, often more *machista* (male-dominant) than others. It tends to be theologically and socially very conservative and anti-ecumenist. It advocates individual piety rather than social transformation. Although I witnessed no counter-revolutionary behavior there, strong nationalist statements were also absent. Lea believed that since no society could be fully of God, it was not worth attempting to transform society. She said, rather let the Christian stay apart, sounding a lot like Niebuhr's "Christ against Culture" model.

With my preconceptions, theological disagreements, and desire to remain the objective researcher, I tried to learn Lea's story without offering any reciprocation. To my surprise, however, I found myself drawn in more than I wanted to be. Perhaps it was because the Spirit of God seemed to move in that place, or perhaps it was just because I found Lea to be a remarkable woman and I wanted to appreciate her perspective. I wanted to know her experience of faith more viscerally, and as a result I came to allow myself to engage more fully with their worship.

What I began to discover, methodologically, was indeed what Rosaldo had learned about the importance of positionality. I had to recognize my social location, my privileged status as a U.S. observer, and my own discomfort due to my own charismatic Catholic history. My prejudice that nothing good could come from a theologically and socially conservative church (what is it they said about Jesus coming from Nazareth?) also thwarted my ability to be a reflexive researcher, at least in the beginning. It was a strange and marvelous thing: These people taught me to listen more carefully, love more deeply, trust more fully in the power of the Christ to transform individual lives. It became clear that these people believed they had experienced miracles.

The scholar of theology needs to take seriously the work of social analysis, which struggles to recognize the positionality of the researcher and the informants. It is of critical importance to recognize that the people can speak for themselves, can interpret their own lives and faith, and can teach "the professionals." If, as scholars, we walk into a religious/church setting without having examined our assumptions, we will surely be unable to acknowledge and appreciate the gifts that the people have to offer. Here Tanner's critiques come to the fore again. What is the history behind a people's social condition? No church or religious culture is uniform; each group, no matter how seemingly homogenous on the surface, has within it gender, class, and age differences that add diversity and create heterogeneity. Each individual has dreams and stories—perhaps tragic ones—that will orient us to know why they are present in this place at this time. The members do not all hold the same beliefs. Lea once told me that although much of her church's focus was on countering Satan's destructive power, she believed that the primary emphasis for believers should be on the power of the triumphant Christ, whose loving Spirit was over all.

Researchers are often told to remain apart, objective. The term "participant observer" is somewhat misleading in that regard, for it implies that one should participate within the culture while observing it with an objective eye. One must learn from the natives, but don't "go native." Keep your distance and don't get too personal. Sometimes it is better to wait for them to come to you, rather than pushing your informants and intruding upon their lives. In contrast, reflexive ethnography privileges the relationship between ethnographer and informant. This relationship is not based solely on speech or dialogue, but incorporates the witness of the life performance of the community. The informant becomes aware, as the outsider, of the power dynamics between the researcher and the informant and the community. The role of the ethnographer shifts from that of participant observer to "participant witness."[29]

> Carrying a host of conflicting associations, including informant, litigant, function of the Holy Ghost, and spectator, a witness is less an observer than a teller—that is, one who translates what s/he sees and hears for an audience. . . . In participant witnessing, the lines between ethnographer and informant blur as each hears the other in a way that encourages self-representation. By portraying themselves as more closely akin to participants witnessing change than to classroom observers, the oral historians mark the instabilities of power dynamics in the project.[30]

Reflexivity occurs when the researcher recognizes and honors the specific knowledge the informant brings to the process. Both the informant and the witness bring their respective skills and knowing into the relationship, privileging neither "learned knowing" nor "cultural knowing," nor differentiating the "better" of the two.

Ethnographer and folklorist Zora Neale Hurston, during a rare interview, was asked how she goes about collecting the songs of the rural South. She answered,

> I learn them. I just get in a crowd with the people and if they're singing . . . I listen as best I can and I start to joining in with a phrase or two. And then, finally, I get so I can sing a verse. And then I keep on until I learn all the songs, all the verses, and then I sing them back to the people until they tell me that I can sing them just like them. And then I take part, and I try it out on different people who already know the song until they are quite satisfied that I know it. And then I carry it in my memory.[31]

What is extraordinary, if not unique, is that in 1935 Hurston had recognized that she needed to modify the objective, scientific methodology used by other ethnographers of that time if she was to succeed as a folklorist with and among the people of Central Florida, where she grew up. One could say that Hurston used a reflexive methodology long before the term for such was coined.

A theologian whose work incorporates a reflexive methodology shares much with the ethnographer. Both write about people and their varying relationships. An ethnographer will listen to the stories of a people or an individual in order to write an accurate ethnographic account of the person or society. A theologian, in order to write convincingly, should know the people, trust the people, and respect the people, or the words on the page will not speak truthfully to their experience of their God. The ethnographer and the theologian should have much in common, for both write about the intersections of culture and belief.

What continues to excite me about ethnography is that in the last twenty years a new breed of anthropologist has arisen, one that seeks to explore not so much the "primitive" or the "other" but the self in relationship with the "other." The "other" could be one's family, one's community, supermarket culture, Barbie culture, *National Geographic* culture, *Sports Illustrated* culture, and so on, sub-cultures located within, or outside, or on the margins of "Western" culture.

An exemplar of this new breed is Ruth Behar, a Cuban-American anthropologist who was brought to the United States as a very young child. She remembers nothing of her island birthplace. For years she avoided research on Cuba, believing that such anthropological work was too solipsistic, too close to home, too personal, not suitable for serious study. She needed to find a culture further afield from her own background for her research to be deemed valid. So she went to a small village in Spain, and then to Mexico to work with a street peddler named Esperanza, whose life offered some parallels with her own. Her book *The Translated Woman: Crossing the Border with Esperanza's Story*[32] received many enthusiastic critical reviews, including one in the *New York Times*,[33] which propelled Behar into academic stardom.

In the closing chapter, Behar writes autoethnographically, reflecting on her own experiences and Esperanza's, naming the struggle she has experienced in the United States as a Latina scholar and within her own family as an adventurous Cubana. Behar's father nearly disowned her, as he felt that through her book she had washed the family's laundry in public. Some in academia strongly criticized her for adding such a personal note at the conclusion of her text, which they otherwise recognized as a brilliant ethnography. On the other hand, some younger ethnographers have taken her work as a license for solipsism. Behar has written many essays since the publication of that text, with its complicating notoriety about the issues surrounding both autoethnography and ethnography within one's own cultural contexts.

In Behar's book of essays, *The Vulnerable Observer: Anthropology that Breaks Your Heart*,[34] she weaves together *autoethnography*, which incorporates the ethnographer's personal context and experiences into the ethnographic process, and *reflexive ethnography*, in which the ethnographer functions as a peer learner in the community being studied.

She writes about the people she knows, how they affect her, and the value of this kind of anthropological scholarship. In the title essay she asks the scholar to move away from being a participant observer, the one who is told to "act like a participant but don't forget to keep your eyes open."[35] Rather, she suggests, the researcher should become the vulnerable observer, the one who throws down her camera, who breaks away from her objective observer pose to get down in the mud to hold the dying child pinned under the rubble of the earthquake.[36]

Having been a pastor for years before entering the academic field of theology, I have often felt the participant-observer dilemma. I have found it nearly impossible to worship in the place where I am responsible for leading worship. I watch the clock at the back of the sanctuary, or the acolytes, or read the bulletin for the next cue, the next moment—making sure the flow is right, the pace is even, the children are not too loud. Because this particular worship service is fluid, allowing for the congregants to express their joys and concerns in a forum-like setting, the worship leader must be alert to keep the service to under one hour and twenty minutes. Sometimes prayer time takes only three minutes; at other times it can last as long as fifteen. While it is extremely difficult for the worship leader herself to worship in this environment, does it by default mean that she cannot be the "vulnerable observer" in her own church?

It is incumbent upon me as a Christian theologian to reflect theologically on contemporary human experience. We need to ask questions about God and the Bible in our contemporary situations. Jesus, as the most important referent for Christians, seems to be the epitome of vulnerability. He opened himself up to listen and respond to the concerns of the people, even when he was tired and hungry. Even when the crowds followed him to the banks of the sea and he wanted to rest, he used that moment to teach his disciples about the power of community. Vulnerability was central to Jesus' being, even to the point of death.

This vulnerability that Behar strives to embody in her methodology, that Jesus embodied in his life, should also be one of the methodological tools in the theologian's handbag. As ethnographers, theologians should reciprocate with the culture they study because they are passionate about the human connections being made, because they care deeply about the people and their culture and want to let the world know how, despite our differences, we are similar. We humans need to hear not only about our difference and diversity, but about our power to respect and love each other just the same.

My mother taught me one of the most important lessons I would need to know about being a pastor. Although I have moved out of that profession to become a scholar, this lesson has continued to be significant. One day when in my first pastorate, preparing one of my first sermons, I got stuck. I telephoned my mother and told her I didn't know where to go with the sermon. I didn't know what the congregation needed to hear. Her sage advice to me was to preach about what I needed to hear; the congregation would in turn hear what they needed to hear. The message was about being vulnerable to life.

The theologian/ethnographer needs to hear the life stories of the people, *los testimonio de la gente,* for these people will bear witness to God's revelation and liberation in their lives. These witnesses tell the stories of human struggle and pain and hope. These witnesses are the ones who can assist in the scholar's transformation from participant observer to vulnerable observer.

After four months living at the Seminario Evangelico de Teología in Matanzas, a place where Rubén and I felt comfortable, where we had made many friends, it was time to move to Santiago de Cuba. There I would work for six weeks with Gabriela, the only woman ordained in Cuba's Eastern Baptist Convention. Many people had spoken highly of her. I'd read her master of divinity thesis and knew that my study would be lacking without her voice. Two days before we were to leave the seminary, I twisted my ankle; however, I didn't realize the extent of the injury. On our way to Santiago, we would spend the weekend in Havana at the National Episcopal Women's Annual Conference. While there, I joined a group walking down to the Malecon to look over the water and sing and dance by the ocean wall. By the evening's end I was in terrible pain and couldn't walk back to my room. Nonetheless, I continued the next day, icing my ankle and managing.

On Sunday morning we arrived in Santiago de Cuba in time for Sunday school at Gabriela's church. After church we walked home, and since I was short on sleep, I asked my new hosts to excuse me for a few hours, as I needed to rest. When I awoke I couldn't walk. The next morning I was no better. I was scared; what would I do now? Gabriela's husband, co-pastor of the church, took me to the hospital, where doctors termed it a sprained ankle, encased my leg in a foot-to-knee cast, and told me to stay off it for ten days. How was I going to do my research? How was I going to get Rubén registered at the local school? Why had I come to Santiago anyway, when I could have stayed in Matanzas surrounded by friends? Feeling vulnerable and frustrated, I was angry with myself and with God for bringing me to this place.

Pura and Paloma, the two elderly sisters with whom we were living, I discovered, were emissaries of the divine. Paloma's son, Omar, registered Rubén at school, claiming to be his uncle, then transported him there every day, including a trip home for lunch. The women cooked for us, which we had expected, but also brought me *un cafecito* every afternoon and attended to my needs for ice, heat, or whatever the doctor ordered. On the second day of what I thought would be my incarceration in the house, Pura told me one of her favorite Scripture passages, "Commit your way to the Lord, trust in God, and God will act" (Psalm 37:5; my translation from Spanish). And beginning that day I immersed myself in reading Scripture, starting with Genesis. I also read a book of scriptural meditations given to me by my best friend at the seminary—the kind for "when you feel sad or depressed or when you're lonely or in love."

Soon I began to understand my purpose in sitting in Pura and Paloma's house in Santiago de Cuba. I'd been too comfortable, and I needed to be dislocated in order to appreciate the dislocation of the people around me. In Matanzas my life was relatively easy; I was fed and cared for, had help doing our laundry. I needed to experience a new reality, closer to the one most Cubans face daily, although still somewhat sheltered. I'd been on the go, listening and learning, taping sermons and classes, hanging out with students and professors, taking life-story narratives and asking probing theological questions, but I hadn't truly lived the difficulties of the *periodo especial*, I hadn't taken the time to sit and reflect, to be vulnerable, and had not fully appreciated the grace of the community, which made it bearable.

At home in the United States I'd read many ethnographies and had talked with both the anthropologist and the ethnographer on my academic committee about fieldwork. They both told me to prepare my questions and expect to change them, to know what I wanted to learn but also to recognize the unexpected epiphanies. Be open to the unforeseen moments when the field offers you nuggets of gold, they advised.

> Epiphanies are understandings that catch us by surprise; they're leaps of the imagination that make sense only when we're on the other side. . . . Fieldwork epiphanies indicate that luck may be involved in getting the necessary pieces in place, but it isn't luck that makes insight happen: you have to be ready for it. . . . The

time we spend seeming to wander in darkness may not be wasted time after all; we are often traveling the right road, but it takes the pain of travel to teach us where we were really going.[37]

Such was Santiago de Cuba. Yes, Gabriela was wonderful, when I finally worked with her. More than that, however, I learned to commit my scholarly way to the "way of the vulnerable observer" so I could begin to write the truth of the people I'd learned to love.

I found that the tools of sensitive theological fieldwork overlapped with the pastoral tools I had already learned. Knowing how to sit across the kitchen table over *café* to hear *un testimonio*, a story of struggle and hope, is a methodological skill that is often not taught to scholars in training. Though anthropologists still grapple with the objectivity question, their new methodologies can help the theologian to better hone her craft. To know ourselves and to recognize that the people we are studying have gifts to offer us, to be vulnerable so we can hear all their stories—these are tasks that resemble the anthropologist's. Theologically, however, perhaps the most important issue of all is the potential for the world to change, sometimes, one life at a time, when we truly recognize the presence of God in the other.

While living at the Seminario Evangelico de Teología, I joined a week-long program for a visiting group of women enrolled in an international program conferring a feminist Doctor of Ministry degree. One aspect of the program was a daily worship service prepared by the students and the faculty. One of those days the Cuban women were to prepare the service, and they asked me to join them in the preparation. The day for our worship service arrived. We had decorated the worship space with colorful fabric, traditional Cuban fruits, a large wooden cross held up by rocks, and many other items from our natural surroundings. We had planned a time of theological reflection, asking each woman to choose a symbol from the worship space and to reflect on her experience of God in Cuba.

Cora, who is the only Cuban woman in Cuba to have a Doctor of Theology degree, stood up. She walked over to one of the large pieces of fabric and proceeded to drape it over the cross, covering it completely. Then she said to us that in Cuba too much time is spent reflecting on the event of the crucifixion of Jesus and its power. Rather, she offered, we should reflect on the women who surrounded the cross. Who were the women, and how were their lives affected by this tragedy? What did they want? What did they need? How did they live? What were their struggles? What were their desires? This, she said, should be our focus; this should be our testimony to the churches. To know the women was to know God.

Notes

1. Kathryn Tanner, *Theories of Culture: A New Agenda for Theology* (Guides to Theological Inquiry; Minneapolis: Fortress, 1997), x.

2. Unless otherwise stated, all interviews were conducted in Spanish, and all translations are my own.

3. H. Richard Niebuhr, *Christ and Culture* (New York: Harper, 1951).

4. Tanner, *Theories of Culture*, 61.

5. Niebuhr, *Christ and Culture*, 11–29.

6. Ruth Behar, "Introduction: Out of Exile," in Ruth Behar and Deborah A. Gordon., eds., *Women Writing Culture* (Berkeley: University of California Press, 1995), 3.

7. Ibid., 4, as paraphrased by James Clifford in his introduction to James Clifford and George Marcus, eds., *Writing Culture: The Poetics and Politics of Ethnography* (Berkeley: University of California Press, 1986).

8. Renato Rosaldo, *Ilongot Headhunting, 1883–1974: A Study in Society and History* (Stanford, Calif.: Stanford University Press, 1980).

9. E. E. Evans-Pritchard, *Nuer Religion* (Oxford: Clarendon, 1956).

10. The term "militant Christian" is used by Cubans who are unwavering in their faith, particularly as they lived through the years between 1962 and 1991, when being a Christian in Cuba was often cause for exclusion from particular vocations, prejudicial treatment, and harassment.

11. In the late 1950s in Cuba, women who married clergy were expected to uphold their husband's career and not to seek a ministerial career of their own. They therefore had neither financial nor ecclesiastical support to seek a seminary degree, even in Christian education, the only degree open to women at that time. Rosa was allowed to study at the seminary only those courses that would enhance her support of her husband's role.

12. Rosa (pseud.), interview by author, Havana, Cuba, 11 March 2000.

13. Tanner, *Theories of Culture*, x.

14. Ibid., 40–42.

15. Ibid., 42–45.

16. Ibid., 45–47.

17. Ibid., 49.

18. Ibid.

19. Ibid., 51.

20. Ibid., 53.

21. Ibid.

22. At the Seminario Evangelico de Teología (SET) students are accepted into the degree program with the minimum of a high-school diploma. In Cuba this is known as a pre-university diploma. SET grants two degrees. A

three-year program leads to the *bachillerato,* or bachelor's degree; some denominations will ordain with this degree. The *licenciatura* or licensure degree, requiring another two years of study and a thesis, is still not equal to a master of divinity degree in the United States. To receive a master of divinity, master of theology, or master of theological studies degree a student must travel to a seminary outside of Cuba.

23. Magdalena [pseud.], interview by author, tape recording, Havana, Cuba, 26 February 2000.

24. Ibid.

25. Renato Rosaldo, *Culture of Truth: The Remaking of Social Analysis* (Boston: Beacon, 1993), 1–21.

26. Ibid., 1.

27. Ibid., 3.

28. Ibid., 19.

29. Deborah A. Gordon, "Border Work: Feminist Ethnography and the Dissemination of Literacy," in Ruth Behar and Deborah A. Gordon, eds., *Women Writing Culture* (Berkeley: University of California Press, 1993), 383.

30. Ibid.

31. Zora Neale Hurston, interviewed by Alan Lomax, audio recording: "You May Go, but This Will Bring You Back," in Robert G. O'Meally, ed., *The Norton Anthology of African American Literature: Audio Companion* (New York: Norton, 1996), PN 10127, compact disc.

32. Ruth Behar, *The Translated Woman: Crossing the Border with Esperanza's Story* (Boston: Beacon, 1993).

33. Nancy Sheper-Hughes, "The Academic and the Witch," *New York Times Book Review,* 5 September 1993.

34. Ruth Behar, *The Vulnerable Observer: Anthropology that Breaks Your Heart* (Boston: Beacon, 1996).

35. Ibid., 5.

36. Ibid.

37. Bruce Jackson and Edward D. Ives, *The World Observed: Reflections on the Fieldwork Process* (Urbana: University of Illinois Press, 1996), xv.

Part Three

□□□

Visions of New Possibility

9.
Womanist Theology as Counter-Narrative

PATRICIA-ANNE JOHNSON

▣▣▣

O ye fairer sisters whose hands are never soiled, whose nerves and muscles are never strained, go learn by experience. Had we had the opportunity that you have had, to improve our moral and mental faculties, what would have hindered our intellects from being as bright, and our manners from being as dignified as yours? Had it been our lot to have been nursed in the lap of affluence and ease, and have basked beneath the smiles and sunshine of fortune, should we not have naturally supposed that we were never made to toil?
—Maria Miller Stewart (African American writer, 1803–1879)

Womanist theory is the "love child" of the civil rights movement of the 1950s and 1960s and the Black Power movement of the 1970s. For Black women, the white feminist movement made clear certain realities. White women could find employment in academia and had indeed done so, but theirs were pretty much the only female faces to be found there. Black women were still standing in line behind their white American sister counterparts.

Similarly, at the close of the 1970s, following the most tumultuous period of social change in contemporary American history, African American women began to name their experiences of discrimination; sexual, heterosexist, and domestic violence; abuse; and disenfranchisement at the hands of Black men. Many African American male clergy and theologians, instead of leading the charge against inhumane and antiquated modes of relationship, carried this type of behavior and exploitation into the seminary environment. Dwight Hopkins tells us that when Black women began to enter seminaries, they were faced with some African American men who resisted their ordination, denied Black women's calling by God, and in some cases abused them sexually.[1]

This scenario speaks to the oppressive climate out of which womanist theory, theology and ethics emerged. It also points to the way womanism functions as a counter-narrative to the sexism of Black movements and the racism of white movements—movements that have critiqued the dominant race, class, and gender system of American society.

The term "womanist theology" came into use following the 1979 publication of Jacquelyn Grant's article "Black Theology and the Black Woman."[2] Grant questioned that theology's most fundamental claim: How could Black theology be dedicated to the liberation of Black people if it remained silent in the face of unrelenting oppression of African American women? Grant also challenged white women's theological stance with regard to racism, but her major goal was to declare a protest against the sexism and chauvinism of the Black theology movement. Due to the chauvinism of African American men in the discipline of theology, she argued, Black women had been rendered invisible. Grant asserted that Black men dare not speak for Black women!

Linda Moody argues that womanism emerges out of the experience of Black women in the United States. Born of the need for a space in which African American women can reflect theologically and ethically on concerns relevant to them, it is distinct from Black male theology, white feminist theology, and third-world theologies of liberation.[3]

Some discern a major difference in the starting points of womanist and white feminist theologies. In Linda Moody's words,

> Whereas white feminist theologies had largely placed sexism at the center of theological reflection, womanist theology does not allow the categories of sexism, classism, and racism to become separated, since each of these categories intersects in the lives of African American women. Womanist theology, instead, wants to address the experience of African American women without relinquishing their relatedness to African American men or to women of other racial and ethnic backgrounds. Womanist theology insists on the interconnectedness of the human race.[4]

First-generation womanist Katie G. Cannon's 1985 article, "The Emergence of a Black Feminist Consciousness," borrowing Alice Walker's term, was the first written text to use the word to identify Black feminist consciousness as "womanist" consciousness.[5] Cannon speaks of a new ethic:

> A womanist liberation theological ethic places black women at
> the center of human social relations and ecclesiastical institu-
> tions. It critiques the images and paradigms that the Black Church
> uses to promote or exclude women. . . . A Black womanist libera-
> tion Christian ethic is a critique of all human domination in light
> of Black women's experience, a faith praxis that unmasks what-
> ever threatens the well-being of the poorest women of color.[6]

Through the term *womanism,* Cannon offered African American
women who were feminist a hermeneutical space conducive to their
own critical literature and commentary. Womanism centers on the
experience of African American women survivors of the African diaspora. Womanist theology also places itself in solidarity with women
of all racial and ethnic origins who suffer oppression. It opposes all
forms of racism, classism, caste discrimination, sexism, homophobia,
and discrimination based on physical disability.

What exactly does it mean to be a womanist? Alice Walker, in *In
Search of Our Mother's Garden,* defines the term in four very distinct
ways. First, "womanist" is from "womanish," denoting a Black feminist acting grown-up, being responsible and in charge. Second, a
"womanist" is "a woman who loves other women, sexually and/or
non-sexually," more broadly, womanists are committed to the "survival and wholeness of an entire people, male and female." The third
aspect of womanism, as defined by Walker, includes a love of life,
music, dance, and the spirit. Womanists are committed to "the folk"
without sacrificing their own sense of self. Finally, Walker declares
that "womanist is to feminist as purple is to lavender." Here she
emphasizes the notion that womanists have their own unique style,
values, and commitments while at the same time sharing some features with white feminists.

Walker's definition of womanism has deeply influenced the work of
Black women theologians. Delores Williams's reflections on it help clar-
ify what womanist theory, theology, and ethics are about, and point to
the evolution of womanist methodology. Womanist consciousness,
says Williams, is informed by the guidance and counsel that mothers
offer their daughters, as suggested in Walker's examples of mother-to-
daughter wisdom. Noting problems with some Black men's preference
for light-skinned women, Williams deems womanist consciousness
"anti-colorist." Womanist consciousness names poor Black folk as the
locus of its values. Womanist consciousness values women as leaders in
the African American community. Womanist consciousness demonstrates a concern for survival and for the building and maintenance of

community. Womanism is concerned about the whole human community. Womanists are reminded to love themselves "regardless." African American women should not bear more than their share of the burden for justice and must be concerned for their own well-being.

Williams affirms womanism's connections to feminism, but with Walker's caution that "womanist is to feminist as purple is to lavender." Womanists do not promote divisions based on homophobia, colorism, or classism. Finally, womanists value mothering and nurturing. These ten characteristics, claims Williams, are intrinsic to the womanist's struggle for selfhood and survival and quality of life among her people.[7]

Womanist Methodology

Womanist methodology lends itself to a holistic approach to the work of theology. Delores Williams suggests a fourfold theological method that is multidialogical, liturgical, didactic, and committed both to reason and to metaphorical language in the construction of theological statements.[8]

Multidialogical intent encourages African American Christian womanists to establish and maintain a diversity of religious, political, and social conversations with persons from many walks of life. *Liturgical intent* advocates for relevant approaches to worship and praxis within the African-American church, approaches in which justice is the starting point of Black church liturgy. *Didactic intent* points to issues of moral and ethical choice as a place of teaching and learning in the Black church, with justice, survival, and quality of life as the central values. *Metaphorical language* commits womanists to a rich linguistic exercise, utilizing female imagination, metaphors, and myths.

Fundamental to womanist methodology are questions of epistemology and praxis, that is, how we obtain knowledge and how we witness to ethical issues. How do womanists know what they know, and how does that knowledge shape womanist praxis? Its epistemological standpoint is what sets womanist theory, theology, and ethics apart from all other forms of theological investigation. For Kelly Brown Douglas, womanists are accountable to poor and working-class women.[9] Dwight Hopkins summarizes Kelly Brown Douglas's vision for womanist theology:

> . . . Three points are important to consider: First, womanists must teach beyond the seminaries and divinity schools and go to

churches and community-based organizations to learn. In her [Douglas's] words "it will be church and community based women who will teach womanist theologians how to make theology more accessible."

Second, if womanist theology is to be accountable to church and community-based women, womanist conversations must take place beyond the academy. Womanist theology must have, as its primary talking partners and location, poor and working-class women in their families, churches, and community organizations. Third, womanist theology must work with church women to help empower them and help them speak their voice so that church leadership will respond and change.[10]

Womanist epistemology and praxis reject the bifurcation between the sacred and the mundane aspects of life. For womanists, God appears in the holy love expressed in the everyday chores of fixing supper and tending sick children just as clearly as God shows up in church on Sunday.[11]

Delores Williams confirms that Black consciousness does not make a dichotomy between the sacred and the secular:[12] "Womanists believe that God exists in places where the word of God is not necessarily mentioned."

Jacquelyn Grant supports this point when she reminds us that Black spirituality makes no distinction between God and Jesus: "The names are used interchangeably and there is often no distinction made between the persons of the Trinity." Jesus *is* God for Black women: "For Christian Black women in the past, Jesus was their central frame of reference. They identified with Jesus because they believed that Jesus identified with them."[13]

Womanist theologians find inspiration in African American women's lives, experience, and culture. Traditional sources such as Scripture and church doctrine, are combined with historical slave narratives, biographies of African American women, spirituals, and liberation theologies. Womanist anthropologist Linda E. Thomas speaks to such methodological possibilities:

We who are womanists concoct something new that makes sense for how we are living in complex gender, racial and class social configurations. We learn from the rituals and techniques which our foremothers originated to survive in hostile environments and from how they launched new perspectives, reconstructing knowledge of a liberative approach to Black women's lives. This self-constituting dynamic is a polyvalent, multi-vocal weaving of the folk culture of African-American women.[14]

Thomas uses ethnography as a tool of theological and methodological analysis. This affords womanist theologians access to the actual communities and spaces where poor Black women, children, and men live in order to create a narrative for the present and the future.[15] For Thomas, womanists must become part of the communities whose stories they tell—stories of the lives of women, the God in whom such women profess to believe, and the children to whom they have given birth. The heart and soul of womanist theologizing lies in the communities out of which they do their work.

Teresa L. Fry Brown has created a splendidly successful womanist praxis model in her organization SWEET (Sisters Working Encouraging Empowering Together). An intentionally womanist venture, the goal of SWEET is to encourage and move Black women toward spiritual and social liberation. Fry combines ethnography, storytelling, worship, feasting, mentoring, study, and discussion to make SWEET a success. Alice Walker's definition of womanism is the group's foundational motif and its touchstone for accountability. In the spirit of Alcoholics Anonymous's "second step," which calls for a belief "that a power greater than ourselves could restore us to sanity,"[16] Fry added to Walker's definition: A womanist believes in somebody bigger than you and me. She possesses a radical faith in a higher power.[17]

Womanist Hermeneutics

The hermeneutics of womanism places Black women's experience at the heart of womanist theological reflection. In Grant's words:

> . . . the source for Black women's understanding of God has been two-fold: *First,* God's revelation directly to them, and *Second, God's* revelation as witnessed in the Bible and as read and heard in the context of their experience. The understanding of God as creator, sustainer, comforter and liberator took on life as she agonized over their pain, and celebrated the hope that as God delivered the Israelites, they would be delivered as well.[18]

The Bible, as central to Black womanist theology, must be read and interpreted by Black women in light of their own experiences of oppression, deliverance, and the ongoing revelation of God. The same is true of womanist liberation ethics. In Katie Cannon's words:

> Black women live out a moral wisdom in their real-lived context
> which does not appeal to the fixed rules or absolute principles of
> the white-oriented male structured society. Black women's analy-
> sis and appraisal of what is right or wrong and good and bad
> develops out of the various coping mechanisms related to the
> conditions of their own cultural circumstances. In the face of this,
> Black women have justly regarded survival against tyrannical sys-
> tems of triple oppression as a true sphere of moral life.[19]

Delores Williams uses the story of Hagar to combine biblical
hermeneutics with womanist liberation ethics to understand the ways
in which God acts in the lives of Black women. But womanist moral
wisdom, biblical hermeneutics, and liberation ethics by themselves
do not save African American female survivors of the African diaspora
from personal and institutional evils. Rather, they uncover the negative ethics that attack and undermine Black womanhood. Cannon
wants to educate Black women about their moral struggle by using
oral tradition and the experience of common people.[20]

Cannon's post-colonial liberation perspective maps out survival
strategies for womanists and calls them to action. Cannon's map contains four main components. The first is pedagogical: womanists must
create educational styles and epistemologies based on Black women's
experiences and epistemologies. Second, Cannon calls for a new paradigm of relationships between Black men and women as well as with
white people. Third, she rejects traditional ethics grounded in European or white American male models. Fourth, using womanist experience as a gauge, Cannon creates fresh ethical perspectives relevant
to Black women's particular existential realities, drawing on the writings of African American women.[21]

Cannon's ethics are grounded in a personal relationship with
Jesus—one that emphasizes family teachings as the bosom out of
which Black women become and remain energized in the struggle to
resist all forms of evil, private and corporate.

Womanist Biblical Interpretation

Renita J. Weems, a womanist professor and scholar of the Hebrew
Bible, examines scripture as a world filled with women of color.
Through the use of womanist imagination, Weems helps students to
understand female roles, personalities, and woman-to-woman rela-
tionships during the time when the biblical texts were written.
Weems sheds womanist light upon such themes as ethnic prejudice

and ethnic cleansing, sexual abuse and incest, economic sovereignty and exploitation, social rivalries and loyalties, friendship and devotion. Like Delores Williams, Weems uses the story of Hagar to articulate a scriptural model of Black women's lives. In Weems's words:

> At some time in all of our lives, whether we are Black or white, we are *all* Hagar's daughter. When our backs are against a wall; when we feel abandoned, abused, betrayed and banished; when we find ourselves in need of another woman's help (a friend, neighbor, colleague, relative, stranger, another man's wife); we, like Hagar, are in need of a woman who will "sister" us, not exploit us.[22]

Weems also explores the chronicles of Ruth and Naomi and Queen Esther as womanist "fictional" stories. In the story of the Book of Ruth, Weems highlights the loving and loyal relationship between two women—a widow and her grieving mother-in-law—that transcends the limitations of ageism, nationalism, and religious orientation. Two women from varying backgrounds find their way to each other without the help of men. They form a reciprocal relationship that endures during the absolute worst of times.

In the tale of Queen Esther, Weems imagines the dilemmas of women married to public figures—that is, the delicate balance they must strike between obedience under the public eye and their own convictions as independent women.[23] Weems explores the image of women as degenerate subjects found in some male prophets' portrayals. Prophetic imagery of women runs the gamut from promiscuous wives to the assertive and savvy Queen defamed as a whore in the character of Jezebel. Weems consistently inverts the discourse by deconstructing these biblical texts and reveals the womanist perspective on the Hebrew Bible.

A constant theme in womanist discourse is the embodiment of God in African American women's lives. Myriad strategies of resistance to historical oppression make Black African American women moral agents who convey what Katie G. Cannon calls "invisible dignity, quiet grace and unshouted courage." Linda Moody speaks to this theme in Cannon:

> In illustrating "invisible dignity" in the lives of Black women, Cannon emphasizes the concept of imago dei. God is a God of equality, intentionality, creating humanity in God's image, male and female as equals meant to walk "side by side." The concept of human dignity cannot be overemphasized in understanding how

Cannon perceives God to be working in the lives of women and men in the Black community.

Cannon offers a second feature of Black women's moral agency, which she terms "quiet grace." Asserting that Black women have never had the option of either becoming immobilized by the terrors of slavery and racist society or of complaining too loudly, Cannon ascribes the term "quiet grace" to the quality of hushed resistance found in the lives of Black women.

Finally, Cannon understands the virtue of "unshouted courage" to be the result of "the forced responsibility of Black women." This courage enables Black women to meet the difficulties of their lives "with fortitude and resistance."[24]

Womanism may be envisioned as a post-colonial discourse that allows African American women to embrace a Jesus and a God free of the imperialism of white supremacy. The God of America's Manifest Destiny, which has allowed white males to claim supremacy, is *not* the God of womanism. Dwight Hopkins speaks to this ideology when he tells us that Jesus has been imprisoned not only by sexism and racism, but also by the privileged classes in their manipulation of the notion of servanthood. For the rich elite, the idea of servanthood has reinforced their impression of the subservience, obedience, and docility of politically oppressed classes and people.[25]

The Black Christ

Womanist theologian Kelly Brown Douglas paints a different portrait of Jesus envisioned as Black. During slavery, Jesus was depicted in two very different ways. Black folk imaged God as powerful, liberative, and sustaining. Whites, on the other hand, understood God as the source of their Manifest Destiny, the God through whom their own privilege, control, and enslavement of other human beings were justified.

According to Douglas and Hopkins, the Black Christ is the Christ who helped the enslaved Black Christians wage resistance against Christian white supremacy, in the material and the spiritual worlds, on earth and in Heaven. The presence of Jesus meant the divine gift of God's freedom to enslaved Black people, a prophetic proclamation and a transformative witness that defined the Black Christ during slavery.[26]

Douglas courageously asserts not only that Christ is Black, but that Christ can be seen in the face of a Black woman (Jacquelyn Grant's view as well). Douglas deals critically with the issues of race, gender, class, and sexual oppression within the gates of the African American community. She questions the Black community for not fighting for sexual and gender equality with the same zeal it has for racial justice and political inclusion. For Douglas, God can be imagined not only as a Black woman, but also a Black man, wherever Black people are struggling to bring their entire community into wholeness.[27]

Womanist ethicist Karen Baker-Fletcher offers five ways of expanding the perimeters of womanist thought. These are the power of voice, the power of making do, the power of memory, the power of holding things together, and the power of generation.[28] The sources suggested by Baker-Fletcher fall under the category of pneumatology—that is, understanding the role of the Holy Spirit—as applied to the lives of Black women. Pneumatology is a still-uncharted realm of womanist theology. Emilie M. Townes and Delores Williams agree that the roles of the spirit, the Holy Spirit and the human spirit, need to be clarified not only in womanist theology but in all constructive liberationist efforts to understand how to live in God.[29]

To live in the spirit of God requires that womanists commit themselves to the search for wholeness—physical and spiritual, concrete and theoretical. As gatherers of knowledge, womanists are dangerous to all forms of hegemony.

> This produces a radical ontology within womanist theology . . . womanist theology has as its primary concern concrete existence, i.e., "lived life," and searches for an impetus for a coherent and unified relationship between body, soul, creation and creator. Womanist theology seeks to uncover and affirm ways in which life itself can be and should be held sacred.[30]

Womanist theology rejects the dualism of Western individualism and insists upon a holistic alternative. Ethicist Emilie M. Townes states that the "subject-other" relationship is held in the web of creation (or, in my terminology, "is-ness"). Such "is-ness" runs counter to the "self-other" opposition of much of Western thought.[31] The womanist search for wholeness is grounded in the deconstruction of the triple oppressions of gender, race, and class. Womanist theory, theology, and ethics, then, is a post-colonial response to the sexism of Black theology and the racism of feminist theology. In Emilie Townes's words:

> Womanist theology challenges the theological presuppositions and assumptions of feminist theology as well. Womanist theology attempts to articulate a theoretical critique of cultural hegemony

through a call for the re-imaging of the roles of men and women in religious practices and also in secular society. Within a theo-ethical framework, it is inductive and based on praxis. The inductive approach taken by womanist theo-ethical reflection stresses experience as opposed to the deductive approach of classical theology.[32]

While Black theology critiqued white racism, it failed to expose its own internal hegemony based on gender discrimination and sexism. Townes speaks directly to this:

> Although womanist theology agrees with Black theology's critique of white racism and the need for Black unity, it also raises an important critique of Black theology. If, in fact, God's action in the lives of Black people is liberating, then all forms of oppression—including those integral to the African American community—are to be exposed and eradicated. Therefore, womanist theology began a critical assessment of the nature of heterosexism, misogyny, sexual abuse, violence and sexism. This was not confined to the history of white male abuse of Black women, but also the abuse Black women experienced from Black men.[33]

Womanist theology and ethics gives Black women the tools to name the systemic oppressions warring against our health and holistic living. Yet, as many African Americans continue to divorce themselves from the African ancestral practice of relationality and drift into an individualistic morality fraught with nihilism, the Black body continues its separation from the Black soul. Townes responds cautiously to this problem:

> However, in its advocacy for relationality, womanist theology must take care that relationality itself does not slip into the miasma of abstractions. Such slippage would lead womanist theology down the path of weak ethical reflection and practice. A womanist theology measures its reflection against the backdrop of the socio-historic reality of Black life in the United States.[34]

African American people have survived fourteen generations of slavery and seven generations of struggle to realize the promise of emancipation. The ethical fitness of the next generations will be determined by the virtues of integrity, hope, sacrifice, courage, and accountability, all of which point toward a different mode of relationality within the Black community. Townes's defining words to us as womanists are:

> To be called Beloved is to ponder these things in our hearts which we are to grow big. Womanist theological reflection demands that we stand up and dance, sometimes, with a twisted hip. The reality of Black folk will give us the music to the song to which we must dance. To be called Beloved is to do theological reflection with the deeply held knowledge that we are not dipped, we are not sprinkled, we are not immersed, but we are washed in the Grace of God.[35]

The task of womanist theologians, ethicists, and theorists must center around a two-part question: First, how do womanists constructively confront the reality of systemic evil as it interacts within the lives of Black African American survivors of the diaspora? Second, in light of the reality of such evil, how do womanists maintain a belief in God as the all-powerful creator and sustainer of the universe? How can an all-powerful, all-good God permit the perpetuation of evil? I would rephrase the question thus: Why has socially constructed evil been allowed to flourish in the name of both "God and country"?

Contributing to the womanist response to this question of suffering and evil, Jamie T. Phelps offers a definition of "social sin."

> Socially constructed evil involves patterns of relationships that are directed towards the denial of the human dignity and value of some human beings for the benefit of other human beings. This dehumanization and marginalization contradicts the reality that all human beings are made in the image and likeness of God and are called by God to eternal communion with the whole human community and the Triune God. Such dehumanization is the source of existential and physical suffering including death. Those who consciously participate in the construction and perpetuation of socially sinful institutions, which mediate existential and physical suffering and death, are participating in what is designated morally as social sin.[36]

A womanist theology of suffering draws upon Black women's experience with pain and suffering. That Black women must resist suffering is a categorical moral imperative. Black women have historically resisted the evils of slavery, Jim Crowism, and the failed promises of the civil rights movement and affirmative action policies. Throughout this process, both enslaved and free, the Black community continues to fashion a distinctive image of itself as moral and ethical human beings, willing and able to judge the world around them.

Womanists have relied on the religio-cultural experiences in their lives. Such experiences helped to ascertain God's revelatory presence and active engagement on behalf of the plight of poor, oppressed, and disenfranchised Black women. Such experiences include psychic moments of transformation, preaching and teaching, rituals of passage and praise, spirituals and shouts and dance, vision and vocation. All of these means allowed the Black community to embrace a hermeneutic of resistance as the linchpin of their faith journey.

Throughout the history of African descendants in America, womanists—though only recently known as such—have lived as witnesses to the power of divine grace, enabling them to create triumph out of victimization. To overcome their anguish, Black women continue to draw strength from hearing and imitating the strategies adopted by their mothers, grandmothers, great-grandmothers, and great-great-grandmothers to handle their own suffering. These stories evoke growth and change, proper outrage and dissatisfaction, and enlarge Black women's moral horizon and choices.[37]

A womanist theology of suffering emerges out of a womanist rejection of traditional Christian paradigms of passive suffering as redemptive and virtuous. A theology of suffering from a womanist perspective sets out several tasks for its practitioners:

1. To re-evaluate the "virtues" of patience, long-suffering forbearance, and love, faith, and hope in light of Black women's experiences. Such re-evaluation engages a hermeneutic of suspicion and a hermeneutic of resistance, rooted in a critical realism that rejects both naive realism and naive idealism as adequate foundations for a theology of suffering.

2. To abandon naive biblicism. The Bible has been a means for those in power to restrict and censure the behavior of African American women. Womanist Christian realism eschews naive biblicism as lacking in relevance to Black women's reality.

3. To draw nourishment from the rich soil of the African American religious tradition and be intimate with the root paradigms of African American culture, African American women's culture in particular.

4. To repel every tendency toward ersatz spiritualization of evil and suffering, of pain and oppression.

5. To remember and retell the lives and sufferings of those who "came through" and those who have "gone on to glory."[38]

Womanist mandates for a theology of suffering require that womanists see themselves as suffering no more. Womanists question all idealization of forbearance, long-suffering patience, and love as cen-

tral motifs of the Christian tradition, most of which have contributed
to the historical abuse of the bodies, minds, and spirits of Black
women. A theology of suffering from a womanist perspective ought to
offer comfort and power to the Black woman.

The Black Church

The concluding word on womanism must speak to the role that the
Christian community in general, and the Black church in particular,
have played in the oppression of African American women. The various manifestations of such oppression are at times overt, at others
subtle and covert. A look at oppression in its many forms within the
Black church is needed.

Are Black men exempt from their responsibilities of "righting the
wrongs" they have historically imposed upon African American
women members of the Christian community? One could argue that,
from an ethical standpoint:

> The dominance and submission mode of gender relations within
> the Black Christian community, as well as the dominant culture,
> meet the criteria for moral evil. One could counter-argue, perhaps,
> that Black men are indeed exempt from the crime of patriarchy
> and the role of oppressor in this definition of evil, based on the
> tenuousness of gender privilege afforded them.[39]

But what of the exercise of gender privilege by Black men, as it contributes to the oppression of Black women? Black theologian James H.
Cone poses the question: "What kind of society do we (Black men)
wish to create? Do we want a genuinely new society, or just the right
to replace white men with Black men?"[40]

How has the Black church colluded with the dominant patriarchy
to perpetuate the violence of sexism and oppression that has defined
Black women's membership within the church? What must womanists do to change this death-dealing paradigm? Womanists know that
whenever an alleged inferior group seeks to define itself on its own
terms, or shift the status quo, a backlash ensues that is intended to
keep the group "in their place."[41]

Womanists understand the difficulty of their task. They must seek
mutuality against the traditional work assigned Black women within
the church of maintaining the idolatrous worship of male domination.

Womanist Black women are called to seek loving relationships
grounded in both equity and parity, unlike the *paterfamilias* model of

the family in which tradition supersedes justice. This phenomenon is clearly demonstrated in the treatment received by Black women Christians forced to take on the prescribed "yoke of salvation." In Jim Cone's words:

> Within the African American church community the silence about the realities of women's experience and how it differs from men's experience has taken the proportions of a version of the "Big Lie," and is a deadly yoke. This yoke consists of silencing, ignoring, degrading, and dismissing women's experiences that reveal the nature and extent of oppression perpetuated against them within the community. Idealization and romanticization of Black women's suffering is as insidious a habit in the African American community as it has been historically in the dominant society.[42]

The idea of the "suffering servant" has been assigned a false nobility for women in the Black church community. To name and complain of Black male insensitivity, abuse, neglect, or dominance as the cause of female suffering is to further marginalize oneself. Consequently, many Black women who risk telling their stories are shamed, denounced, and treated as pariahs rather than prophets. The yoke of silencing, degrading, ignoring, or dismissing women weighs down the Black Christian community in a conspiracy against its own total liberation.[43]

Womanists must continually seek to challenge the African American Christian and lay communities and to turn their gaze inward and put their own houses in order. Looking inward demands that we no longer exploit the concept of solidarity to mask bigotry.[44] This is particularly true for the African American community, as men of color have much to lose by dismantling their own sexism, and therefore no incentive to do so. Black men continue to benefit from patriarchy. Womanists demand that Black men stop placing Black women on the pedestals that only serve to mythologize and romanticize their unequal status within the community. Womanists challenge the motives behind such unjust practices.

Womanists remember that, when Black men and women worked side by side during slavery as oppressed folk, issues of gender were secondary. Today's realities, however, require a different set of problem-solving skills that utilizes critical analysis of gender hierarchy. In so doing, we must demythologize the notion that African American women and men working side by side in the cotton rows automatically has translated into gender equality.[45]

Black men must be made to understand that they should and will be held accountable for the perpetuation of oppressive and dehumanizing behavior toward women. The Black women who choose to name themselves as womanists and feminists are not suffering from some disease caught from white women, but rather are women engaged in wrestling with both the awful truths and the awesome power of their lives. It is ironic at this juncture in American history that Black Americans are, rightfully, so critical of the hegemony of white Euro-American society, while the injustice that besets their own community in the form of sexist bias goes unchecked. The *metanoia,* or repentance, that must now take place has to occur within the heart of the Black community.

What is required to live and flourish in the Black Christian community as a whole? Genuine mutuality of healthy female and male subjects seeking to know and love God is key. To be in the spirit demands risk, the risk of examination and reconciliation, of challenge and of change. The sexist apartheid within the Black church must be dismantled. The radical vision of equality that has historically inspired the Black church in its struggle with racism must be applied equally to sexism. In Frances Wood's words: "We must all repent from the idolatrous worship of maleness . . . women from silence and complacency . . . men from the castrating yoke of sexism."[46]

Notes

1. Dwight N. Hopkins, *Introducing Black Theology of Liberation* (Maryknoll, N.Y.: Orbis, 1999), 131.

2. Jacquelyn Grant, "Black Theology and the Black Woman," in Gayraud S. Wilmore and James H. Cone, eds., *Black Theology: A Documentary History, 1966–1979* (Maryknoll, N.Y.: Orbis, 1979), 412–33.

3. Linda A. Moody, *Women Encounter God: Theology across the Boundaries of Difference* (Maryknoll, N.Y.: Orbis, 1996), 81.

4. Ibid., 82.

5. Katie G. Cannon, "The Emergence of Black Feminist Consciousness," in *Feminist Interpretation of the Bible,* ed. Letty M. Russell (Louisville, Ky.: Westminster, 1985), 40.

6. Cited in Moody, *Women Encounter God,* 82.

7. Ibid., 83–84.

8. Delores S. Williams, "Womanist Theology: Black Women's Voices," in *Black Theology: A Documentary History, 1980–1992,* ed. James H. Cone and Gayraud S. Wilmore (Maryknoll, N.Y.: Orbis, 1993), 269.

9. Kelly Brown Douglas, *The Black Christ* (Turner Studies in North American Black Religion 9; Maryknoll, N.Y.: Orbis, 1994), 114.

10. Hopkins, *Introducing Black Theology,* 135.

11. Cited in Moody, *Women Encounter God,* 86.

12. Ibid.

13. Jacquelyn Grant, *White Women's Christ and Black Women's Jesus: Feminist Christology and Womanist Response* (Atlanta: Scholars, 1989), 212.

14. Linda E. Thomas, "Womanist Theology, Epistemology, and a New Anthropological Paradigm," *Cross Currents* 48:4 (Winter/Spring 1998–99): 492.

15. Ibid., 488–89.

16. The Hazelden Foundation, *The Little Red Book* (New York: Harper & Row, 1987), 23.

17. Hopkins, 137. See also Teresa L. Fry, "Avoiding Asphyxiation: A Womanist Perspective on Intrapersonal and Interpersonal Transformation," in *Embracing the Spirit: Womanist Perspectives on Hope, Salvation, and Transformation,* ed. Emilie M. Townes (Maryknoll, N.Y.: Orbis, 1997), chap. 6, and Teresa L. Fry Brown, *God Don't Like Ugly: African American Women Handing on Spiritual Values* (Nashville: Abingdon, 2000).

18. Grant, *White Women's Christ,* 211.

19. Katie G. Cannon, *Black Womanist Ethics* (Atlanta: Scholars, 1988), 4.

20. Hopkins, *Introducing Black Theology,* 139.

21. Katie G. Cannon, *Katie's Canon: Womanism and the Soul of the Black Community* (New York: Continuum, 1995), 70.

22. Renita J. Weems, *Just a Sister Away: A Womanist Vision of Women's Relationships in the Bible* (San Diego: Lura Media, 1988).

23. Hopkins, *Introducing Black Theology,* 142.

24. Moody, *Women Encounter God,* 99–101.

25. Hopkins, *Women Encounter God,* 145.

26. Ibid., 150.

27. Douglas, *The Black Christ,* 109–10.

28. Karen Baker Fletcher, *A Singing Something: Womanist Reflections on Anna Julia Cooper* (New York: Crossroad, 1994), 185–206.

29. Moody, *Women Encounter God,* 106–7.

30. Emilie M. Townes, "Womanist Theology: Dancing with a Twisted Hip," in *Introduction to Christian Theology: Contemporary North American Perspectives,* ed. Roger A. Badham (Louisville, Ky.: Westminster John Knox, 1998), 215.

31. Ibid.

32. Ibid., 218.

33. Ibid.

34. Marcia Y. Riggs, "The Logic of Interstructured Oppression: A Black Womanist Perspective," in *Redefining Sexual Ethics: A Sourcebook of Essays, Stories and Poems,* eds. Susan E. Davies and Eleanor H. Haney (Cleveland: Pilgrim, 1991), 99–100.

35. Townes, *Womanist Theology,* 223.

36. Jamie T. Phelps, "Joy Came in the Morning, Risking Death for Resurrection: Confronting the Evil of Social Sin and Socially Sinful Structures," in

A Troubling in My Soul: Womanist Perspectives on Evil and Suffering, ed. Emilie M. Townes (Maryknoll, N.Y.: Orbis, 1993), 48–49.

37. Ibid., 124.

38. The five components mentioned were outlined by M. Shawn Copeland in the aforementioned article, pages 122–24.

39. Frances E. Wood, "Take My Yoke upon You: The Role of the Church in the Oppression of African American Women," in *A Troubling In My Soul: Womanist Perspectives on Evil and Suffering*, ed. Emilie M. Townes (Maryknoll, N.Y.: Orbis, 1993), 38.

40. James H. Cone, *My Soul Looks Back* (Maryknoll, N.Y.: Orbis, 1986), 123.

41. Wood, "Take My Yoke upon You," in Townes, ed., *A Troubling in My Soul*, 39.

42. Ibid.

43. Ibid.

44. Ibid., 45.

45. Ibid., 43.

46. Ibid., 45.

10.

Claiming the "Fearsome Possibility"
Toward a Contextual
Christology of Disability

KIMBERLY ANNE WILLIS

◻◻◻

Crippled. Handicapped. Handicapable. Handicopeable. Challenged. Impaired. Disabled. Differently abled. While numerous terms have been developed to refer to persons with disabilities, there is a lamentable paucity of critical theological scholarship addressing the human experience of disability, even as the number of persons with disabilities continues to increase. In 1989 the National Organization on Disability (NOD) reported that figure at 35 million Americans; in 1990, the year the Americans with Disabilities Act was signed into law, it stood at 43 million, or about one in six. In 2002 NOD estimates 49.7 million North Americans are living with a disability, reflecting an increase of 6.7 million persons with disabilities over twelve years.[1] Broader definitions of disability and technological advances in medicine are just a few of the factors that ensure the number of persons with disabilities will continue to rise.

But the experience of disability is certainly not confined to the United States. The United Nations estimates that there are over 500 million persons with disabilities worldwide. Thus, approximately 10 percent of our global population is a part of this growing minority group. Of this 10 percent, an estimated two-thirds live in developing countries.[2] Many of these persons live in rural areas where limited access to medical care and necessary resources substantially increases their likelihood of long- term disability.

Yet we must also acknowledge the innate limitations of such numbers. Numbers are not people. They cannot tell us their stories of living with a congenital disability, acquiring a disability through injury or disease, or shifting between the states of temporarily able-bodiedness and disability. Numbers may reveal how many persons with disabilities attend a religious service, but they cannot disclose how persons with disabilities incorporate their experience of disability into their understanding of God, themselves, and the world. And numbers provide little insight into the persistent social and theological marginalization that, when mixed with the yeast of fear and anxiety in our churches, rises and exiles persons with disabilities from the community called to embody the very One who is the Bread of Life.

Postmodern feminist Christology, through its emphasis on embodiment, provides a critical foundation for establishing an alternative Christology inclusive of the experience of disability. Addressing five aspects of this perspective, this chapter will (1) discuss the need for contextual Christologies, (2) examine two central issues both women and persons with disabilities confront regarding embodiment, (3) identify four unique theological and social issues confronting persons with disabilities, (4) propose that the image of Jesus Christ as the Disabled God represents a biblically grounded and theologically sound contextual Christology, and finally, (5) address how this Christology can promote a shift from the so-called religious and medical models of disability to the transformative "social interaction" (or "minority") model.

The Multiplicity of Human Experience: Claiming a Contextual Christology

Julie Hopkins, a researcher and lecturer in feminist theology, proposes that diverse cultural and socioeconomic factors influence our individual understandings of Jesus Christ, and thus our Christologies must be relativistic. It is these diverse factors that also present us with unique existential questions.[3] Thus, the work of theologians such as Gustavo Gutiérrez, Mercy Amba Oduyoye, and Chung Hyun Kyung has helped shape new Christologies capable of embracing the multiplicity of our human experiences. This pluralism of Christologies both expresses the realities of those who have been silenced for too long and challenges the reign of those who have enforced this silence.

Feminists ardently endorse the validity and necessity of recognizing the unique experiences and perspectives of women. Elizabeth Johnson identifies three steps in forming a feminist Christology: (1) uncovering the sexist readings of the narratives, symbols, and doctrines of Jesus Christ, (2) searching for alternative interpretations in Scripture, tradition, and women's experience, and (3) proposing new images of Jesus the Christ according to the feminist model of inclusion and reciprocity.[4] This process includes the presence and contributions of women to the Christian tradition, and also proposes a christological image in which women are able to fully participate. This paradigm provides a useful example for developing christological models inclusive of the lived realities of persons with disabilities.

Common Oppression: Women and Persons with Disabilities

Women and persons with disabilities (of both genders) are communities mutually oppressed by an exclusive dominant standard. They thus share important common experiences. Two of these experiences are directly related to embodiment and provide insights for formulating a Christology inclusive of disability. These common experiences include: (1) being perceived as deviant from societal norms and (2) prohibition from participating in the *imago Dei*.

Deviance from Societal Norms

History abounds with accounts of women being perceived as deviant from accepted societal norms. Aristotle expressed it vividly: ". . . the female is as it were a deformed male; and the menstrual discharge is semen, though in an impure condition; i.e., it lacks one constituent, and one only, the principle of Soul."[5] Other key thinkers such as Plato, René Descartes, Immanuel Kant, and George W. F. Hegel have perpetuated similar misogynistic views. Hegel states, "Women are capable of education, but they are not made for activities which demand a universal faculty such as the more advanced sciences, philosophy and certain forms of artistic production. . . . Women regulate their actions not by the demands of universality, but by arbitrary inclinations and opinions."[6] These are but two examples of the social, economic, and interpersonal standards that have adamantly proclaimed and reinforced the myth of female inferiority.

Just as women have been deemed deviant from the male norm, persons with disabilities have been deemed deviant from the able-bodied norm. Regardless of the specific disability, differences in bodily form are equated with deviance. While society is increasingly obsessed with the ever-elusive "perfect body," persons with disabilities are increasingly viewed as an intolerable deviation:

> . . . the concept of disability unites a highly marked, heterogeneous group whose only commonality is being considered abnormal. As the norm becomes neutral in an environment created to accommodate it, disability becomes intense, extravagant, and

problematic. Disability is the unorthodox made flesh, refusing to
be normalized, neutralized, or homogenized.[7]

It is this unorthodoxy of disability that threatens the stability of the
able-bodied orthodoxy and cries out as an embodied testimony to our
universal human frailty and vulnerability. It is this fleshly unorthodoxy that cries out for an alternative contextual Christology.

Finding a Place in the *Imago Dei*

Historically, women have been denied their rightful place within the
imago Dei. Mary McClintock Fulkerson defines *imago Dei* as "the
attributes of human being that make it capable of relationship with
God. Most important, it conveys the theologically appropriate affirmation of the goodness of finitude—of creatures. There is, then, an
incipient universal referent to the *imago*; by definition, to be crea-
turely is to be worthy of regard."[8] Yet when women have tried to
claim their place they have met adamant resistance deeply rooted in
patriarchy and theological rhetoric. Yet despite the risks and the
opposition, they have persevered in the struggle. For women, claiming an innate worthiness means rejecting the inherent oppressiveness
of patriarchal norms that aim to relegate them to inferior levels and
shackle them there.

Persons with disabilities are similarly oppressed by a temporarily
able-bodied norm that deems disability as antithetical to participation in the *imago Dei*. As is true for women, dominant norms restrict
the participation of persons with disabilities in society and potentially
diminish an individual's sense of self-worth. The theological implications of this temporarily able-bodied norm are clearly depicted
through the personal narratives of persons with disabilities who have
been deemed innately unfit to participate in the *imago Dei*.

In 1950 disability activist Diane DeVries was born without lower
limbs and with stumps for upper extremities. Her grandmother told
DeVries her disability was the result of her mother fornicating with
the devil. Her grandmother thus deemed DeVries "the devil's daughter."[9] DeVries was repeatedly subjected to similar diatribes that
claimed her very existence embodied the "sin" of her mother in an
illicit affair with the devil. It is a deeply disturbing and theologically
perverse scenario. But perhaps even more disturbing, such accounts
are not unfamiliar to many persons with disabilities.

Tammie, a young blind woman, recalls the story of the events following her birth:

Mom told me that Aunt Lou confronted her after delivery asking her if I was my daddy's. "Did you sleep with someone else? Why else would she be blind? God probably made her blind so she didn't have to look at your sin while she was in the womb." And she's not a crazy religious fanatic or anything. She just came up with this thing.[10]

While Tammie's aunt just "came up with this thing," such narratives voice a deeply ingrained and exclusive able-bodied bias that cannot incorporate disability without creating elaborate, if distorted, theological scenarios to account for its existence.

While both accounts seek a "reason" for the existence of a disability, both also assume that disability results from moral failure or sin. These convictions, however, preclude recognizing that disabled bodies can actually facilitate, rather than innately prohibit, participation in the *imago Dei*. Nancy Eiesland, writing out of her own lifelong experience of disability, boldly proclaims, "Our bodies participate in the *imago Dei*, not in spite of our impairments and contingencies, but through them."[11] Yes! This attitude also recognizes that the body does not have to be rejected in favor of a disembodied spirituality. Rather, it affirms the internal wholeness of people with disabilities and affords them authentic participation in the *imago Dei*. It is this wholeness and inclusivity that was embodied in the earthly ministry of Jesus Christ.

Dual Challenges: Women with Disabilities

Surveying two themes shared by women and persons with disabilities, we see an obvious overlap: women with disabilities are members of both communities. This "dual citizenship" subjects them to oppression based on both criteria. Obviously women are subject to oppression based on a wide variety of factors (such as ethnicity, age, sexual orientation, and class). Yet for at least some of these dual citizens, gender becomes subservient to their disability. In many ways this is not surprising; our culture tends to rate women as more "socially acceptable" than persons with disabilities. Rosemarie Thompson recalls the anger of disability rights activist Judy Heumann upon her realization that "when I come into a room full of feminists, all they see is a wheelchair."[12] Such "selective vision" is not uncommon as it accurately reflects our immersion in the dominant, temporarily able-bodied, norm of our culture.

Toward a Christology of Disability

In addition to the injustices they may share with women—being perceived as deviant; being unwelcome in the *imago Dei*—persons with disabilities also encounter some unique challenges that necessitate an alternative contextual Christology. Some of these challenges include: (1) the causal relationship others sometimes draw between sin and disability, (2) the social fear and anxiety related to disability, (3) the lack of appreciation for the diversity in the circumstances of disability, and (4) the multidimensional experiences of pain.

Sin and Disability

As previously depicted in the birth narratives of Diane and Tammie, there is a pervasive tendency in some circles to establish causal relationships between sin and disability. In such circles it is commonly believed that if someone commits a sin, that individual—or perhaps someone they love—is given a disability as a punishment. Too often Scripture has been interpreted in ways that both attribute disability to the sin of a specific individual and promote the further marginalization of persons with disabilities. Eiesland notes:

> It cannot be denied that the biblical record and Christian theology have often been dangerous for persons with disabilities. Nor can the prejudice, hostility, and suspicion toward people with disabilities be dismissed as relics of an unenlightened past. Today many interpretations of biblical passages and Christian theologies continue to reinforce negative stereotypes, support social and environmental segregation, and mask the lived realities of persons with disabilities.[13]

Lamentably, those with this antiquated perception of disability tend to use Scripture as a weapon of blame and guilt rather than as a source of spiritual nourishment and strength. What about the unwavering scriptural commandment that demands justice for the oppressed? How do we interpret such passages in light of the oppression and marginalization experienced by so many persons with disabilities? No longer can we ignore the impact that distorted and selective scriptural interpretation has upon our willingness and ability to welcome all persons into the body of Christ.

Fear and Anxiety

Encountering a person with a disability, especially a visually shocking one, produces fear and anxiety in us. We are uncertain how to act. We don't know what to say. We fear being offensive. We tell our children not to stare. We are curious about the specifics of the disability but tell ourselves we shouldn't be curious. And perhaps we are fearful because somewhere in the depths of our being we know that we too could instantly become "one of them." And we are right; disability is as close as the drive home or that lingering illness or pain that refuses to go away. It is intimately close to us, but we refuse to accept its presence as an integral aspect of the human experience. This inability creates an overwhelming fear of disability that leaves us feeling threatened by its very existence. Jürgen Moltmann offers the following revealing statistics: 90 percent of the general population claim they do not know how to act toward those with disabilities, 56 percent would not want to share a house with a person with a disability, and 70 percent report feeling fearful when they see persons with disabilities.[14] Given the likelihood that most of us will experience either short-term or long-term disability sometime in our lives, the implications seem clear: we will probably enter into our own experience of disability feeling ignorant, awkward, and fearful about joining the ranks of those whom our culture has so marginalized.

Robert Murphy, while serving as chair of the anthropology department at Columbia University, was diagnosed with a spinal tumor that resulted in a ten-year descent into quadriplegia. In a highly poignant and perceptive ethnography, he describes the fear of those around him:

> People recoil from us, especially when there is facial damage or bodily distortion. The disabled serve as constant, visible reminders to the able-bodied that the society they live in is shot through with inequity and suffering, that they live in a counterfeit paradise, that they too are vulnerable. We represent a fearsome possibility.[15]

Disability is indeed a "fearsome possibility" for us. It is fearsome because it represents the absolute antithesis of all our deeply embedded cultural norms. It is fearsome because it dramatizes the fact that our bodies are highly contingent entities. It is fearsome because it reveals the mortality we are so conditioned to deny. People with disabilities must daily contend with the reality that they embody a "fearsome possibility" that the temporarily able-bodied majority refuses to accept.

Diversity within the Disability Community
Nor does our culture easily acknowledge the differences in disabilities and the circumstances of their onset. There is a pervasive tendency to speak of "persons with disabilities" as a uniform sub-group of society,

without realizing that the rather tenuous common factor in this community is that some part of the body, at some point in time, for some reason, ceased to function "properly" and resulted in either a temporary or permanent disability.

This community is composed of persons with myriad disabilities (such as emotional, mental, developmental, physical, and learning) that are manifested in a variety of ways: some are obviously present; others are "invisible" but nevertheless disabling for the individual; some appear sporadically and to varying degrees. While there are definite similarities, there are also important differences between and within these groups that must be acknowledged. John Hull, for instance, comments on the different ways that blind people and deaf people perceive physical space:

> If blind people live in time, deaf people live in space. Deaf people measure time by seeing movement. If, however, deaf people gaze out upon a world in which there is no movement, such as the stars, a deserted street, or some mountain scenery, then there is a quality of permanence, of static consistency. In losing this kind of awareness of space, blind people have less awareness of change-ability. The world of blind people is more ephemeral, since sounds come and go.[16]

Disabilities are acquired in a variety of ways and last for varying periods of time. They can be acquired congenitally, by accident, disease, or injury. A disability may also be either permanent or temporary. Perhaps more important, this community is composed of men, women, and children from every imaginable category. When examining a particular tile of the disability experience, we must not mistake a single tile for the entire colorful and diverse mosaic that is the disability community.

Multidimensional Experiences of Pain

For many persons with disabilities, pain is a constant companion that refuses to be silenced, and its scope may not be limited to the physical. Some persons with disabilities experience little or no physical pain, while others must daily contend with its presence. But whether it is the physical pain of a specific disability or the emotional pain of relentless discrimination and the sense of "otherness," living with a disability can be a profoundly painful experience.

This multidimensional aspect of pain is similar in important ways to the Korean experience of *han*. Theologian Andrew Sung Park defines *han* as "the collapsed pain of the heart due to psychosomatic, inter-personal, social, political, economic, and cultural oppression and repression. The reality of *han* is the emotional, rational, and physi-cal suffering of pain rooted in the anguish of the victim."[17] Notably, this concept emphasizes oppression and anguish rather than sin. This is crucial. *Han* denotes a highly contextual and person-oriented understanding of pain and anguish that can serve as a powerful impetus for transformative change. Similarly, disability requires a contextual Christology capable of incorporating a multitude of diverse experiences.

The Disabled God

In many ways, the contextual Christology of the Disabled God extends several key themes present in feminist Christologies to include disability. Many persons with disabilities who feel relegated to the margins because they contradict societal norms or are seemingly unable to participate in the *imago Dei* find their experiences reflected in the Disabled God. The Disabled God celebrates both the God who becomes disabled on our behalf and the God who refuses to abandon those on the margins. Eiesland depicts the Disabled God as:

> the experience of Christ from below as a corporeal experience. The power of the disabled God is the seemingly inherent contra-diction that God embodies. This revelation of God disorders the social-symbolic order, and God appears in the most unexpected bodies. The disabled God does not engage in battle for dominance or create a new normative power. God is in the present social-symbolic order at the margins with people with disabilities and instigates transformation from this de-centered position.[18]

This Christology has a strong scriptural basis that is centrally, though not exclusively, located in John 20:19-30, which depicts the interac-tion between the risen Christ and Thomas. This passage reveals an often overlooked reality: Jesus is resurrected as the Disabled God. His body reveals the marks of the nails and the gaping wound in his side. It is a tragic irony that our faith communities, whose existence is grounded in a God who became disabled and was resurrected disabled on our behalf, persist in the sinful exclusion and oppression of per-sons with disabilities.

The classical Western tradition professes that in the incarnation, God becomes fully human in the person of Jesus Christ. While this was a debatable issue in the early church, it is now a bedrock tenet of Christianity. Our redemption, despite the pluralism of atonement theories, involves God as fully human and fully divine enduring a tortured, bloody death on our behalf. We cannot deny the blood or ignore the disabling death, for the cross will not afford us such an illusory luxury. But if the Disabled God is left on the cross, Christianity ends with the murder of God. It is not just that God in Christ endures a tortured and disabling death on our behalf, God in Christ *survives* that death:

> What is the significance of the resurrected Christ's display of impaired hands and feet and side? Are they the disfiguring vestiges of sin? Are they to be subsumed under the image of Christ, death conqueror? Or should the disability of Christ be understood as the truth of incarnation and the promise of resurrection? The latter interpretation fosters a reconception of wholeness. It suggests a human-God who not only knows injustice and experiences the contingency of human life, *but also reconceives perfection as unself-pitying, painstaking survival.* [italics mine][19]

I believe that there is a sustaining strength in this christological image for persons with disabilities. The Disabled God embodies pure and complete Emmanuel—God with us. In the midst of extreme human pain and suffering, God is physically broken—but never defeated. God defeats death—but doesn't stop there. The image of the Disabled God as "painstaking survivor" speaks not only to overcoming death; it also speaks to painstaking authenticity in life. Disability and death do not prevent Jesus from manifesting his authentic self and becoming who he was called to be. He is the embodiment of painstaking authenticity that survives and thrives in the midst of relentless oppression and brutality.

This authenticity is also central to the christological image of the Disabled God. This authenticity requires that we see in scenes such as Jesus in Gethsemane the real manifestations of Jesus' fear, sorrow, desire, and need for companionship. The account in John 20 thus depicts the authenticity of both Jesus' and Thomas's experiences. Jesus is not resurrected in a state of able-bodiedness. The holes and the gaping wound in his side proclaim the marks of his disabling death.

This passage also reveals Thomas's demand to encounter the authenticity of the risen Jesus: "Unless I see in his hands the print of the nails, and place my finger in the mark of the nails, and place my hand in his side, I will not believe." Thomas must have known about crucifixion and understood its effects on the human body. While the text does not reveal whether Thomas actually touched the wounds, he was the first person to acknowledge the risen Christ not only as the Lord that lived, ministered, and was crucified in their midst, but as the God who defeats death through the resurrection. He was the first person to proclaim that "one may address Jesus in the same language in which Israel addressed Yahweh."[20] Thus, we can ask the question: would Thomas have made this bold declaration if Christ was raised in a state of able-bodiedness? While any answer is admittedly conjecture, posing such a question does reinforce the scriptural witness that Thomas's proclamation arose from a transformative encounter with the Disabled God.

The Disabled God and Conceptual Frameworks of Disability

But what are the implications of a contextual Christology grounded in this image of the Disabled God? What impact can it have on our contemporary understanding of disability? Answering these questions requires that we understand and reflect upon three primary models used to conceptualize the experience of disability, known as the religious, medical, and social interaction models. Each of these models provides a unique lens for viewing the experience of disability. No mere academic theories, these models form, whether we realize it or not, the foundation of our own images about disability.

The "religious model" focuses on the spiritual realm. Accordingly, disability is viewed as being inflicted on the individual due to divine disfavor or retribution. The religious model localizes disability within a person's physical body. Given the supernatural "origin" of disability, its "solution" is also spiritual. Typically this "solution" will be a form of repentance, of deciding to again obey God. John Hull recounts an incident in which a fellow Christian he calls Mr. Creswell told him that he received word from the Lord that Hull should carry a pocket Bible with him at all times. Hull reflects that:

> Mr Creswell . . . told me roundly that God was telling me the simple thing that I should now do in order to have my sight back and if I were not prepared to obey him then I should not be surprised if my sight were not restored. Sin was the cause of blindness, as of all illness, and sin lay in the resistance and pride of men in refusing to obey the word of God, and to do the simple things God said.[21]

This is a painfully accurate depiction of the religious model of disability. While this model proposes that the "solution" is within the control of the individual, only God can effect a cure. In a seemingly
formulaic way, God will decide whether to cure or not to cure, based
on the particular actions of the person with a disability.

In many ways the medical model supercedes the religious model.
While retaining the same perspective on the location of disability,
this model reflects the advancement of technology and conveys
Godlike power to the physician. The medical model, rather than
attributing disability to divine disfavor or retribution, defines it as
abnormality. Anyone who fails to meet certain medical standards for
normalcy is deemed deviant and thus abnormal. Thus, the "solution"
for disability is medical cure, to return the individual to as "normal"
a state as possible. And of course it is physicians, with their medical
expertise, who are to make this happen.

The social interaction model (also known as the social minority or
social construction model) depicts disability in a substantively different way. Disability is not construed as divine retribution or abnormality, but rather as simply different from the average, "average"
being a relative state variously defined within different contexts.
Rather than being negative, the state of disability is deemed neutral.
It is neither innately bad nor good. Rather, it neutrally describes one
aspect, among many others, of a person. Perhaps one of the most revolutionary and potentially transformative characteristics of this
model is its location of disability. It does not reside within the body of
the individual; rather, the experience of disability lies in the interaction between a person with a disability and the broader society. This
extricates the experience of disability from being a static entity within
the individual to being a fluid and transformative relationship
between individuals. Thus the "solution" for disability lies not within
the physical brokenness of my body; it lies within that liminal space
of my interaction with you. How do you react to my bodily presence?
Do you ignore me or interact with me? Do you respect me as an individual or pity me as a disabled person? Do you recognize my wholeness or claim only my brokenness? Will you empower me and allow
me in turn to empower you?

Extricating disability from being a static bodily defect to being a
relational dynamic between persons necessitates a substantive shift in
deciding who can effect change. No longer is the "solution" for disability dispensed solely by God or the medical professional; everyone
who interacts with a person with a disability can now effect powerful
change. You can personally influence how society depicts disability

by reflecting on and transforming your attitudes and actions toward persons with disabilities. It is that simple, and it is that complex.

This social interaction model proposes that disability is a highly dynamic and relational encounter between persons. It is in this encounter that fear can be overcome and respect and dignity conveyed. Thomas will not believe the disciples' story of the risen Christ until he personally encounters that God for himself. It isn't even enough for Thomas to be able to see the wounds. He needs to touch them: "unless I put my finger into the place where the nails were, and my hand into his side, I will not believe it" (John 20:25). So the risen Christ comes to him and invites Thomas into a powerful and transformative encounter: "Reach your finger here; see my hands. Reach your hand here and put it into my side" (John 20:27). It is this encounter that results in Thomas's bold proclamation that deems Jesus "My Lord and my God!" Encountering the Disabled God empowers Thomas to declare Jesus' authenticity. We know and are known through our encounters with one another.

A contextual Christology of Christ as the Disabled God necessarily depends on the free will of Christ. If Jesus were an automaton subject to the control of a tyrannical God, then our redemption is a farce. It can only be the final act of a well-rehearsed drama in which God is a strict and bloodthirsty director. It is crucial that Jesus was able to make choices—to heal or not to heal, to love or hate, to submit or rebel against God, to accept or reject people, to die or not to die. Is this not the Good News we as Christians proclaim? Not that God devised a preprogrammed scheme, sent his Son to earth and demanded his blood to atone for sinful humanity, but that out of overwhelming love for humanity, in spite of our sinful nature, Jesus freely chose to offer himself for us on the cross—to endure a bloody and tortured death and become literally disabled on our behalf.

There is no question that Scripture and the central tenets of the Christian faith demand justice for the oppressed. It is not a question of scriptural interpretation; it is a question of whether we are both willing to acknowledge our complicity in oppressing persons with disabilities and refuse to participate any longer in their systematic oppression. We too have a choice. Disability rights activist James Charlton states:

> While religion hosts a panoply of reactionary ideas about disability, the institutional church may be worse. Throughout the world, the role of the church has been tied historically to colonial wealth and support of the existing social order. . . . If one wants change, any kind of change, support cannot be found within the tradi-

tional religious institutions. . . . They represent and reflect the status quo, both past and present.[22]

Charlton is right; the institutional church is guilty of the sin of complicity in the face of the oppressive status quo. This has been our historic choice, but it does not have to be our future choice. We have
been given free will and we can decide to make another choice. The
Christology of the Disabled God provides an insightful alternative
Christology capable of both incorporating the lived experiences of
persons with disabilities and transforming our perception of the disability experience.

Whether we are temporarily able-bodied or live with a disability,
we all share the state of human embodiment. Women and persons
with disabilities continue to recognize and celebrate the human body
as central rather than peripheral to their identity. Feminist Christologies reflect this critical element of women's experience. Similarly, an
alternative contextual Christology of disability acknowledges both
that it was through the authentic marks of disability that the risen
Christ was known, and that the lived experiences of persons with disabilities can be effectively incorporated into an image of God. It is this
Disabled God who invites us into intimate and transformative encounters that challenge us to break down barriers, overthrow stereotypes,
confront our fears, and commit ourselves anew to embodying the
Gospel in this world. May we take the risk to seek the companionship
of the One who is the Disabled God and to overcome the fear and
ignorance that is dismembering the body of Christ.

Notes

1. The source of these statistics is the National Organization on Disability's
website, http://www.nod.org.

2. United Nations Division for Social Policy and Development, *The United
Nations and Disabled Persons: The First 50 Years*; available from
http://www.un.org/esa/socdev/enable/dis50y01.htm.

3. Julie Hopkins, *Towards a Feminist Christology* (Kampen: Kok Pharos,
1994), 11–12.

4. Elizabeth Johnson, "Redeeming the Name of Christ," in *Freeing Theology:
The Essentials of Theology in Feminist Perspective*, ed. Catherine Mowry
LaCugna (New York: HarperCollins, 1993), 116.

5. Aristotle, *Generation of Animals*, trans. A. L. Peck (Cambridge: Harvard
University Press, 1943), 2:175.

6. George W. F. Hegel, *The Philosophy of Right,* trans. T. M. Knox (New York: Oxford University Press, 1973), 263.

7. Rosemarie Garland Thomson, *Extraordinary Bodies: Figuring Physical Disability in American Culture and Literature* (New York: Columbia University Press, 1997), 24.

8. Mary McClintock Fulkerson, "Contesting the Gendered Subject: A Feminist Account to the *Imago Dei,*" in *Horizons in Feminist Theology: Identity, Tradition, and Norms,* ed. Rebecca Chopp and Sheila Greeve Davaney (Minneapolis: Fortress Press, 1997), 107–8.

9. Nancy Eiesland, *The Disabled God: Toward a Liberatory Theology of Disability* (Nashville: Abingdon, 1994), 33.

10. Nancy Eiesland, "Barriers and Bridges: Relating the Disability Rights Movement and Religious Organizations," in *Human Disability and the Service of God: Reassessing Religious Practice,* ed. Nancy Eiesland and Don Saliers (Nashville: Abingdon, 1998), 220.

11. Eiesland, *The Disabled God,* 101.

12. Thomson, *Extraordinary Bodies,* 26.

13. Eiesland, *The Disabled God,* 74.

14. Jürgen Moltmann, "Liberate Yourselves by Accepting One Another," in *Human Disability and the Service of God: Reassessing Religious Practice,* ed. Nancy Eiesland and Don Saliers (Nashville: Abingdon, 1998), 112.

15. Robert Murphy, *The Body Silent* (New York: Henry Holt, 1987), 117.

16. John M. Hull, *On Sight and Insight: A Journey into the World of Blindness* (Oxford: Oneworld, 1997), 86.

17. Andrew Sung Park, *The Wounded Heart of God: The Asian Concept of Han and the Christian Doctrine of Sin* (Nashville: Abingdon, 1993), 16–17.

18. Eiesland, *The Disabled God,* 100.

19. Ibid., 101.

20. William Foxwell Albright and David Noel Freedman, eds., *The Anchor Bible: Gospel of John* (New York: Doubleday, 1970), 1026.

21. Hull, *On Sight and Insight,* 77.

22. James Charlton, *Nothing about Us without Us: Disability Oppression and Empowerment* (Berkeley: University of California Press, 1998), 64.

11.

The Nature of Nature
Ecofeminism and Environmental Racism in America[1]

RITA LESTER

◻◻◻

A political advertisement on British late-night television opens with a newborn baby alone in a nursery at night while a storm rages outside the window.[2] A white woman in a nightgown enters and cradles the pinkish baby protectively. Then a fully clothed, white businessman enters the nursery, apparently the father, and the commercial concludes with the reassuring message that the Conservative Party would stop the threat of environmental destruction that hangs over us all.

Although this advertisement is British, its assumptions are not dissimilar to those of mainstream American culture, and we might ask: What does this ad suggest about the relationship between social locations and understandings of nature? The white mother and child signify ideas about nature, womanhood, and race.[3] Is the middle-class nuclear family indispensable to the survival of the "natural" world? What is meant by the call of some ecological (and political) movements to save the world for "our children," and whose children does this refer to? How do the woman's whiteness and motherhood function in this political ad? What about its use of the phrase "our children" and the image of the white baby, signifying an apparently white future in the face of threatened environmental destruction?

The way a person thinks and speaks is grounded, shaped, and limited by one's personal experience. That experience is influenced by one's gender, race or ethnicity, socioeconomic status, and so on; in other words, one's social location. Not only in the humanities, but even in the so-called hard sciences, questions are raised about who is doing the research, who is included in the study, and how racist and sexist biases might impact the scope, method, and validity of the study.[4] Issues of identity and social location shape peoples' understandings of nature and therefore should be considered in environmental discussions. The "nature" environmentally concerned people work to "save" depends on whose understanding of nature is being invoked and for what purpose. What counts as nature or natural? Whose nature is protected and whose is not? When is nature a commodity? For whose children are "we" saving the earth?

How have environmental issues been determined, defined, and constituted in the United States, and with what assumptions about nature, race, and gender? The assumptions embedded in today's mainline or popular environmentalist movements can be traced to four periods in American environmental thought: the colonial period, the nineteenth century, the Progressive Era of the early twentieth century, and modern environmentalism in the last third of the twentieth century.

Racism and environmental exploitation shaped the Euro-American colonists' relationship to Native Americans, African Americans, and the land. On the American continent, the nonnative immigrants created an ecological shift, through colonialism and capitalism, that was both material and ideological.[5] The Native American populations considered land sacred and inviolable, and nature as a community to which humans as well as nonhuman living things belonged.[6] Human life was embedded in and dependent on nature, as can be seen in Frank Linderman's interviews for *Red Mother*. Prettyshield, a Crow woman born in 1850, told Linderman that her people could tell the number of winter moons left until summer by counting the grooves in the tongue of a chickadee. The Crow would not hurt the bird in the process of this counting and would then quickly let the bird go. Though Linderman considered himself an expert on the chickadee because he had written many stories about it, he did not know about the split or grooved tongue that developed in accordance with the seasons. Linderman saw the bird as an artifact of nature, whereas Prettyshield saw the chickadee as a vital member of her Crow community and history.[7]

European immigrants, on the other hand, interpreted land as a gift from God for the satisfaction of human desires. Their fenced fields, domesticated animals, and concepts of land ownership radically altered the ecosystems of North America. Two themes stand out in early immigrants' understanding of natural resources in the so-called new world: they believed that humans were commanded by God to subdue and have dominion over the earth, and that the American wilderness, as promised land, was given to the settlers as a chosen people, as an exodus people. Roderick Nash, professor of history and environmental studies at the University of California, Santa Barbara, writes that "for most of American history, Christianity provided the intellectual lubrication for environmental exploitation."[8] Alfred Crosby, winner of the 1987 Ralph Waldo Emerson Prize, terms as "ecological imperialism" this movement of people from England and Europe into temperate zones like North America, where they displaced and replaced native peoples and bio-diversity.[9] When Frederick Jackson Turner bemoaned the disappearance of the frontier, he did so out of a longing for the myth that only through returning to wilderness could people be restored to the innocence of their youth.[10]

The early immigrants' attitude toward the land and its resources was paralleled in their attitude toward the native peoples. Native Americans, and, with the institutionalization of slavery, Africans, were often perceived of as wild or uncivilized savages, like untamed nature, and in need of domestication.

The enslaved "other" is often depicted as a resource of mere bodies, or even of untamed, uncivilized animals to be used, "developed," or exploited. It is instructive to examine the ways in which America's white ancestry, and its often racist treatment of Native and African Americans, shaped the vision of its later environmental movements.

The European conquest of the Native peoples of the Americas was founded upon and served to legitimate the conviction that white, Christian, European civilization was culturally and theologically superior to any other human community.[11] Native Americans were considered "heathens" and "savages" of the wilderness; that is, they belonged to a realm outside of redeemed civilization. In this context, wilderness itself was considered unredeemed and uncultivated earth; wilderness was "empty" and available for possession. Colonists rationalized the dispossession of Native Americans from the land through the language of labor and discipline. Historian David Roediger writes that settler ideology held that improvident, sexually promiscuous, "lazy Indians" were failing to "husband" or "subdue" the resources God had provided and thus should forfeit those resources. It was only through the labor of animals and humans that earth was turned into desirable land, according to John Locke in his *Second Treatise of Civil Government;* labor turned land into valued property, and only white men were properly "property owners."[12]

Unlike the image of the African American slave, male or female, the mythical image of the Native American, male or female, was of independence, a symbol of American freedom. Roediger posits that it was this mythical independence, as well as the disappearing of Native populations, that prevented white working-class men in the nine-teenth century from speaking of being a "wage Indian." Instead, they adopted the term, "wage slave."[13] A white working-class man could not complain of having to "work like an Indian," but could and did complain of having to "work like a slave." Blackness was almost com-pletely linked to servitude. The use of the word *slave* took on special meaning in America, with its actual history of black slavery.

In the South, most whites interacted with blacks only within the confines of the institution of slavery. And, like Natives, blacks were associated with nature and animals. But instead of being linked with wild animals, as Natives were, slaves were more likely associated with work animals and beasts of burden. Like animals, or even worse than animals, slaves were worked constantly, regardless of weather and per-sonal safety, coerced into harvesting profitable commodities from the property they were not allowed to own.

African American women in particular were exploited not only for their labor of production, but for their reproduction as well. These women were not seen as human mothers but as "breeders." Breeding slaves was less expensive for white owners than buying new slaves, and breeding was regularly practiced after the early 1800s when the external slave trade to the South was legally halted.

Black slave women were expected to give birth, the labor of repro-duction, without interrupting their other labor, the labor of produc-tion. Delores Williams compares this practice of breeding female slaves to strip-mining, which exhausts the earth's body. Slavery and the plantation system led to agricultural methods that exhausted the soil.[14] Without crop rotation or diversification or the capital to invest in fertilizer, the land had to be worked harder and harder for smaller yields, a financial problem offset only by a dependence on more intensive labor supplied by the slave trade. Black women and men, and the very earth they cultivated, were worked at an intensive, destructive, and unsustainable rate—unsustainable for both workers and the land. Delores Williams writes: "Just as technology's rapid and often unchecked contribution to the destruction of nature is rational-ized on the basis of technology providing greater profits, comfort, and leisure for more Americans, the exploitation of the black woman's body was rationalized to the advantage of white slave owners."[15]

Never benefiting from the Lockean precept of land ownership as due reward for working the earth, these laborers did not gain the own-ership of the land they worked. Black women in particular were vul-nerable to those who owned the means of production, and they were objectified accordingly. They demonstrated that womanhood was not weakness, marriage was not protection, motherhood was not an exemption from work, and survival was not passivity.

Though the Southern model of racism, shaped by slavery, is more obvious than the Northern, both the Southern and Northern models of the relationship between women and nature were shaped by racism and were environmentally destructive. Both Northern and Southern models denied land ownership to non-Europeans. Both denied or could not perceive the intrinsic value of the natural world. Both ideologically separated white women from other women, while still seeing all women as closer than men to the evils or potential chaos of nature.

So, although men would dominate the study of nature, by the close of the nineteenth century there was a spectrum of images of womanhood, and each image demonstrates a different projection on the relationship between nature and race. Native women understood nature as a place of freedom because of its role in their sense of community and spirituality. African American women lived with domesticated nature, in the fields or in the kitchen, processing the fruits of the fields into food. Because of their oppression and exploitation, it is unlikely that African American women saw nature itself as a place of liberation, though it might have been a refuge from the racism of "civilization." Southern planter women oversaw gardens but did little of the work, nor did they turn the fruits of the field into food themselves. Wealthy, genteel Northeastern women tended gardens, encouraged nature appreciation, and painted landscapes as kind of a natural history meets romanticism but were removed from nature.

There were glimmers of nineteenth-century federal concern for the environment; for example, in the 1870s Secretary of the Interior Carl Schurz, a German American trained in scientific forestry, was not indifferent to forest conservation.[16] At the time, anxiety over the disappearing frontier influenced conservation interests; so did U.S. imperialism and restrictions on immigration. The conservation movement, represented in persons and institutions such as Gifford Pinchot, Theodore Roosevelt, John Muir, and the United States Forest Service, was rooted in a liberal tradition of conservation as democratic, efficient, and aesthetic. This progressive conservationist agenda promoted national strength and growth through the use of natural resources to serve human economic needs. Pinchot wrote that "the first great fact about conservation is that it stands for development . . . [that is] the use of the natural resources now existing on this continent for the benefit of the people who live here now."[17]

This legacy persisted in the work of the Tennessee Valley Authority, the Civilian Conservation Corps, and the so-called beautification project of Lyndon B. Johnson. Initially, this "wise-use" utilitarianism appeared both patriotic and ecologically beneficial, but progressive conservation efforts were aimed solely at the protection of specific nonurban wilderness areas and represented the interests of the limited, privileged segment of the population that approaches nature as a recreational or aesthetic resource for spiritual regeneration. Definitions of nature and subsequent agendas are embedded in social and class assumptions, and the flexibility of these definitions is lost if we don't ask, "Beautification, or recreation, for whom?"

The progressive conservation movement of the 1920s, for example, was closely linked to eugenics, white-supremacy, and anti-immigrant sentiments. These sentiments were also shaping the social sciences and the philosophy of museums such as the American Museum of Natural History in New York. One trustee of that museum, Madison Grant—a successful lawyer, cofounder of the California Save-the-Redwoods League, an advocate for national parks, and secretary of the New York Zoological Society—was also a white supremacist author.[18] Madison's racism was apparently not much of a problem to his contemporaries at the American Museum of Natural History or the Redwood League. The father of primatology in the United States, Robert Yerkes, was a leader in the so-called "social hygiene" movement. Haraway writes that the social hygiene movement advocated both eugenics and conservation and promoted itself as "all in the service of science."[19] But the so-called progressive conservation of the early 1900s would give way to a different kind of environmentalism by mid-century.

The shift from progressive-conservation economics, which Samuel Hayes labeled the "gospel of efficiency,"[20] to a fully developed environmental ethic was occurring in the written works of Aldo Leopold in the 1940s. As early as the 1930s and 1940s, American churches were lending liturgical support to such various land celebration observations as Arbor Day, Rogation Day, Rural Life Sunday, and Soil Steward Sunday. But environmental ethics did not fully emerge into mainstream American culture until the 1960s and 1970s with the anti-pesticide work of Rachel Carson, the 1965 Presidential Science Advisory Committee statement on pollution, Paul Ehrlich's thesis on the population bomb, and the 1970 State of the Environment report from the Council on Environmental Quality.

In the 1970s environmentalism became a major preoccupation addressing air and water pollution, depletion of energy resources, the destruction of wilderness areas, the ravages of pesticides, and nuclear waste. The 1980s saw an explosion of environmental consciousness and the greening of religion at a time when questions of gender and race had become topics of social, historical, and ethical consideration and were entering the field of environmental theory as well.

What's Race, Gender, and Class Got to Do with It?

In the 1970s and 1980s, America's professional mainstream ecological movement did not reflect the concerns of racial minorities in its membership, staffing, leadership, or agenda prioritizing—in spite of the research suggesting that African Americans, for example, have higher rates of voluntary association in social, political, or religious organizations than their white counterparts.[21] If environmental groups and academic disciplines were to address social locations issues such as race, class, and gender, they would have to expand their agendas from traditional conservation goals to social justice and public health goals. Their focus would have to shift from an emphasis on wildlife and wilderness to concern for the environment of daily life, including the urban settings, the home, and the workplace.

In regard to gender, the trends toward professionalization in the environmental establishment, along with its implications for tactics, ethics, and personnel structures, may be making environmental organizations less friendly to women, particularly minority women. Although a grassroots environmental group is often organized and initially run by women who might be called amateurs, the larger the organization becomes, and the more financial resources it commands, the more it is run like a big business (with boards of directors, corporate officers, large staffs, and even large budgets), and the more likely it is to be run by men.[22] This process occurred in Greenpeace, the Sierra Club, the World Wildlife Club, and the National Wildlife Federation. Although each of these saw their membership rolls double in the 1980s, the representation of women in these organizations did not grow proportionately.

The mainstream environmental movements of the 1980s shared the agendas of older, more traditional conservation groups concerned largely with the maintenance of recreational hunting and fishing, a largely middle-class, male-oriented agenda. When wildlife experts surveyed environmental groups about their agenda priorities in the late 1980s, they concluded that these priorities were strongly influenced by gender, particularly in regard to animals. Specifically, men showed a greater willingness to exploit animals, usurp wildlife habitat, and gain greater personal satisfaction in the mastery and control of animals through "harvesting" than did women.[23]

Human health was also a low priority within most mainstream environmental groups, particularly health issues that bear directly on the lives of women and the lives of urban and minority youth. One in nine white women, one in eleven African American women, and one in twenty Hispanic and Asian American women in the United States will develop breast cancer.[24] Women's traditional work environments, including the home, are dangerous due to indoor pollution. But indoor pollution does not receive the attention, concern, money, or staff time from environmental organizations that public pollution receives. The health of children, particularly urban children, is also a low priority in mainstream environmental movements, despite the fact that minority children are at greater risk than their white counterparts for environmentally influenced diseases like lead poisoning. Unfortunately, as the environmental movement becomes more professional, more respectable, and more middle-class, it may increasingly shift its agenda from social and structural change to blaming individuals, particularly individual consumers who purchase for the private sphere, that is, the traditional space of women, the home.

Shopping and buying are considered to be in the traditional domain of women, particularly since consumption loomed larger in the life of the post–World War II family. Advertisers aim their sales pitches at women, and women consequently tend to be a majority in the ranks of consumer movements. The power of consumer movements may reside in their ability to turn an often trivialized act—shopping for household goods—into an important job in which women exert control over a serious economic-environmental unit: the home.[25]

But the politics of environmental consumption are more complex than they may initially appear. "Green" consumers, usually women who purchase for the private sphere, are beginning to acknowledge strategies learned from other arenas of social activism and political change. Women have found that when they do not shape the agenda of social movements, they are blamed for any failures; when they do, they get little of the credit for any successes.

In defense of ecologically unsound production or packaging practices, industry often blames the consumer by arguing that it only produces what consumers want. Therefore, the argument goes, industries will not detoxify or recycle if consumers do not call for it. The flip side of this, an argument also used to scapegoat private sphere consumers, is that if consumers do not jump on the "green" consumer bandwagon, they are made to feel guilty for not providing a healthy home and supposedly not caring for the planet and future generations.

The campaign against disposable diapers is an example of a scapegoating practice in the green movement. The manufacture of disposable diapers, a paper product, creates dioxins through bleaching, and also uses forest resources. Disposable diapers became the target of environmental campaigns in the 1970s and 1980s as a major contributor to the eco-crisis and as a symbol of a throwaway society. Not only did this campaign typify the gender bias of consumer blaming, it also may have overstated its case. Diapers comprise only 2 percent of American's total garbage (17 percent is yard waste, 30 percent is plastic, and 40 percent is paper, all wastes associated with the outdoor or public spheres of society), yet were a main source of waste targeted for criticism.[26]

Consumerism is a double-edged sword manifested in the "green consumer." America has often seen the ultimate purpose of its economy as the production and consumption of as many goods as possible. Green consumers buy environmentally friendly products and are label-readers who try to exert political influence through purchase power. They choose products that are produced and packaged with little waste; for example, some consumers might buy non-hybrid grain cereals in bulk, stored in reusable containers, or cotton clothing that is not bleached with toxic formaldehyde. Such products often cost more than those in chain grocery or department stores, and consumers often rely on the information provided or advertised by the manufacturer. But consumer-based solutions being promoted to and by middle-class North Americans only perpetuate global economic injustice and gender and class privilege.

At the same time, "green" consumerism leaves untouched major environmental abusers, such as the military and multinational corporations. Because green products cost more and are only available in limited areas, green consumers tend to be middle- or upper-class. Therefore, the so-called proper consumer behavior pushed by a middle-class environmental movement leaves out a critical class analysis and ends up blaming those least able to participate in a consumer movement, the working poor. A just environmentalism would entail a critique of the economy of hyper-consumption, including marketing and advertising practices. An environmental ethic needs to be cautious about cozying up to industries that reduce "green" to a marketing strategy.

Environmental Justice

The racist treatment of Native and African Americans has so shaped the vision, goals, and practices of the contemporary environmental movement that it is hardly surprising that ecological degradation disproportionately affects America's minority communities, both urban and rural, particularly in the South and on Native American reservations.

The environmental justice movement in contemporary America is a loose collection of recent social movements responding to specific abuses of industrialization and urbanization.[27] According to an environmental justice analysis, environmental degradation is tied to the deeper inequalities of capitalism and corporatism, institutional racism, militarism, sexism, neocolonialism, and the exploits of the so-called free market economy. Whereas contemporary mainstream environmental movements have traditionally focused on habitat protection and consumer rights, the environmental justice movement has stronger historical and ideological ties to the civil rights and anti-nuclear movements. As Richard Hofritcher has suggested, environmental justice groups use these ties to redefine the scope of the environmental movement to include social conditions that people experience in everyday life. They address such topics as unsafe and/or unhealthy working conditions, the geography of residential and occupational racial segregation, militarism, the crisis of labor in a pro-corporate world, economistic thinking (profits over people, the environment, and so forth), and the eroding economic base of disadvantaged communities.

One example of an environmental justice concern is environmental racism. In the United States, people of color are more likely than people of European descent to be victims of pollution, toxic waste, and ill health due to environmental factors. This inequity has been named "environmental racism" and motivates a large part of the environmental justice movement.

Environmental racism has three components. First, there is racial discrimination in environmental policymaking and enforcement of regulations and laws. Second, there is deliberate targeting of communities of color for placement of toxic waste facilities and official sanctioning of life-threatening poisons and pollutants present in communities of color. Finally, there is a history of excluding people of color from leadership and decision-making in the environmental movement.

The national geography of pollution and hazardous waste reveals the danger faced by African Americans as well as other minorities.

Racial minorities are disproportionately victimized by residential and occupational environmental health hazards. As of 1987, three out of every five African Americans (that is, fifteen million) live in communities with abandoned commercial toxic-waste sites, with three of the nation's five largest landfills located in predominantly African and Latino American communities. The largest hazardous waste dump in the country, which receives waste from nearly all fifty states, is located in a predominantly African American county in Alabama. The population of the corridor between New Orleans and Baton Rouge, Louisiana, known as Cancer Alley because of its one hundred chemical companies and refineries, is predominantly black. Whether in the south side of Chicago, rural Alabama, or South Central Los Angeles, people of color suffer disproportionately from environmental abuse and its ensuing health hazards. In its landmark study *Toxic Wastes and Race*, the Commission for Racial Justice of the United Church of Christ found race to be the most important factor in the location of abandoned toxic-waste sites, more important than factors such as income, home ownership rates, or property values.[28]

The struggle for environmental justice by African Americans is not an innovation of the 1990s, but is interwoven with the more widely recognized civil rights struggles of the 1960s.[29] Although these struggles were not framed as "environmental," the movements for civil rights addressed and redefined environmental issues. For example, the discovery of the systematic and deliberate neglect of garbage collection and sanitation services in African American neighborhoods contributed to urban riots of the 1960s. Martin Luther King Jr.'s 1968 trip to Memphis was undertaken to resolve an environmental justice dispute, that of African American sanitation workers. In this way, African American scholars and activists such as Robert Bullard and Benjamin Chavis have argued, environmental justice is historically and politically related to the civil rights agenda.

City planning and zoning are not determined by environmental soundness, but by social power, or more correctly, by lack of social power. The mainstream environmental movement has not sufficiently addressed these social justice issues. Social inequality and imbalances of social power are at the heart of environmental degradation, resource depletion, and pollution. Despite federal laws designed to eliminate racial discrimination in the areas of housing, employment, and education, the government has largely failed to address discriminatory environmental practices. Whites, regardless of class, are less likely to be exposed to environmental hazards than African Americans.

Native American reservations have also become prime targets for environmental injustices. For example, waste disposal firms target reservations because they are not covered by state environmental regulations. The American government uprooted Natives, denying them rights to the very earth they had tended for generations, then placed them on federally controlled, undeveloped, and undevelopable land. In addition, reservation lands have never been truly owned by Native tribes; they are held "in trust" by the United States government through the Bureau of Indian Affairs.[30] This pseudo-independence places reservation land and resources in a precarious position: they are rarely genuinely controlled by Native governing bodies, nor are they protected by United States laws, policies, or agencies such as the Environmental Protection Agency. Indigenous people can be relocated for hydroelectric dam projects; the Cree and Inuit peoples still battle over James Bay in Canada. Further evidence of the contempt Euro-Americans have for Natives and their industrially undeveloped land can be seen in the government's practices of toxic dumping and experimental bombing that occurs solely on Native lands in this country.[31]

The legacy of racism in the U.S. has allowed those who benefit the most from the exploitation of persons and land to bear the least burden, literally dumping that burden on those with less social power. Though the nature/culture dichotomy itself still exists, a shift has occurred in the valuing of nature and culture: instead of seeing nature as unredeemed chaos, the white middle class (and other socioeconomic racial strata influenced by this ethos) now consume nature for recreational or aesthetic, spiritual reasons. Its primary purpose is to provide escape from the chaotic, unredeemable city, which houses mostly minorities. Meanwhile, through public policy, zoning, residential segregation, and high-risk occupations, environmental issues disproportionately affect African Americans and other minorities who reside in urban areas.

Native Americans have sustained successful, long-term battles to defend treaty rights and homelands, increasingly with the aid and advice of environmental groups such as Greenpeace and the Sierra Club. Such groups are redefining their own focus to include what could be called the "resource wars." Some indigenous communities are effectively refusing the toxic by-products of industrialization as well as the rhetoric of "jobs versus the environment," even in the face of continued grim economic prospects on reservations without gambling casinos.

Since the 1872 founding of Yellowstone National Park, conservationists and Native peoples have often been at odds. This adversarial relationship has partly been the result of conservationists' designating as natural parks areas in which Native peoples live, thereby forcing changes in their residence and livelihood. Natives have suffered starvation, disease, and cultural disintegration as a result.

Environmental groups such as Greenpeace have begun to realize that the defense of Natives' treaty rights is an integral part of an environmental protection strategy. For example, when the Chippewa Indians decided to oppose Exxon's plans to mine on their reservation in 1976, they stood alone. But by 1986, the Chippewa, under the leadership of Winona LaDuke, had assembled a successful broad-based coalition of Natives and environmental groups in Wisconsin.

Because treaties often allow for Natives of the Northwest to exercise the right to fish, some tribes such as the Sauk of the Skagit River have argued successfully in court that that right means nothing if the fishing habitat is so degraded as to deprive the tribes of their modest subsistence needs. In 1980 Judge William Orrick ruled in Phase II of the case of *United States v. Washington* that treaty tribes have the implicit right to have their fishery habitats protected. This ruling, supported by non-Indian groups such as Skagitonians Concerned About Nuclear Plants, has successfully halted or delayed half of the proposed nuclear installations in Wisconsin. Thus Native activism, in cooperation with non-Native environmentalism, intertribal coordination and resources co-management, has prevented some reservation lands from becoming national sacrifice zones—that is, areas degraded to the extent that they cannot be reclaimed. In this way, Native activism has raised the critical question: Sustainability of what and for whom?

Women have also been politicized because of environmental concerns.[32] Women, particularly working-class women, regardless of race, have a high affiliation rate with environmental justice groups at the grassroots and local neighborhood level. Like Lois Gibbs at Love Canal, these women—often mothers in a residential community—are initially mobilized to protest around a single issue. But often these groups branch out to address multiple issues. For example, Mothers of East Los Angeles (MELA) stormed into the political arena by opposing a proposed state prison, participating in the Coalition Against the Pipeline, and spearheading the defeat of a proposal by the California Thermal Treatment Services to locate an incinerator in a nearby community.[33]

Started by Juaua Beatriz Gutiérrez, a mother and housewife, and supported by her pastor, Father Luis Carbo of the Santa Isabel Church, and Father Morreta of Resurrection Parish, MELA lobbied the state assembly, conducted fund raisers, and worked to defeat proposals that would degrade the environment of their neighborhood. Winning the respect of Greenpeace and the Natural Resources Defense Council, MELA grew from six women to three thousand persons in six years.

When so-called "traditional" women move to grassroots protest and make the connection between their health and their government's policymaking process, they mobilize to confront inequalities.[34] Ideologies of motherhood, in this context, are not merely privatized or domesticated; they are a foundation for resistance that transcends the private/public sphere dichotomy. In order to protect the domestic sphere, women move into the public sphere and in the process can become politicized.

Because the leadership and agendas of mainstream United States environmental groups continue to be overwhelmingly white, male, and middle-class, black women call for the reprioritization of ecological ethics. There are important examples of African American women activists' success in redefining ecological/environmental ethics from which all concerned persons can learn and draw hope, faith, and courage. The beautification efforts of the Magnolia Tree Earth Center in New York City's Bedford-Stuyvesant area, which for fifteen years has planted trees in Brooklyn, is one of the oldest organized efforts of African American women to restore natural beauty and cleaner air to inner-city neighborhoods.

In 1986 Concerned Citizens of South Central Los Angeles successfully organized and defeated the Los Angeles city council's efforts to locate a thirteen-acre incinerator, which would have burned two thousand tons of waste daily, in low-income black and Latino neighborhoods. Concerned Citizens is largely composed of black women and has continued to employ a nonhierarchical, rotating leadership model. Rachel Bagby and the Philadelphia Rehabilitation Corporation, with its five thousand resident members, advocates and exemplifies communal living, recycling efforts, urban gardening, and literacy and employment programs for its community and surrounding area.

In Chicago, Hazel and Cheryl Johnson of Altgeld Public Housing organized and continue to head People for Community Recovery (PCR). The group was formed in response to the fact that public housing in Chicago is most often built directly over public landfills; of the nation's landfills, Chicago's have the highest concentrations of hazardous waste. PCR has successfully fought the Chicago Housing Authority, forcing the removal of asbestos from public housing and lobbying for a moratorium on new landfill permits in the city. Other efforts, like the National Black Women's Health Project, SisteReach, and Luisah Teish in New York City have organized urban gardens, holistic healing initiatives, and grassroots efforts to prevent gentrification.

Occupational health issues, from an eco-justice perspective, should also not be a top-down approach. Modern "rationality" has held that experts speak to the issues better than those who are most affected and emotionally involved, but are deemed unqualified to determine appropriate working conditions. Environmental justice efforts challenge this modern rationality by refusing to leave the areas of health and safety regulations to the sole control of experts.

Gender, race, and class experiences and social locations shape definitions of nature and, therefore, influence what areas of the world and what quality-of-life issues will be addressed as environmental concerns. The more diverse people involved in defining environmental concerns, the less likely the environmental agenda will reproduce the classism and sexism of society. Without attention to the diverse understandings of what counts as "nature," the best efforts at "saving the earth" for "our children" may not lack passion, but they will lack justice.

Notes

1. This chapter is based on a presentation to the Chicago Academy of Science for the "Questions of Nature" series at the Peggy Notebaert Museum in Chicago, 17 February 2000.

2. This advertisement is discussed in Vron Ware, *Beyond the Pale: White Women, Racism and History* (New York: Verso, 1992), i.

3. In addition to such factors as skin pigmentation, language, and culture, facial appearance and even dress can play a role in inter-group racial differentiation, as in the case of Jews and Arabs in the Middle East. Post-structuralist African American literary theory on this point has been influenced by the French Antillean psychiatrist Frantz Fanon, as well as by Anthony Appiah and Henry Louis Gates Jr. For Fanon, the black subject is not biologically determined but culturally determined; see Frantz Fanon, *Black Skins, White Masks* (London: MacGibbon and Kee, 1968). Appiah interprets "race" as a fiction with no scientific basis in "The Uncompleted Argument: Du Bois and the Illusion of Race," *Critical Inquiry* 12:1 (Autumn 1985): 21–37. Gates also sees "race" as a trope, an arbitrary signifier, though a powerful one, in "Writing 'Race' and the Difference It Makes," *Critical Inquiry* 12:1 (Autumn 1985): 1–20. As Diana Fuss suggests, race is a political concept that we can use as a biological fiction without denying its real material effects in history. Diane Fuss, *Essentially Speaking: Feminism, Nature and Difference* (New York: Routledge, 1989), 91.

4. See Sandra Harding's *Whose Science? Whose Knowledge?* (New York: Cornell University Press, 1991); Mary Jacobus, Evelyn Fox Keller, and Sally Shuttleworth, eds., *Body Politics: Women and the Discourses of Science* (New York: Routledge, 1990); and Donna Haraway, *Primate Visions: Gender, Race, and Nature in the World of Modern Science* (New York: Routledge, 1989).

5. Carolyn Merchant, in *Ecological Revolutions: Nature, Gender and Science in New England* (University of North Carolina Press, 1989), describes two American ecological revolutions, one colonial, occurring roughly between 1600 and the American Revolution, and one capitalist, which took shape between the revolution and 1860. She also suggests that a third ecological revolution is at hand, a global revolution.

6. John G. Neihardt, *Black Elk Speaks: Being the Life Story of a Holy Man of the Oglala Sioux* (Lincoln: University of Nebraska Press, 1961), 1–3, 198–200, 203–4, 217–18.

7. Prettyshield was in her seventies when Linderman interviewed her for his book *Red Woman* (New York: John Day, 1932), reissued as *Prettyshield: Medicine Woman of the Crows* (Lincoln: University of Nebraska Press, 1972). See Vera Norwood, *Made from This Earth:* American Women and Nature (Chapel Hill: University of North Carolina Press, 1993), 175–77.

8. Roderick Nash, ed., *American Environmentalism: Readings in Conservation History* (New York: McGraw-Hill, 1990), 9.

9. See Alfred Crosby's *Ecological Imperialism: The Biological Expansion of Europe, 900–1900* (Cambridge University Press, 1986.)

10. Donald Worster, *Under Western Skies: Nature and History in the American West* (New York: Oxford University Press, 1992), 7.

11. This legacy of an anti-ecological Christianity persists. Albanese examines the disparity that some religious groups and people, particularly Goddess feminists such as Charlene Spretnek, feel is an unbridgeable chasm between Judeo-Christian religions, which they see as in opposition to ecological wisdom, and religions that embody ecological wisdom. Catherine L. Albanese, *Nature Religion in America: From the Algonkian Indians to the New Age* (Chicago: University of Chicago Press, 1990), 175.

12. John Locke, *Second Treatise of Civil Government* (Buffalo, N.Y.: Prometheus, 1986), 28.

13. David Roediger, *The Wages of Whiteness: Race and the Making of the American Working Class* (New York: Verso, 1991), 9.

14. Eugene Genovese, *The Political Economy of Slavery* (New York: Random, 1967), 27.

15. Delores Williams, "Sin, Nature, and Black Women's Bodies," *Ecofeminism and the Sacred* (New York: Continuum, 1993), 24.

16. *Annual Report of the Secretary of the Interior on the Operations of the Department for the Fiscal Year Ended June 30, 1877* (Washington, D.C.: U.S. Government Printing Office, 1877), xv–xx.

17. From Gifford Pinchot, *Breaking New Ground* (New York: Harcourt Brace Jovanovich, 1947), 320–26.

18. Madison Grant, *The Passing of the Great Race.* See Donna Haraway's "Teddy Bear Patriarchy" in *Primate Visions,* 57.

19. Ibid.

20. Samuel Hayes, "Conservation as Efficiency," in *American Environmentalism: Readings in Conservation History,* Roderick Nash, ed. (New York: McGraw-Hill, 1990), 102–4.

21. Robert Bullard, *Dumping in Dixie: Race, Class, and Environmental Quality* (Boulder, Colo.: Westview, 1990), 12.

22. See Joni Seager, *Earth Follies: Coming to Feminist Terms with the Global Environmental Crisis* (New York: Routledge, 1993), 190.

23. See table, "Priorities on the Agenda of the Eco-Establishment," in *Inside the Environmental Movement*, ed. Donald Snow (Washington, D.C.: Island, 1992), as reprinted in Seager, *Earth Follies,* 180.

24. See Women's Information Network Against Breast Cancer's website: http://www.winabc.org/newweb/breast-health/about-breast-cancer.htm.

25. Suellen Hoy speculates on the links between the middle-class emphasis on cleanliness, the gender implications of consumerism and cleaning, and the ideal of a clean that is "whiter than white," and how these are influenced by "green" housekeeping. See Suellen Hoy, *Chasing Dirt: The American Pursuit of Cleanliness* (New York: Oxford University Press, 1995), 151–78.

26. Seager, *Earth Follies.* See also Michael de Courcy Hinds, "Do Disposable Diapers Ever Go Away?" *New York Times,* 10 December 1988.

27. Robert Bullard, "Environmental Justice for All," in idem., ed., *Unequal Protection: Environmental Justice and Communities of Color* (San Francisco: Sierra Club Books, 1994), 3–22. Also see preface by Benjamin F. Chavis Jr. and foreword by congressman John Lewis.

28. Commission for Racial Justice, *Toxic Waste and Race in the United States: A National Report on the Racial and Socioeconomic Characteristics of Communities with Hazardous Waste Sites* (New York: United Church of Christ, 1987).

29. See introduction to Richard Hofrichter, ed., *Toxic Struggles: The Theory and Practice of Environmental Justice* (Philadelphia: New Society, 1993), 1–2.

30. Al Gedicks writes that as recently as 1970, practically all Indian mineral and energy resources were effectively controlled by large multinational corporations through lease agreements with the Bureau of Indian Affairs. Al Gedicks, *The New Resource Wars: Native and Environmental Struggles against Multinational Corporations* (Boston: South End Press, 1993), 42. Also see Phillip Jorgensen, "A Century of Political Economic Effects on American Indian Society, 1880–1980," *Journal of Ethnic Studies* 6 (1978): 51.

31. Six hundred bombs have been detonated on Shoshone land. Winona LaDuke, "A Society Based on Conquest Cannot Be Sustained," foreword to Gedicks, *The New Resource Wars.*

32. Celene Krauss, "Blue-Collar Women and Toxic-Waste Protests: The Process of Politicization," in *Toxic Struggles,* 107–17; Cynthia Hamilton, Environmental Consequences of Urban Growth and Blight," in *Toxic Struggles,* 67–75.

33. Gabriel Gutierrez, "Mothers of East Los Angeles Strike Back," in Bullard, ed., *Unequal Protection,* 220.

34. Celene Krauss, "Women of Color on the Front Line," in Bullard, ed., *Unequal Protection,* 256–71.

12.

"To Make the Wounded Whole"
Womanist Explorations of Reconciliation

STEPHANIE Y. MITCHEM

▣▣▣

"There is a balm in Gilead, to make the wounded whole."
—Negro spiritual

The Ku Klux Klan staged a march and rally a few years ago in Ann Arbor, Michigan. Since Ann Arbor is reputedly one of the most liberal cities in America, the anti-Klan protestors showed up too. One of the Klan marchers—a white male—was isolated and attacked by a crowd of black and white anti-Klan protestors. Television cameras captured a black woman throwing her own body between the protestors and the Klansman, who by now was on the ground. When asked later why she shielded the Klansman, the woman told of her concern that if police were to intervene, the attackers' own safety might be jeopardized. The image of this woman fending off the mob is seared into my memory; I am struck by both the incongruity and the "normality" of her action. It was incongruous because she protected someone who would have, quite likely, never reciprocated the favor. Yet it was "normal" because of black women's sociocultural training, which burdens them with saving just about everybody (especially other black people) with the glaring exception of themselves.

The image of that woman's body as a shield continues to cause me discomfort, but more for its normality than its incongruity. Her work at that moment inspires this chapter, since I contend that she was involved in a radical act of reconciliation. In that act, her body, like that of so many black women, was normally expected to be in jeopardy even as it served as protection for the Black community by warding off retaliatory attack from whites. The gesture expressed the typical pattern of Black women's mediating role.

Reconciliation aims toward making that which has been wounded or fractured whole again, with a wholeness encompassing body and spirit. The conventional theological notion of reconciliation is eschatological in tone, salvific in theme. Both endings and beginnings are held within such a notion. In this chapter, I will begin to develop a womanist construction of reconciliation in its social and theological contexts.

Womanist theology is by and for black women, particularly in the United States, and presents a unique view that is both distinct from and informed by black theology and feminist theology. Womanist theology has been in development since the 1980s, as black women realize that they have been rendered invisible even as their bodies are on the firing lines. This is not news: the shocking "normality" of that shielding gesture follows naturally from the historical realities of black women's raced and gendered and classed oppressions. If that woman's story is made up of intertwining rhythms, then we can hear in it the contrasting rhythms of Ida B. Wells and the figure of Mammy. Indeed, both of those rhythms speak to the idea of womanist reconciliation.

The first rhythm is that of Ida B. Wells, who worked in the 1890s to end the horrors of lynching. Many black men and some black women were lynched throughout the South in this form of social control following the emancipation of the enslaved Africans. Black people were kept in place with fear, intimidation, and death. Joining the black community's tradition of activist black women, Wells used words and political savvy to fight for an end to these horrendous acts. Yet Wells, like other black women activists, had to behave strictly within the constraints of Victorian womanhood. In this way, Wells could secure the social protection and approbation offered to women while avoiding public censure. "Wells' experience suggests that the dynamics of gender protection were a critical if submerged part of African American women's lives. . . . To affirm themselves and their vision of social justice, black women used humor, reticence, anger, or strictest decorum."[1] Was the contemporary black woman's protection of the Klansman related to this rhythm—both risky and traditionally mothering? Did she expect her gender to serve as her own protection?

The second rhythm is heard in the continued expectation that black women will gladly give "service." The figure of Mammy represents a grotesque caricature of the caring African American woman. In the slave era, the mammy happily cared for a white family's needs ahead of those of her own family. "Perhaps the most cynical aspect of the relationship is that the black mammy was responsible for orienting white children into the oppressive culture designed to keep the black mammy system in place."[2] Could this stereotype of black-woman-as-caretaker have influenced the anti-Klan marcher as she protected the Klan member? Was her use of her body to shield him part of this rhythm, this unfortunate tradition? These two rhythms or traditions of black womanhood—that of Ida B. Wells and that of Mammy—open the exploration of the question: What is a womanist theological construction of reconciliation?

In the past few years, as research on African American women's spirituality has grown, I have begun to consider the relationship of spirituality to healing practices and to salvation. While most theologies *name* reconciliation as involved in salvation, African American women *enact* a theology of reconciliation. Healing, or making the wounded whole, becomes intimately related to reconciliation and salvation in African American women's epistemological frameworks.

Healing, both personal and communal, is one of the themes of this chapter. The theme of reconciliation recurred often in interviews I conducted with several members of the Detroit Metropolitan Black Women's Health Project (hereinafter referred to as DMBWHP). Its members' linkage of health with healing and spirituality with wholeness shows how reconciliation is enacted in black women's lives. The power of these women's words underscores the rich spirituality and the refrain of healing that infuse the lives of black people.

This chapter considers both the social contexts of womanist reconciliation, such as the DMBWHP, and the theological contexts, especially those that inform womanist theology. Black women's holistic spirituality becomes the linking consideration for the chapter's last section, on the movement toward a womanist statement of reconciliation.

Reconciliation: The Social Contexts

Often, Western theological doctrines and pastoral practices of reconciliation reflect primarily personal activity: *I* sin, *I* seek forgiveness, *I* reconcile. The communal dimension is only indicated in an individual's relationship to some nebulous social contract. Embedded in this conceptualization is a denial: if *I personally* have done nothing wrong, I have no reason to enter a process of reconciliation. Spiritualized theologies that divorce body and soul also help deny the need for reconciliation of "earthly" matters. Such understandings elide the existence of social sin and negate the individual's responsibility to society. From positions of privilege, particularly, it is possible and desirable to view the world only in terms of individual actions and consequences. However, life contains other realities. For most African Americans, the discussion of reconciliation must include social contexts. For a people who have lived through lynchings, stereotypes, many forms of discrimination, and continued Klan marches, how could it not? The complex issues of race, gender, and class shape much of that discussion.

Race is a reality of life in America, and racial reconciliation has long been a theme of some social activists in the United States. Gender and class become factors that inflate the controlling power of race. Race undeniably impacts the way that black people can live in this country. Experiencing oppression because of one's race, gender, or class can motivate the desire for reconciliation.

In a socially grounded picture of reconciliation, personal commitments are analyzed in light of social responsibility. The ethical category of "ought" analyzed by black people calls whites in the dominant society to recognize their participation in social injustice and names the many benefits of privilege. These moral and ethical discussions become painful in a society of denial. Those who are oppressed fall into defensive positions; those who oppress attempt to justify the injustices.

The United States' political and economic global dominance creates a climate in which continuation of the status quo is desirable to some. Difference from the dominant "norms" itself can be viewed as betrayal of some nonexistent, fictional "normality." When a "normality" is accepted that excludes and denigrates others on the basis of race or gender, those barriers become embedded in contemporary social constructions. These barriers are not easily breached, since it is so easy to believe that they are natural: after all, many learn exclusion as a value in the context of family.

Legal scholar Patricia Williams has pointed out some ways in which divisive practices are taught, within family settings, as acts of love. She reached the conclusion, "Hate learned in a context of love is a complicated phenomenon. And love learned in a context of hate endangers all our family."[3] Black women often face this love-hate struggle. For instance, the stereotype of the care-giving Mammy, which is inflicted onto black women, is caught in this dangerous web. This milieu of "kind and gentle oppression," which is sometimes no more than another name for hate, has informed America's sense of itself for too long. This sense of "kind hate" is reflected in the historical postcards of lynchings that appear in the 1999 collection *Without Sanctuary;* these cards were mailed to white friends and family members with the message, "Wish you were here."[4] Analysis of the root causes of oppression is an integral component of social and personal reconciliation.

Large-scale social movements have sought some forms of racial reconciliation, as was found in some aspects of the civil rights movement. Yet in order to begin the movement toward a womanist theology of reconciliation, another analysis is necessary: of black women in social contexts. In a social climate imbricate with race, class, and gender oppressions, the Black Women's Health Project operates on national and local levels and helps black women navigate the terrain of injustice in order to find new sources of reconciliation.

The DMBWHP is a chapter of the National Black Women's Health Project (NBWHP). Begun in the 1980s, the Project defines itself as an organization

> committed to defining, promoting, and maintaining the physical, mental, spiritual, economic, and emotional well-being of Black women. Therefore our mission is to facilitate the empowerment and wellness of women of African descent, their families, and future generations and communities globally. For us, health is not merely the absence of illness, but the active promotion of wellness.[5]

A parallel statement in *Vital Signs* reads:

> *Such wellness is impossible without individual and group empowerment. Such personal and collective empowerment is essential to the redefining and reinterpretation of who Black women are, were, and can become.* (emphasis mine)[6]

This activist work of black women is part of a social reconciliation and encompasses a unique sense of the communal. Darlene Clark Hine, in her own research as a historian, wrote of her discovery of the communal dimension of black women's work.

> "Making community" means the processes of creating religious, educational, health care, philanthropic, political, and familial institutions and professional organizations that enabled our people to survive. . . . Black women created essential new communities and erected vast female networks during the transitions from slavery to freedom, from farm to city. It was through "making community" that Black women were able to redefine themselves, project sexual respectability, reshape morality, and define a new aesthetic.[7]

Community building is central to the meaning of the Project, local and national. The expectation of camaraderie rings through the history of black women's networks. Acceptance and support are given as gifts that black women do not experience in many places. Project members constantly challenge each other to focus on saving self. This is not as simple as it seems. Sometimes the members worked against their own socially learned survival methods. In these methods, secrecy, silence, and denial of self become ways to keep moving in the face of social assaults. These methods make sense in disempowered and disenfranchised communities, such as a "Jim Crowed" or enslaved world. However, these forms of survival are ultimately not healthy for the individual or the community.

Darlene Clark Hine terms this survival method, used to protect the inner person and values, a black women's "culture of dissemblance." In many ways, she contends, the ability to dissemble has become self-destroying denial. "Only with secrecy, thus achieving a self-imposed invisibility, could ordinary black women acquire the psychic space and gather the resources needed to hold their own in their often one-sided and mismatched struggle to resist oppression."[8] The deeper needs and health of black women themselves were discounted in such a structure. The Project, in its social healing dimensions, works against this culture of dissemblance. In the DMBWHP, there is genuine intent to reach black women and to effect changes in lives.

From 1996 to 1998, I attended meetings of the Detroit chapter and conducted interviews with several of the members. [9] Its members included Mattie, Nefertiri, Quincy, Azana, Lisa, Frances, Melody, and P'jazz. Some are quoted here; some names are pseudonyms to protect individuals' privacy. In many ways, the work of the Project and the words of its members reflect both social and personal reconciliation. Social and personal dynamics of healing are seen in the development of informational networks, combating denial on many levels, and identification of personal strengths.

The unwholesome fracturing of self is apparent when the women discuss their lives at chapter meetings. Entering their sacred meeting space, some are personally fragmented from the experiences of daily life. Melody stated:

> You have to constantly live in two different worlds. If you work around whites, then you're home with your family. That's where internal healing comes in, because you have to find a way to work and proceed in this world, know who you are, and know that the change is so gradual, so gradual, it probably won't happen in your lifetime.

Health, or wellness, became a goal to bring these fragments of self back into wholeness. Melody defined health as "Being safe. And happy. . . . Let me talk a little about safety. It means being safe in your body and your mind and being happy with who you are."

Frances answered the question "What is illness to you?" this way:

> Ah! Do you know some of the early theologians who talk about illness being a separation from self, a separation from society? That kind of isolation, that kind of non-communal-ness, is a state of ill health that gets manifested in all kinds of ways. We talk about the whole mind-body dynamic. . . . I also believe that we, depending on how we care for ourselves will determine our vulnerability.

Frances later defined healing as "the integration of the self."

For Lisa, healing is physical, mental, and spiritual:

> And everything else I can think of. Healing means knowing myself enough to know when something's wrong. It means loving myself to give myself permission to do all the things I need to do to get well, which means rest, which means crying, which means writing, which means people to hug me, which means access to the foods and herbs which help me balance myself which means I don't have to kill another thing to stay alive, which means I want to live in a symbiotic relationship with the earth. It means acknowledging everything I know about black female religion. Healing means learning.

Community building, anti-dissemblance, personal and social empowerment, self-discovery, advocacy—all these reflect reconciliation in the work of the DMBWHP. The women's words also reflect the healing dimension of reaching for new self-understandings, which must involve stating their own personal realities. Health becomes a doorway to restating the place of self in the world, to redefining the boundaries of life. These social contexts of womanist reconciliation open to a discussion of its theological contexts, which also inform the epistemological framework of black women.

Reconciliation: Theological Contexts

The words of the women of the Health Project, the social contexts, the possibilities of personal meanings—all give rise to new doctrinal understandings of reconciliation. Womanist theology revisits Christian doctrine with black women's lives as the point of departure.

Salvation, in a womanist theological construct, can be understood as born of the struggle to reconcile the places assigned to black women and their communities with their seemingly irreconcilable hopes, engaging a variety of activisms to alter these complex social dissonances. As a result, reconciliation and salvation, in black women's frameworks, are intimately connected with healing. Health is not an abstract issue or an idealized goal; for black women, health is a spiritual ordering of life linked with reconciliation and salvation.

The context for the prophetic womanist theological task and also the concepts of reconciliation are both embedded in black communities and are central to black theological construction. Black women's theoretical groundedness is often rooted in the black communities in which we find ourselves. From community building to self-discovery, the social context remains central to the development of womanist theological understandings of reconciliation. A few examples will demonstrate this theological context.

Jeremiah A. Wright Jr., pastor of a church in the Chicago area, was a contributor to a volume on black faith and public theology.[10] Wright terms the spiritual formation developed in some black churches "an underground theology," and this sociospiritual development is central to understanding reconciliation. Such formation teaches "resistance and refusal" to accept negative and limiting social definitions. The black church has the power to create an alternative social milieu in which resistance stories can be heard and refusal strategies taught.

Certainly, not all black church communities have this kind of spiritual formation, as James Cone points out. Cone is a preeminent theologian whose work has led to a stronger development of black theology. Healing the acts and effects of racism requires a radical race critique that some black theologians do not want to attempt. Aiming for reconciliation within black communities, and between black and white communities, Cone argues for communal adoption of the attitudes of both Martin Luther King Jr. and Malcolm X.

> Malcolm alone makes it too easy for blacks to go it alone and for whites to say "Begone!" Martin alone makes it easy for whites to ask for reconciliation without justice and for middle class blacks to grant it, as long as they are treated specially. Putting Malcolm with Martin enables us to overcome the limitations of each and to build on the strengths of both.[11]

The ideal of racial reconciliation drives much African American social and theological exploration. The healing of social divisions, the tasks of self-definition, and forms of critical analysis become other ways of expressing this aim for racial reconciliation. Theologians must also attend to the social dilemmas posed by all oppressions. Cone continues with pointed statements about the possibilities of racial reconciliation. "There can be no racial healing without dialogue, without ending white silence on racism. There can be no reconciliation without honest and frank conversation."[12]

Catherine Meeks, a professor at Mercer University, writes that she is pessimistic about options for racial reconciliation in the United States because of the difficulties and pain inherent in such a process. Like Cone, she states that both black and white Americans are invested in "not rocking the boat." As a Christian, she says: "Only out of the biblical mandate for reconciliation between god and human beings can racial reconciliation grow. All of us must confront our places of darkness and light so that we can become convinced of how short we have fallen in this regard."[13]

The processes of "transforming" society involves both reconciliatory and transgressive acts—those that move one beyond one's assigned place or help one recognize the meaninglessness of that place. Both offer ways of seeing through the social illusions.

In her ethnographic study *African American Women Quitting the Workplace*,[14] Dorothy Pennington found that women's relationships to their jobs were personal. Resisting narrow definitions, they found ways to expand beyond boundaries. For those in the study, this involved quitting particular workplaces, and sometimes starting new, very experimental business ventures. Several of the women in the study had advanced degrees, and departed from solid, business-school career paths. Each woman cited God or the universe as her motivation and encouragement to take the step.

In other words, the religious context was not viewed as separate from the social, and the professional was not divorced from the personal. A relationship with the divine was somehow in active conversation with life decisions. This is not a recent phenomenon among African American women. Two historical examples and the contemporary words of DMBWHP members will underscore the holistic, active spirituality of black women.

Holistic Spirituality

For most African American women, their quests for personal and social healing are components of their activism. Barbara Essex, an ordained minister, wrote: "The women who gave birth to me transformed society's norms into something that would work for them. . . . They made a life for themselves and their children. . . . They refused to be fenced in . . . when they hit a brick wall, they tore it down."[15] In such a view, the theological context is not separate from the social, and this yields a holistic view of the world. This perspective gives rise to a holistic spirituality.

God, by many names, has been understood by African American women as in the midst of daily life, not in the confines of a church or a heaven. This attitude is not new; it has been documented back to the lives of enslaved African women. In a groundbreaking study, Joan Martin explores the work ethic of enslaved Christian women and notes one among other components: "Black women's theological and ethical understanding of God to slavery [was] as the God of freedom, shelter, protection, and abundant life."[16] It is reconciliatory to understand God, in the midst of oppression, as good: this is a radical statement. Such a statement can be easily misunderstood. If an alternative set of operative values and another view of faith are not appreciated in this statement, the enslaved women's faith in God seems no more than theodical madness.

Karen Baker-Fletcher has extensively studied the work of Anna Julia Cooper, a nineteenth-century black writer. Baker-Fletcher cites one of Cooper's poems:

> God—is not afar!
> The simple may know:
> The Hereafter is here;
> Eternity is now.
> And myself am Heaven or Hell.[17]

Baker-Fletcher stated that Cooper understood heaven and hell as in people, to be revealed in their daily choices; justice was a lived experience, thus yielding relationship with God. Baker-Fletcher concludes, "We live into the hereafter."

The DMBWHP's members who were interviewed also demonstrated this relationship of life to faith in understandings of healing, faith, and spirituality. As they described healing, they often moved into reconciliatory and faith talk.

Quincy, an older woman and one of the Detroit chapter's original organizers, discussed faith as integral to healing. "When someone says something about healing, I immediately think about spirituality. Church. I've seen people healed. I believe in people being called to heal. I believe in the word of God."

Mattie, a member in her sixties, commented on the healing dynamics of faith from her own experience with cancer treatment. Mattie viewed God as directly answering prayer. God can heal body and spirit, but there is still human responsibility.

> Healing, to me, come by the grace of God. . . . You got to get it for yourself; you got to believe God is able. . . . I get up in the morning and I say, "Lord, I want to thank you for getting me through the night. Put your shield around me. Lord, I want to thank you." And I do my exercise.

Lisa is no longer Christian, especially because of her childhood experiences of religion in a "town steeped in denial." Christian religions, she maintained, are intended to

> keep black people out of power. . . . Religiosity is the guise. . . . I remember so clearly, as a child, being told by a woman, "Wearing lipstick is a sin, and you wouldn't want Jesus to come back right now and see you," and we had just left our mothers, putting on lipstick.

Lisa posited the idea of something more efficacious for her, "black women's religion." She knows herself as "spiritual" in a bodied and grounded way. As a result, Lisa described spirituality as

> part of our connection with magic. We are a magical force. Magic is the energy we create with unconditional love and that is a powerful creative force. It's not leaving it to something out there because spirit is in here. It's surrounding us, it's in us. . . . It's what makes us strong when we're not supposed to be here anymore.

Each of these examples indicates a lived experience of reconciliation, which is enacted by many black women in the wider world and in their own bodies. A womanist theology of reconciliation must embrace these complex values that black women consciously and unconsciously hold.

Toward a Womanist Statement of Reconciliation

Reconciliation is affiliated with salvation, especially as seen in the shape of black women's lives. Justice with love becomes a central configuration in womanist theoethics. Katie Cannon, a womanist ethicist, draws from the literature and folk wisdom of African American

women to explore the dimensions of spirituality. Among her conclusions is that

> African American women's spirituality as expressed in literature . . .
> does not begin with questions about the omnipotence, omni-
> science, and omnipresence of God and then move to justify God's
> goodness in the face of evil. Rather womanist protagonists con-
> tend that God's sustaining presence is known in the resistance to
> evil.[18]

Her exploration of resistance to evil, as part of the agenda of womanism, is intended to "stress the urgency of the African American
women's movement from death to life." Movement from death to life
is a healing activity, complex and multi-layered in black women's
understandings.

When issues of body, spirit, or community are raised, healing itself
becomes a form of reconciliation. As the women who were interviewed stated, illness is influenced by one's mind, spirit, and relationships. The importance of healing could be considered reflective of
African cognitive frameworks, which focus on connections of persons
with each other, within self, with world.

Emilie Townes's explorations of womanist spirituality as social witness are consistent with this value base. Townes writes: "The task of
womanist spirituality is to illuminate and question the oppression,
and then begin the eradication of radical oppression and devaluation
of the self and the community in the context of structural evil."[19]
Townes calls this a wholesome yearning for a new heaven and earth,
"a world crafted on justice *and* love that holds us all in God's creation
rather than in a hierarchy of oppressions." These monumental tasks
are activities of healing and reconciliation of personal, communal,
and spiritual brokenness. These tasks are not merely survivalist, but
can be understood as gateways for liberation.

One hears of reconciliation as a spiritual value of black women
throughout the writings of womanist ethicists and theologians.
Health Project members, too, witness to and affirm this value through
their networking processes. Working for the wholeness of black
women and men through reconciliation is a spiritual task reflecting
the unique history and rhythms of African American communities.

Today's black women shape their own life meanings contrary to
public opinions, and the interplay of the social and the personal
weaves new tales. This networking ritualizes reconciliation in black
women's lives, while stories yield new expressions of liberation theol-

ogy. Linda E. Thomas, a womanist theologian who has done ethnographical research on black women in the United States and South Africa, writes: "A practical liberation theology has to embrace a prominent role for healing of the broken-hearted through the implementation of ritualized acts of spiritual discipline. To heal ourselves is fundamentally a spiritual exercise upon our real bodies."[20]

Healing the broken-hearted and ritualized acts of spiritual discipline must be informed by love, both of self and the wider community. Womanist theologian Diana Hayes defines the concept of *agape* as "the soul-stirring, gut-wrenching active force that is at the basis, the very foundation of our faith. We must find, in the words of Martin Luther King Jr., 'the strength to love' not just those who are like us but especially those who are unlike us."[21]

Reconciliation is the lens through which black women's approaches to suffering are comprehensible. Suffering is not salvific. But the analysis of suffering is practical and grounded in real life experience. Reconciliation is one name for black women's practice of working toward salvation. Salvation points toward healing and wholeness, for self and community, and further resists suffering. There are intricate and dynamic exchanges among experiences, analysis, assessments, and actions, all of them informed by black women's spirituality. The spirituality that informs African American women's reconciling efforts may sometimes be Christian but is just as likely to be formed by a "black women's religion," as was Lisa's.

Reconciliation does not imply that scars are magically removed, that some imagined lost innocence is regained. Instead, reconciliation works with the challenge that the repaired and the healed have their own strength and meaning. Forgiveness is part of the process; forgetting is not. The personal and the communal are both part of the content of reconciliation.

Womanist reconciliation, then, aims toward personal and communal wholeness; it remains centered in, and informed by, spirituality. This aim for wholeness is not separate from the wholeness of the divine, nor is it religion-in-the-abstract. As Karen Baker-Fletcher writes:

> God is present in our everyday lives, and infinite possibilities for healing and wholeness are in our midst. For womanists, God is neither simply that ultimate ground of being by which we are grasped in moments of mystical experience nor some ultimate point of reference whom we come to understand primarily by reason. It is in our human bodies, souls, and minds in our everyday lives that we *experience* and *reason* about the sacred.[22]

So a womanist theology of reconciliation encompasses the reconciliation of humans with each other and with God, reconciliation of persons and of institutions.

Jacquelyn Grant issues a deeper challenge. Womanist theology is a corrective one; it challenges the existing theological systems that deny the humanity of black women and men and continue to oppress peoples considered "inferior" in the maintenance of hegemony. Says Grant, "The entire system of religious/theological language needs to be transformed."[23] This is the deeper, ongoing process womanist theology undertakes.

Carolyn Medine, a womanist cultural historian, draws from the narratives of black women and men to develop more fully the theological concept of *logos* or the "word." *Logos* is tied to imagination, which deconstructs and reconstructs in ways not initially considered possible. The aim of her understanding of *logos* is peace, which reimagines reality but does not level difference. Differences are held in polyphony.[24]

"To make the wounded whole" is to learn to live in polyphony, to cherish and nurture self and community. In a womanist theological construction, reconciliation is an opening to deeper healing. The anti-Klan marcher, like many black women putting their bodies on the line for justice, is best understood as drawing from this rhythm, this healing instinct. In such a holistic view, reconciliation challenges all oppressive, dehumanizing systems, not merely restoring to former order, but rebalancing the old so that a new heaven and earth can begin.

Notes

1. Patricia A. Schechter, "'All the Intensity of My Nature': Ida B. Wells, Anger and Politics," *Radical History Review* 70 (Winter 1998): 66.

2. Jacquelyn Grant, "Servanthood Revisited: Womanist Explorations of Servanthood Theology," in Dwight N. Hopkins, ed., *Black Faith and Public Talk: Critical Essays on James H. Cone's Black Theology and Black Power* (Maryknoll, N.Y.: Orbis, 1999), 130.

3. Patricia J. Williams, "The Ethnic Scarring of American Whiteness," in *The House that Race Built*, ed. W. Lubiano (New York: Pantheon, 1997), 263.

4. James Allen et al., *Without Sanctuary: Lynching Photography in America* (Santa Fe, N.M.: Twin Palms, 2000).

5. Mission Statement, Detroit Metropolitan Black Women's Health Project, 1996.

6. *Vital Signs* 11:3 (July–September 1995), 3.

7. Darlene Clark Hine, *Hine Sight: Black Women and the Re-Construction of American History* (Brooklyn, N.Y.: Carlson), xxii.

8. Ibid., 41.

9. Stephanie Y. Mitchem, "Getting Off the Cross: African American Women, Health, and Salvation" (Ph.D. dissertation, University of Michigan, Ann Arbor, 1998).

10. Jeremiah A. Wright Jr., "An Underground Theology," in Hopkins, ed., *Black Faith and Public Talk*, 96ff.

11. James H. Cone, "Looking Back, Going Forward," in Hopkins, ed., *Black Faith and Public Talk*, 256.

12. Ibid.

13. Catherine Meeks, "Rage and Reconciliation, Two Sides of the Same Coin," in *America's Original Sin: A Study Guide on White Racism* (Washington, D.C.: Sojourners, 1993), 161.

14. Dorothy L. Pennington, *African American Women Quitting the Workplace* (Lewiston, N.Y.: Edwin Mellen, 1999).

15. Barbara Essex, "Some Kind of Woman," in Emilie M. Townes, ed., *Embracing the Spirit: Womanist Perspectives on Hope, Salvation, and Transformation* (Maryknoll, N.Y.: Orbis, 1997), 203.

16. Joan M. Martin, *More Than Chains or Toil: A Christian Work Ethic of Enslaved Women* (Louisville: Westminster John Knox, 2000), 143.

17. Karen Baker-Fletcher, "The Strength of My Life," in Townes, ed., *Embracing the Spirit*, 131.

18. Katie G. Cannon, *Katie's Canon: Womanism and the Soul of the Black Community* (New York: Continuum, 1995), 111.

19. Emilie M. Townes, *In a Blaze of Glory: Womanist Spirituality as Social Witness* (Nashville: Abingdon, 1993), 67.

20. Linda E. Thomas, "Emancipatory Christianity" in Hopkins, ed., *Black Faith and Public Talk*, 187.

21. Diana L. Hayes, "My Hope Is in the Lord: Transformation and Salvation in the African American Community," in Townes, ed., *Embracing the Spirit*, 22.

22. Baker-Fletcher, "The Strength of My Life," in Townes, ed., *Embracing the Spirit*, 131.

23. Grant, "Servanthood Revisited," in Hopkins, ed., *Black Faith and Public Talk*, 135.

24. Carolyn Medine, personal conversation.

Bibliography

Allen, James, Hilton Als, John Lewis, and Leon F. Litwack. *Without Sanctuary: Lynching Photography in America*. Santa Fe, N.M.: Twin Palms, 2000.

Baker-Fletcher, Karen. "The Strength of My Life," in Emilie M. Townes, ed. *Embracing the Spirit: Womanist Perspectives on Hope, Salvation, and Transformation*. Maryknoll, N.Y.: Orbis, 1997. 122–39.

Cannon, Katie G. "The Dance of Redemption," unpublished paper.

———. *Katie's Canon: Womanism and the Soul of the Black Community*. New York: Continuum, 1995.

Collins, Patricia Hill. *Fighting Words: Black Women and the Search for Justice.* Minneapolis: University of Minnesota Press, 1998.

Cone, James H. "Looking Back, Going Forward," in Dwight N. Hopkins, ed. *Black Faith and Public Talk: Critical Essays on James H. Cone's Black Theology and Black Power.* Maryknoll, N.Y.: Orbis, 1999. 246–60.

Essex, Barbara. "Some Kind of Woman," in Townes, ed., *Embracing the Spirit,* 203–11.

Grant, Jacquelyn. "Servanthood Revisited: Womanist Explorations of Servanthood Theology," in Hopkins, ed., *Black Faith and Public Talk,* 127–37.

Hayes, Diana L. "My Hope Is in the Lord: Transformation and Salvation in the African American Community," in Townes, ed., *Embracing the Spirit,* 9–28.

Hine, Darlene Clark. *Hinesight: Black Women and the Re-Construction of American History.* Brooklyn, N.Y.: Carlson, 1994.

Martin, Joan M. *More Than Chains or Toil: A Christian Work Ethic of Enslaved Women.* Louisville: Westminster John Knox, 2000.

Meeks, Catherine. "Rage and Reconciliation, Two Sides of the Same Coin," in *America's Original Sin: A Study Guide on White Racism.* Washington, D.C.: Sojourners, 1992. 160–61.

Mission Statement. Detroit Metropolitan Black Women's Health Project. 1996.

Mitchem, Stephanie Y. "Getting Off the Cross: African American Women, Health, and Salvation." Ph.D. dissertation, University of Michigan, Ann Arbor, 1998.

Pennington, Dorothy L. *African American Women Quitting the Workplace.* Lewiston, N.Y.: Edwin Mellen, 1999.

Schechter, Patricia A. "'All the Intensity of My Nature': Ida B. Wells, Anger and Politics." *Radical History Review* 70 (Winter 1998).

Thomas, Linda E. "Emancipatory Christianity," in Hopkins, ed. *Black Faith and Public Talk,* 178–89.

Townes, Emilie M. *In a Blaze of Glory: Womanist Spirituality as Social Witness.* Nashville: Abingdon, 1995.

Vital Signs 11:3 (July–September 1995), 3.

Williams, Delores S. *Sisters in the Wilderness: The Challenge of Womanist God-Talk.* Maryknoll, N.Y.: Orbis, 1993.

Williams, Patricia J. "The Ethnic Scarring of American Whiteness," in W. Lubiano, ed., *The House that Race Built.* New York: Pantheon, 1997. 253–63.

Wright, Jeremiah A., Jr. "An Underground Theology," in Hopkins, ed., *Black Faith and Public Talk,* 96–102.